Beginner's Guide to Woodturning

Beginner's Guides are available on the following subjects:

Audio
Building Construction
Cameras
Central Heating
Colour Television
Computers
Digital Electronics
Domestic Plumbing
Electric Wiring
Electronics
Gemmology
Home Energy Saving
Integrated Circuits
Photography
Processing and Printing
Radio
Super 8 Film Making
Tape Recording
Television
Transistors
Woodturning
Woodworking
Video

Beginner's Guide to

Woodturning

Frank Underwood
and Gordon Warr

Newnes Technical Books

Newnes Technical Books
is an imprint of the Butterworth Group
which has principal offices in
London, Sydney, Toronto, Wellington, Durban and Boston

First published 1981

British Library Cataloguing in Publication Data
Underwood, Frank
Beginner's guide to woodturning.-
(Beginner's guides).
1. Turning - Amateurs' manuals
I. Title II. Warr, Gordon III. Series
684.'08 TRT202

ISBN 0-408-00507-6

Photoset by Butterworths Litho Preparation Department
Printed in Great Britain by
The Whitefriars Press Ltd, London and Tonbridge

Preface

Whenever woodturning is demonstrated, a crowd will gather, fascinated by the sight of wood spinning in the lathe, ribbons of shavings hissing over the gouge or chisel, and beautiful shapes quickly being formed from a plain block of wood. Turning is an occupation which provides an outlet for manual skill, artistic talent, and creative desire. That is why so many people are taking it up as a hobby. Many others make the hobby pay its way by selling their wares. May we persuade you to join them?

First, we will outline the development of woodturning from crude and simple lathes to modern machines, and explain the functions of the parts of the lathe and its attachments. Then we will discuss the tools used, their maintenance and handling. We will show you how they are used and explain the various techniques for making bowls, platters, and many simple, everyday things.

This book is not large enough to cover the subject fully; indeed, a whole series of large volumes would still leave much unsaid. Woodturners are always learning: new ways of doing a job, new ideas in design, new uses of tools and accessories. But the basic skills remain the same, as they have for many years. So we will guide you along the way to acquiring those basic skills and developing others. Be patient, persevere, and keep your tools sharp!

Frank Underwood
Gordon Warr

Contents

1 Introduction

The craft of woodturning is nearly as old as that of carpentry and has origins going back to the times of the earliest recorded history. One primitive type of lathe was rigged up between a pair of suitably placed trees (*Figure 1.1*), each acting as a support for the wood being turned. A piece of cord was then fastened to a conveniently overhanging and springy branch, wrapped a couple of times around the wood to be turned, then tied in a loop, a little above ground level. The turner would stand before his lathe, place his foot in the loop, and apply downward pressure, thus causing the wood to revolve. On releasing the pressure, the resilience of the branch would bring the workpiece and the cord back to their original positions. And so the wood was made to revolve forwards and backwards, the turner being able to use tools and remove wood only on the forward revolutions. Sometimes a simple treadle would be incorporated (*Figure 1.2*).

Another early source of motive power was a strung bow. The bowstring would be wrapped around the workpiece and, as the bow was moved to and fro across the work, the wood was spun forwards and backwards. This type of lathe required an assistant to work the bow or a highly skilled turner who could operate the bow with one hand and control the turning-tool with the other. Such lathes were still used in the Middle East until at least the 1940s.

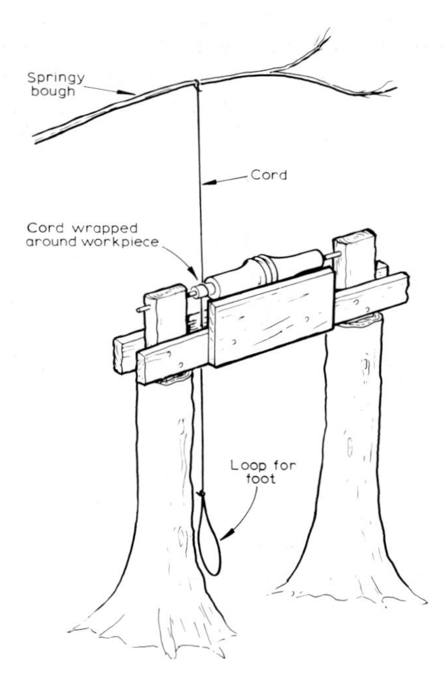

Fig. 1.1. Early pole-lathe

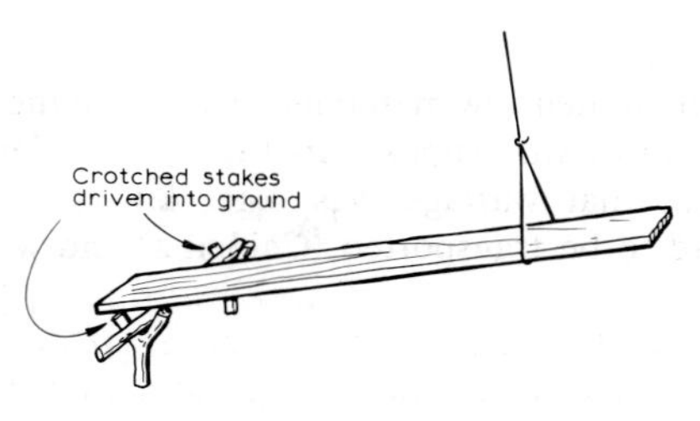

Fig. 1.2. Pole-lathe provided with simple treadle

Both these patterns of lathe were crude but effective, and their operators were highly competent. Both gave only five or six revolutions each way and, as the turner was restricted to removing wood on the forward movement, he had to time the manipulation of his gouge or chisel to coincide with the direction of rotation.

Springy pole-lathes, little different from the oldest known types, were in fairly common use in England up to the outbreak of the second world war. Indeed, a few survived until the 1950s, but pole-lathes now exist only in museums. The operators were known as 'chair bodgers' and were centred on the furniture-making town of High Wycombe.

Bodgers were itinerants, who would move into beech forests of the Chiltern Hills and set up portable shelters. They used an ash sapling about 10ft to 12ft long as the spring (*Figure 1.3*).

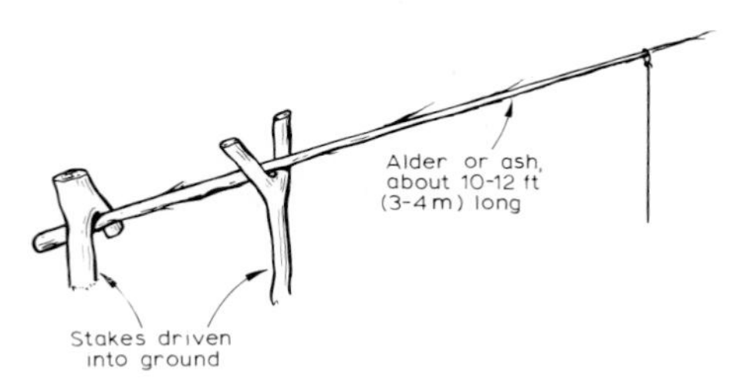

Fig. 1.3. Typical method of support for spring pole

Because the lathes were restricted in size, and the tools used were fairly limited in number, it was easier for bodgers to move to the source of their raw materials than to take the heavy logs to established town workshops. Another reason for this way of working was that wastage was high, and only the finished turnings had to be transported. Chippings and waste were left behind or, more likely, used as fuel for fires.

Trees were felled and crosscut to the lengths required. These short sections, called 'billets', were split or cleft with a handled wedge, and struck by a 'beetle', which was a large and heavy mallet. The billets were then roughly trimmed octagonal with a broad-bladed hatchet known as a 'side-axe' or with a draw-knife. The wood was turned while green (or unseasoned), then the turned parts were stacked and allowed to dry. (A piece of wood turned when unseasoned to a perfect circular section will, on drying, become slightly oval but on work of small size this distortion is very small and could be detected only by using callipers.)

The bulk of the bodgers' vast output was turned legs, rails, and spindles for chairs – particularly Windsor chairs (*Figure 1.4*). A bodger could completely turn a chair-leg in under two minutes.

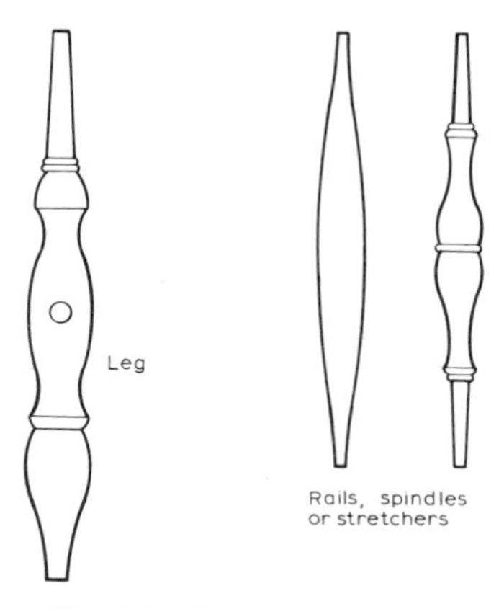

Fig. 1.4. Chair bodger's work

So great was the individual output and so well trained the bodger's eyes that identical turnings would be produced with negligible checking or measuring.

The carpenters' shops which were to be found in villages and towns – particularly during the heyday of the carpenter in the 18th and 19th centuries – were often equipped with lathes. These lathes had wooden beds consisting of a couple of planks up to 9 in by 3 in in section. One of the advantages of the wooden bed is that the length, and therefore the turning capacity, could be very large. The headstock and tailstock were known as 'puppets' and were made of wood, as was the toolrest. On these early lathes, only the actual centres on which the wood revolved were of metal, being the product of the local blacksmith. With the introduction of cast iron, head- and tail-stocks and toolrests began to be made from this material, but the wooden bed

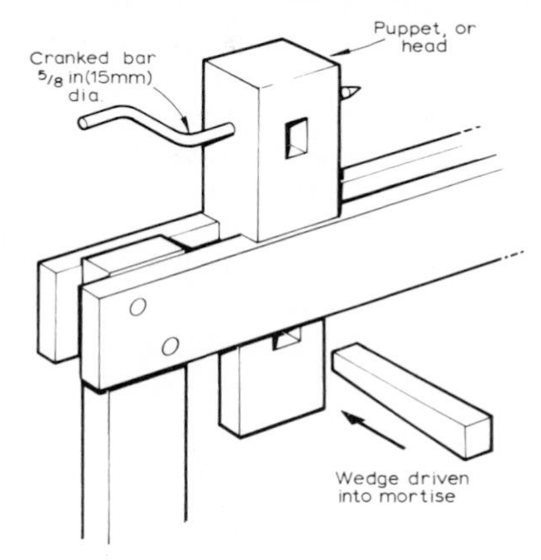

Fig. 1.5. Adjustable wedge-held puppet

remained a feature of such lathes, which are still to be found in old woodworkers' shops.

Sometimes the power-supply was a waterwheel, but more often it was manpower. A wheel, 6 ft or 7 ft in diameter, was set up on a spindle supported by a couple of trestles. To the wheel was fixed a crank, or handle, and a belt ran from the rim to the headstock pulley. The large wheel not only provided the right ratio of diameters to give a reasonable speed to the lathe but also created sufficient momentum to overcome the slowing effect of a heavy cut. One man provided the power to keep the work revolving, while another did the turning.

This type of lathe was an essential part of the wheelwright's shop, in particular for turning the hub, or nave, of the traditional cartwheel. Elm was used for these parts, the resistance to splitting given by its interlocked grain making it specially suitable. For a large wheel, a block for a nave would start off at about 15 in cube and with a weight of about 84 lb.

Until recently, a great deal of woodturning was carried out in West Wales. Here the work was largely for dairy farmers and the domestic trade, the wood used invariably being locally-grown sycamore, which is an excellent choice for anything connected with food. Bowls, ladles, spoons, breadboards, and rolling-pins were typical products of the Welsh turners' shops, as were rollers for mangles. Some bowl-turners could, from one block of wood mounted on the lathe, turn up to four bowls, each bowl being made from the hollow of the next larger one.

The 20th century saw the introduction of the all-metal lathe with a bed of cast iron. Power-operated lathes became the rule rather than the exception, although – as with most other machinery – the motor was separate from the machine and power was transmitted to the headstock by belts, pulleys, and shafting. Variable speeds were introduced by having pulleys of different diameters.

The treadle-operated machine also appeared. Operating the treadle caused a fairly heavy flywheel to rotate. The flywheel provided continuity and smoothness of rotation and momentum, imparting a steady speed to the work through a flat or round belt from the rim of the flywheel to the headstock pulley.

The post-war years have seen a great revival in woodturning, both in small professional shops and by the amateur, and turned ware is again to be seen in shops and market places. Now the emphasis is on its beauty and individualness. Many amateurs, although they do not earn their living from the lathe, seek a market for their wares. So a lathe can often be thought of as an investment that can be made to pay for itself. One Cotswold schoolboy works on his father's lathe; his speciality being lacemakers bobbins (*Figure 1.6*). He earned enough during one summer to buy himself an expensive cricket bat. Another acquaintence of the authors turns floats for angling from light, clean woods such as red cedar, obeche, and balsa. He sells them through tackle shops.

Useful and decorative items can be produced more quickly on a lathe than by any other form of woodworking, and the lathe can therefore be a most convenient way of making economical presents.

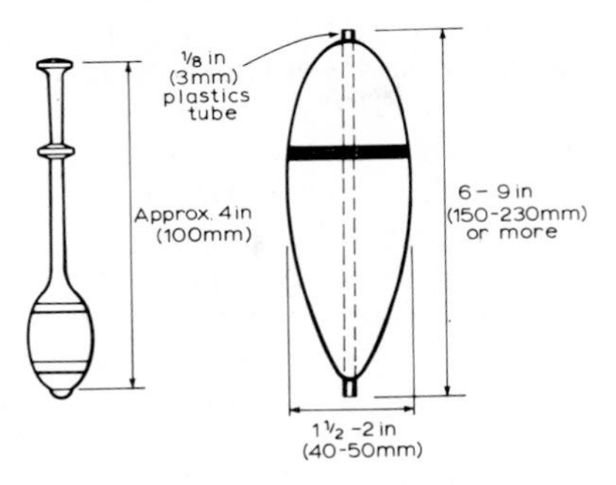

Fig. 1.6. Left, lacemaker's bobbin; right, sea-fishing float

The modern woodturner is more fortunate than those of earlier generations. There are many well-engineered lathes for him to choose from, and all he needs by way of power is a supply of electricity. Turning-tools are readily available, and methods of holding the workpiece in the lathe have been vastly improved in recent years. For the woodturner to exploit his craft to the full, an assortment of sundries and fittings is essential, and tiles, clock faces and movements, glass dish-inserts, peppermill mechanisms, and cigarette lighters are among the items which can be purchased from specialist suppliers. There has been a big growth in suppliers of turnery equipment, lathes, tools, and timbers over the last few years. These suppliers advertise widely in craft and similar magazines, and as most firms offer a postal service, the amateur need never be stuck for supplies.

2 The basic lathe

The modern lathe is still simple in principle. The techniques involved in woodturning have remained unchanged over the centuries, and so have the essential features of the lathe: headstock, tailstock, bed, and toolrest. The important characteristic of modern lathes is that nearly all are motorised: that is, an electric motor provides the driving power and is fitted as part of the machine. There are exceptions, the main ones being lathes which are designed as attachments for other machines, such as a circular saw or a combination or 'universal' machine which can perform several different woodworking operations. These should not be confused with another type of machine: this is basically a lathe, complete with its own motor, on to which can be fitted attachments such as planer, circular saw, mortiser, belt-sander, and so on. (It is, incidentally, easy to devise and make a disc sander to fit almost any lathe.)

Another small group of lathes consists of those designed as attachments for portable power-drills. These are necessarily small in the capacity of work they will accommodate, which is governed by the limited power of the drill motor. A typical lathe of this type will take work up to approximately 24 in (610 mm) in length or turn bowls and similar work up to about 5½ in (140 mm) diameter. It is important with such an attachment to use a drill from the same manufacturer. Apart from the possible difficulty of fitting a drill of one make to an attachment of another, some makes of drill have bearings which will not stand up to the considerable side thrust imposed by turning.

For the man who wants to set himself up with a lathe and yet keep costs down, there is an alternative to buying a complete machine. It is still possible to make a small lathe of the type popular around 80 years ago – one with a wooden bed and cast metal parts. Headstock, tailstock, toolrest, and saddle are bought as machined castings, complete with bearings, mandrel, and faceplate in the headstock, which is provided with a four-step vee-pulley, and barrel in the tailstock. The constructor supplies wood for the bed, which can be any length within reason. This type of lathe will tackle faceplate work up to 9in (228 mm) on the right-hand side of the headstock and even larger diameters on the left-hand side. (Turning on the left-hand side is known as 'rear turning'.) It is up to the person making the lathe to provide a power-source.

Lathe size

The size of a lathe is specified by two main dimensions. The first is the length of timber that can be turned: that is, the distance from headstock to tailstock or, more accurately, the distance 'between centres'. Typical capacity between centres is 30 in (735 mm); this can be thought of as standard, since it corresponds to the height of a table and so table-legs can be produced on such a lathe.

The second dimension used to specify the capacity of a lathe is the maximum workpiece diameter it will take. This is governed by the height of the centres above the bed and is called the 'centre-height'. Sometimes the term 'swing' is used: this means the maximum diameter which can be accommodated and is double the centre-height. Typical centre-heights are 4 in to 5 in (102 to 127 mm).

A lathe will not necessarily cope with a piece of wood which is at the maximum dimensions for both length and swing. This is because the toolrest support and saddle are usually located above the bed of the lathe, and so at this point the capacity of the lathe in terms of workpiece diameter is restricted.

Mounting

A study of the literature issued by lathe manufacturers will show that a lathe may be available either as a bench model or mounted on its own base – which, these days, is invariably in the form of a cabinet. With a bench model, it is up to the purchaser to provide either a bench-top or an independent cabinet and to set up on this not only the lathe but also the motor and its platform, the electric wiring, and the starter switch. Some lathes have rear turning facilities secured to the headstock casting, others have them as a completely separate unit which will also need to be secured in place. If a base is to be made for the lathe, it will need to be of substantial construction. An average lathe, with motor and sundry parts, is likely to weigh between 100 and 200 lb (45 to 90 kg), and those which carry attachments can weigh considerably more. It is not just the dead weight of the lathe which has to be considered but also the forces created by rotation and by vibration in the early stages of turning.

Headstock

The principal components of a typical lathe are shown in *Figure 2.1*. While they all have their part to play, the headstock (A) can be regarded as the heart of the machine. It is usually a casting of iron or aluminium alloy and carries the main mandrel (B) and (C). The mandrel is mounted in bearings, and provision is made for lubrication. It may be solid or hollow, the advantage of a hollow mandrel being that centres and similar accessories can be easily removed by tapping them with a steel rod through the hole. The mandrel is threaded at both ends if it is designed for rear turning, the thread being to mount faceplates and similar holding devices. The outer thread (B) is a left-hand one. This is because it is essential that the direction of rotation of the lathe should always tend to tighten anything mounted on the mandrel nose. (Naturally, the threads of the attachments must match.)

Even if the mandrel is not hollow, the right-hand end will have a tapering hole drilled part-way into it. This is known as a 'Morse

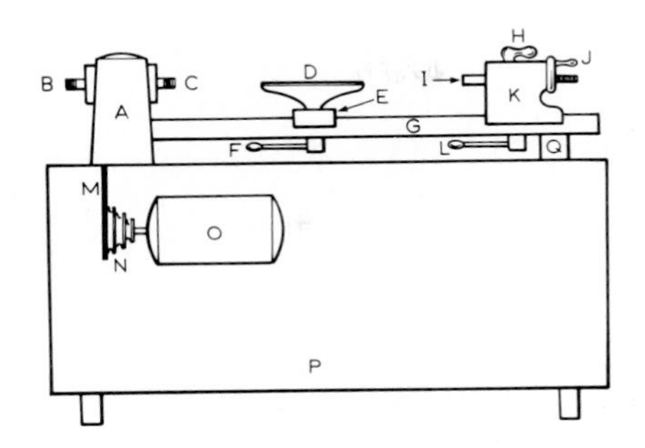

A	*Headstock*	*J*	*Barrel advance wheel*
B	*Mandrel, outer end*	*K*	*Tailstock*
C	*Mandrel, inner end*	*L*	*Tailstock locking lever*
D	*Toolrest*	*M*	*Drive belt*
E	*Toolrest saddle*	*N*	*Multi-step pulley*
F	*Saddle locking lever*	*O*	*Motor*
G	*Bed*	*P*	*Cabinet*
H	*Tailstock barrel lock*	*Q*	*Leg*
I	*Tailstock barrel*		

Fig. 2.1. Parts of the lathe

taper'. Various components have tapered plugs to mate with the mandrel and hold entirely by friction; the greater the pressure on the mating parts, the better the grip. Morse tapers should never be oiled, but must be kept clean for maximum efficiency. Morse tapers are of standard form and range in size from No. 1 upwards. The vast majority of lathes available to amateurs are drilled for a No. 1 taper; only on much larger machines do the makers move up to No. 2 or No. 3.

Rear turning

Because the maximum diameter which can be turned is limited, even on a lathe with a generous centre height, many lathes have the facility already mentioned for 'rear turning' work of large diameter. This is usually provided on the left-hand side of the headstock, where there is no restriction by the bed. Maximum diameter is limited here only by the rigidity of the whole lathe, the robustness of the bearings, and the provision for holding the toolrest.

Typical maximum diameter for rear turning is around 20 in (508 mm), although a limiting factor is the thickness of the workpiece and hence its weight. Another critical point is the speed of revolution, as diameter of work and revolutions per minute (r.p.m.) are interrelated; speeds are discussed later.

Although it is of little interest to the amateur, it is possible to obtain a type of lathe known as a 'bowl-turning head'. This is essentially a headstock only – no bed and no tailstock – and is intended for faceplate turning only.

One leading British manufacturer has solved the problem of limited swing in a different way. The whole headstock, together with the rear-mounted motor and its platform, can be made to swivel through 180 deg. This is a unique feature of most of the machines produced by the company. They can have attachments added to undertake many other woodworking operations, and the swivelling headstock is particularly useful when using the saw or planer attachment in a restricted space.

The same manufacturer also produces a lathe of very much smaller capacity than the average already referred to – 12 in (305 mm) between centres and centre-height of 3½ in (89 mm) – but, as it incorporates the swivelling headstock, its maximum diameter for faceplate turning is 14 in (365 mm). This is an ideal machine where both capital outlay and space are limited, and where the turner is likely to limit his work to bowls, reading-lamps, egg cups, and similar small items. (In practice, while a large lathe will cope well with small items, the bulk of turnery is small so do not buy the biggest lathe you can find.)

Pulleys

On the central part of the mandrel is mounted a stepped pulley, which receives the power from the motor (0) transmitted by the belt (M) from another stepped pulley (N). There are usually four steps on the pulley, to give four different speeds, but on some lathes there are three or five.

There is (at least) one make of lathe where the pulley incorporates an indexing mechanism consisting of 24 holes drilled around the side of the large pulley, and a plunger in the headstock is located so as to line up with and engage in any one of the holes. The mandrel and workpiece can thus be locked in any one of 24 positions. This is useful when, for example, the piece being turned has flat surfaces which have to be worked on when in a locked position. The plunger also acts as a convenient way of locking the headstock when removing a faceplate from the mandrel nose.

Toolrests

Toolrests (D), rectangular on plan, are from about 6 in (152 mm) in length. Most lathes are supplied with one of this size and another about 12 in (305 mm) long. Toolrests over this size usually have two mounting-pins and so require two toolrest supports.

The sectional shape of toolrests (*Figure 2.2*) is a matter of controversy, even among experts. In practice, one gets used to

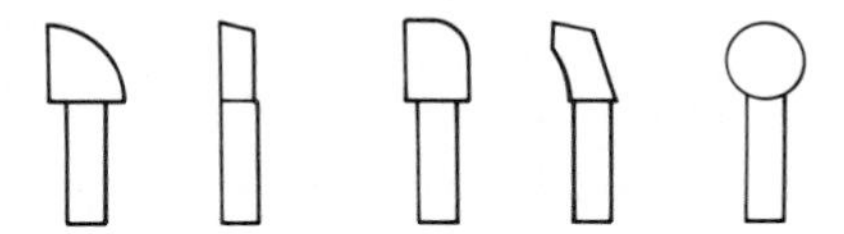

Fig. 2.2. Typical toolrest sections

what one has, but to some extent the choice of shape depends on whether a lot of large-diameter work is to be tackled: the larger the diameter, the greater the upward angle of the turning tool, and increasing this angle changes the point at which the tool is supported. Normally, this point, or fulcrum, needs to be as near the work as possible.

Toolrests can also be obtained which are curved in plan. One such rest approximates to a quarter-ellipse about 6 in (152 mm) in length, and has the mounting-pin set at one end of the curve.

This pattern is designed for bowl-turning: when hollowing the inside (*Figure 2.3*), the curved rest fits a typical bowl far better than a standard straight one and thus enables the tool to be supported close to the work, which is essential.

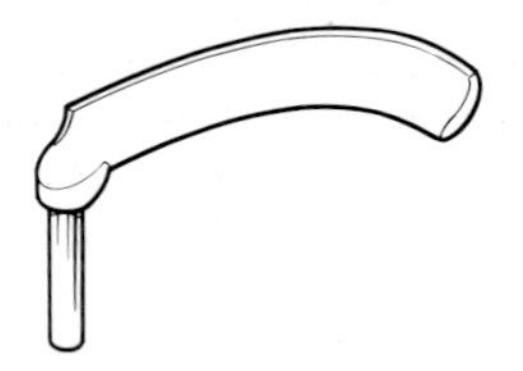

Fig. 2.3. Toolrest for bowl-turning

Toolrests and their supports were at one time often held by what was in effect a nut and bolt. Though this system worked satisfactorily, it required a spanner every time the toolrest had to be re-positioned. In some types of turning, particularly faceplate work, frequent resetting of the toolrest is essential and the need for a spanner is a nuisance. Most modern lathes now incorporate a tightening system with a built-in lever, so that toolrest adjustment is quick and simple (F, *Figure 2.1*).

Bed

There is a wide variety of different sections for the bed of a lathe, and a selection is shown in *Figure 2.4*. The tubular one has been used for many years by one well-known manufacturer: the slot at the top allows for connecting up with the toolrest saddle and the

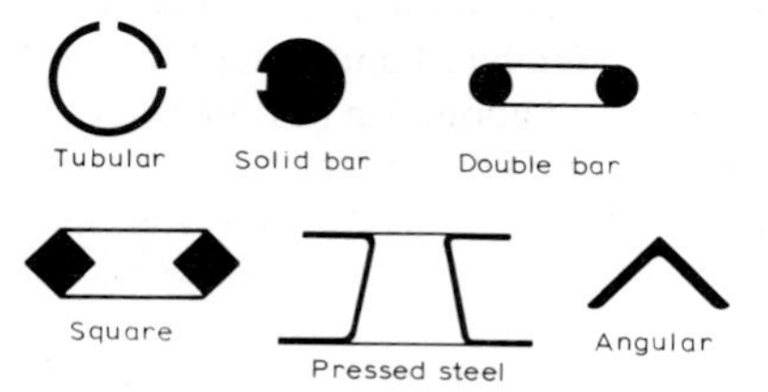

Fig. 2.4. Typical bed sections

tailstock, while the tightening levers act through the side slot on clamping blocks within the tube. The arrangement works well, with the possible disadvantage that the tube needs to be cleared of chippings from time to time.

The solid bar with the locating groove is the pattern used by the manufacturer of the lathes with swivelling headstocks. The system of holding toolrest saddle, tailstock, and other attachments is both simple and ingenious. They fit completely around the bar and are tightened by levers. A spring-loaded plunger at the rear of the component engages with the groove on the bed, and allows the component to be moved laterally. By releasing the plunger and slackening the lever, the component can be swung round, out of the way.

The other sections shown are used by different manufacturers. Note how the square bar is at 45 deg. This effectively increases the sectional height of the bar and thus its ability to resist deflection about this axis. The pressed-steel bar is used for power-drill attachments and also by overseas makers of lathes offered as attachments for basic woodworking machines.

Even in small machines of the heavy-duty type, the beds may be made of cast iron. Generally there is a leg, or foot, at the right-hand end of the bed, so that the whole lathe is supported horizontally (Q, *Figure 2.1*).

Tailstock

The tailstock (K, *Figure 2.1*) is usually a casting, the important part of the assembly being the barrel (I) which is an accurately machined steel bar which slides in a hole in the body. The sliding movement is controlled by a handwheel (J). It is desirable for the barrel to be capable of about 3 in (76 mm) travel, mainly because a chuck and bit are often held in the tailstock and used for boring a workpiece rotating on the headstock mandrel, and this requires a generous amount of movement. (Chapter 10 deals with boring on the lathe.)

The barrel can be locked in place in the tailstock by the clamping lever or barrel-lock provided in the top (H) or side of the tailstock, and the whole tailstock unit can be moved to any position along the bed (G), then locked to it by tightening the locking lever (L). The barrel is similar to the mandrel in that it may be hollow or solid and the left-hand end is bored out to a Morse taper. Headstock centre and tailstock centre should be exactly in line when checked either from the front or the top, but, unlike a metal-turning lathe, a certain amount of inaccuracy will not affect the work.

Better-quality lathes have a tailstock feature known as a 'self-ejecting barrel'. This means that as the barrel is withdrawn through the tailstock body by turning the handwheel, whatever is inserted in the taper within the barrel is automatically ejected.

Motor

A machine which is first and foremost a lathe rather than an attachment is almost certain to have its own motor. However, most lathes are supplied without the motor and one has to be bought separately. It is usual for the lathe manufacturer to provide some sort of platform or mounting for the motor, which is usually placed either behind or below the lathe.

The lathe manufacturer is likely to recommend a suitable motor, specifying its horsepower rating and armature speed. For most lathes of the size we are discussing, a ½ h.p. motor, with a speed of 1425 r.p.m., is the one usually recommended. Where a lot of large-diameter work is envisaged, a ¾ h.p. motor will have the extra reserve of power.

It is also likely that the lathe manufacturer will supply the pulley which has to be mounted on the motor spindle. Motor spindles differ in size, although ½ in (12.5 mm) and ⅝ in (16 mm) are the most common. This should be borne in mind when obtaining the motor as, obviously, the hole in the pulley and the spindle of the motor must fit precisely. With a motor of fairly low power, the usual method of securing the pulley on the spindle is by means of a setscrew of a pattern for which a socket-wrench or Allen key will be needed. The motor spindle will have a flat on it, and it is essential that the setscrew tightens on to this. Steps on the motor pulley will match those on the mandrel pulley.

If possible, a motor of the 'totally enclosed' type should be fitted. Woodturning creates a lot of fine dust, especially during glasspapering, and this dust can find its way into motors of the vented type, where it can become a fire hazard.

Belt

Transmission of power from motor to mandrel is almost certain to be by belt, and the type favoured by most lathe makers is the vee-belt (*Figure 2.5*). Because of its tapering section, this acts

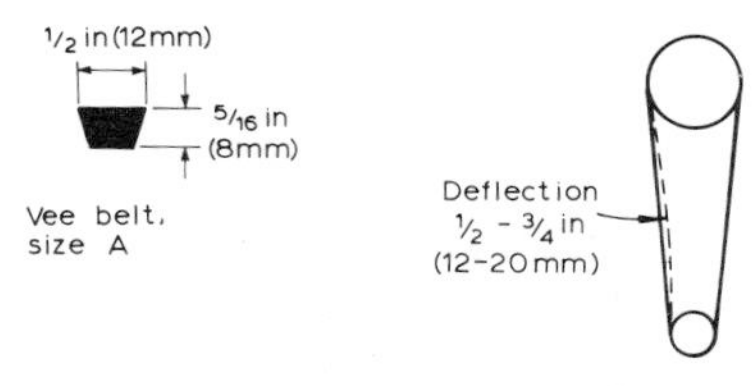

Fig. 2.5. Vee-belt dimensions and tension

rather like a wedge in the pulley; the greater the load, the more the belt is pulled into the groove and so the better the grip. The grip also depends on such factors as belt tension, condition of belt and pulleys, and the resistance imposed on the transmission. Vee-belts are made in a wide range of lengths, the circumference of the belt being the dimension specified. They are also made in three popular sections, referred to as M, A, and B in ascending order of size. The section normally used on lathes is A, which is ½ in (12.5 mm) across at the widest part.

At least two lathe manufacturers, one British and one Scandinavian, are using a belt system known as the 'Poly-V' belt. This belt is essentially flat in section, but on the inner surface is a series of small raised ribs of vee shape. Likewise, the pulleys have an overall flat profile, but with small vee grooves formed in the periphery. Thus the belt can be thought of as being like a number of miniature vee-belts, side by side and fixed together –

hence its name. It is claimed that the power-loss with this system is very low and that the belts are better able to negotiate small-diameter pulleys without slip or excessive flexing – and hence wear – of the belt.

Correct tensioning of the belt is important. If it is too tight, the result will be excessive wear of bearings and belt, overheating, and the risk of a damaged motor. If too slack, then belt-slip is likely, with loss of power and speed. For most installations, where the distance apart of the pulley-centres does not exceed 20 in (508 mm), the amount of distortion of the belt from a straight line, when pushed sideways by hand, should be about ½ in to ¾ in (12.5 to 16 mm), as in *Figure 2.5*.

Lathe speed

The importance of the speed of the lathe should be well understood by the turner, although it is often overstated: after all, most old lathes operated at a single speed and that was fairly slow. Certain types of turning, however, are best carried out at a particular speed, albeit approximate, which is why lathes should be capable of different speeds.

Modern lathes are made to operate over a range of speeds, expressed in terms of r.p.m. In practice, this is usually from about 700 to 3000. However, it is not the rate of revolution which is necessarily the critical factor, but the speed at which the wood passes the cutting tool, and this is a linear measurement. Consider the two following examples, assuming in both that the r.p.m. are 1000. First, a piece of wood 1 in (25 mm) across is being turned. Its circumference is approximately 3 in (76 mm), therefore peripheral speed is 1000 × 3 in, or 250 ft per minute. In the second case, the diameter of the wood is 12 in (305 mm) and so its circumference is approximately 38 in (965 mm). Speed at the periphery is 1000 × 38 in, which is 3166 ft per minute – that is, 12 times the peripheral speed of the 1 in diameter wood.

So in order to arrive at peripheral speeds which are approximately similar, the optimum r.p.m. depend on the diameter of the work being turned. However, the usual piece of turning is rarely as simple as a plain cylinder, whatever its diameter. A piece being turned between centres, for example, might have a diameter of 3 in at its greatest and 1 in at its minimum girth (*Figure 2.6*).

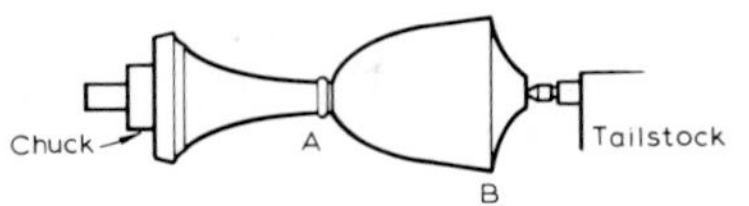

Fig. 2.6. Spindle-turning. Diameter at B is greater than at A, so different peripheral speeds for the same revolutions per minute are inevitable

With bowl or faceplate turning, the situation is even more variable. For any given r.p.m., the linear speed of a point on the wood increases as the point moves further from the centre. When turning a piece with a diameter which is at the maximum capacity of the lathe, the speed at the periphery could be as much as 20 times that at a point near the centre (*Figure 2.7*).

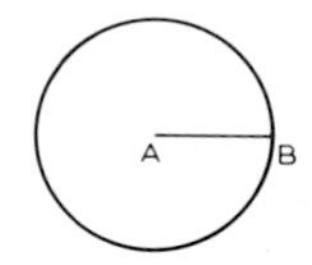

Fig. 2.7. Faceplate turning. The peripheral speed increases from A to B in direct proportion to the diameter for any speed of rotation

The following points summarise the practical application of these principles.

Use the highest speed for work of small diameter – up to, say, 1½ in (38 mm).

Use the low speed for large-diameter work, which can be defined as anything greater than the swing of the lathe.

It is often useful to start a piece of turning at a low speed and turn it to a cylindrical shape. Even a carefully prepared block of wood is not likely to be completely symmetrical when first mounted in the lathe, so, when first rotated, it will probably be out of balance, even if only slightly. This means that the roughing-out gouge will be cutting in a 'hit-and-miss' way to begin with, and it is better and safer if this happens at a low rather than a faster speed. An out-of-balance workpiece will also set up unequal forces about the centre of rotation and this will cause vibration. Excessive vibration puts a strain on the headstock bearings, and also on the mounting of the wood. The higher the speed, the greater the centrifugal effect if the wood is out of balance, and this could cause the wood to fly out of the lathe. A low initial speed is more important when turning large items where the effect of being out of balance is also more critical. Once the work has been made cylindrical, and so in balance, the speed can often be stepped up.

Low speed combined with too fast a sideways movement of the cutting tool can cause a spiral effect on the work. When working at a low speed, whatever the diameter of the work, lateral movement of tools – gouges in particular – should be slow and steady.

Too high a speed and incorrect tool manipulation can result in dust being removed from the wood instead of shavings. This is particularly so in faceplate work when a scraper is being used. Too high a speed when scraping can also cause excessive dulling of the tool's cutting edge.

From the above it will be realised that there is rarely an ideal speed to use, as a typical workpiece has a multiplicity of diameters on it. On a lathe with a four-speed headstock, the third highest speed will be found to be the one most often used for spindle work and the second highest for faceplate work. As with a lot of craftwork, personal experience becomes the best guide, given that the principles are understood.

Faceplate

Faceplates (*Figure 2.8*) are standard parts supplied with the basic machine. Average size is around 6 in (152 mm) in diameter, although both smaller and larger sizes are available for many machines. A faceplate is drilled through for screw-fixing purposes, and it often has a series of shallow vee-rings machined into its front surface to help in centralising the workpiece when mounting it. A faceplate should be mounted on the mandrel nose only when a fibre washer, or one of similar material, has been slipped over the mandrel screw, behind the faceplate.

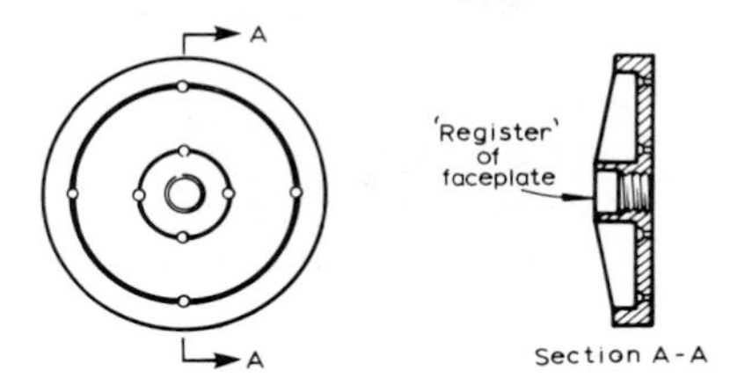

Fig. 2.8. Typical faceplate, about 6in (150mm) diameter

Failure to use such a washer can make it difficult to remove the faceplate. This is particularly so if the lathe is started without the faceplate having been fully screwed on to the thread, as starting the motor creates a snatching, and therefore a locking, effect. In any case, a faceplate should have some provision for removal when tight. This may be a hole in the centre part through which a tommy-bar can be passed, or a couple of flats machined on the same part, allowing the use of a spanner; hence the value of a locking mandrel.

Very large pieces of wood need careful preparation and mounting in the machine. The larger the workpiece, the greater is the risk of vibration, especially in the early stages of removing wood before the work has been made truly cylindrical. Hence the importance of careful preparation of large pieces before they are mounted in the lathe and of making them approximately cylindrical or at least symmetrical.

Centres

In turning between centres, the wood is mounted between headstock and tailstock. A live, or driving, centre is used in the headstock (*Figure 2.9*) and a dead centre in the tailstock (*Figure 2.10*).

There are different patterns of driving centres, of which three are illustrated. All have a central point and two or more sharp flanges which bite into and grip the wood. Both driving and dead

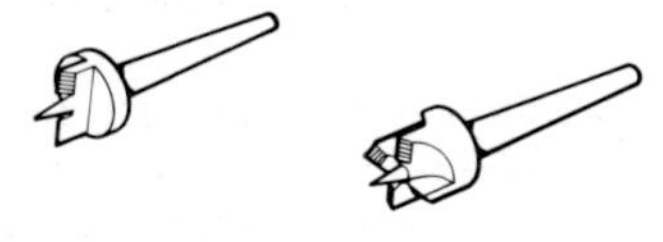

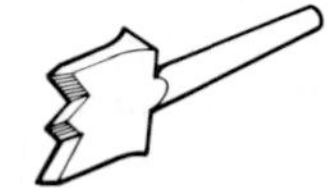

Fig. 2.9. Live, or driving, centres

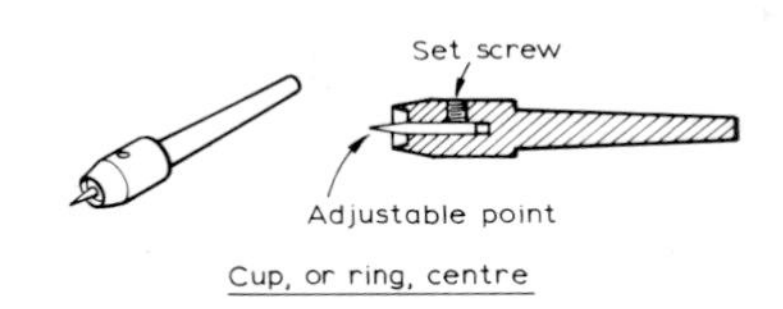

Fig. 2.10. Dead, or tailstock, centres

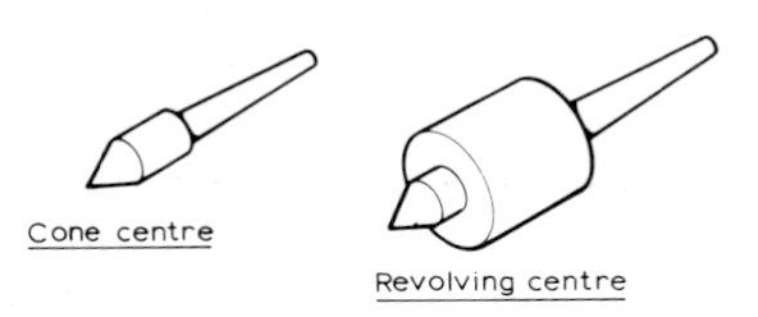

centres have a shank of No.1 morse taper, which fits into the head- or tail-stock.

The most common pattern of dead centre is the cone centre, which is simple but effective for the bulk of spindle turning. The ring, or cup, centre is also shown. This has a small central pin and a sharpened rim which is about ⅜ in (9.5 mm) in diameter. The central pin is for location only, the main support coming from the rim, which forms a shallow groove in the end of the wood. Cup centres can have either a fixed pin or one which is adjustable and is locked in position by a small setscrew in the side.

There is a slight tendency for a cone centre to act like a wedge in the end of the wood, and this can lead to splitting. The cup centre does not have this disadvantage because the support comes from the annular rim. This centre is useful, therefore, for turned items which are very slender at the end, and for laminated turnings where the cone centre's wedge effect could cause problems on the glueline.

A type of tailstock which originated on engineering lathes is the revolving centre. As the name suggests, the cone on which the wood is supported rotates with it, as it incorporates a ball-race, and so friction and burning are eliminated. This centre is also essential when using the turning mandrels described later.

Should an old lathe of the heavy-duty pattern ever be obtained secondhand, the mandrels might be bored out for No. 2 morse tapers. It is possible to obtain sleeves which convert a No. 1 taper component, such as a centre, to fit a No. 2 taper mandrel.

Grinding

An attachment which is not used in turning but is indirectly essential is a grinding wheel (*Figure 2.11*). So important is it to the turner that most lathe manufacturers offer some sort of grinding facility to be fitted as an attachment to the basic lathe.

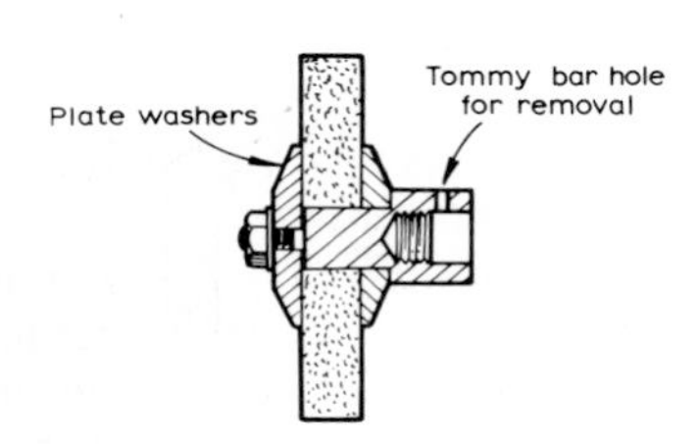

Fig. 2.11. Grindstone attachment. Section through mandrel assembly for left-hand mounting

Modifications

There are two modifications which can be carried out on standard lathes to improve versatility considerably.

Lever tailstock

Some tailstock barrels are operated by revolving a plain hand-wheel. On more elaborate machines, the barrel mechanism has a lever handle, or pair of handles, as well as the wheel. When work involves a lot of boring with a chuck and bit in the tailstock, a lever-operated tailstock is clearly more satisfactory than the plain handwheel.

The tailstock of a lathe can be modified for a lever operation, as shown in *Figure 2.12*; only limited metalworking skills are

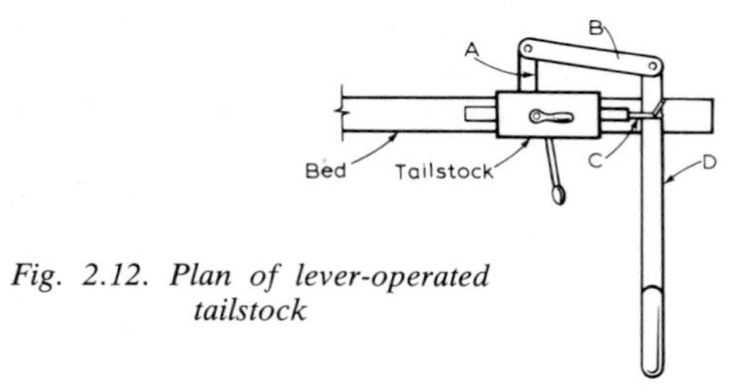

Fig. 2.12. Plan of lever-operated tailstock

needed. The modification in no way impairs the basic functioning of the tailstock, and reverting to operation by wheel is a matter of one or two minutes only. Cross-sectional sizes of the parts are only approximate, and so are the other dimensions, as they depend on the make of lathe.

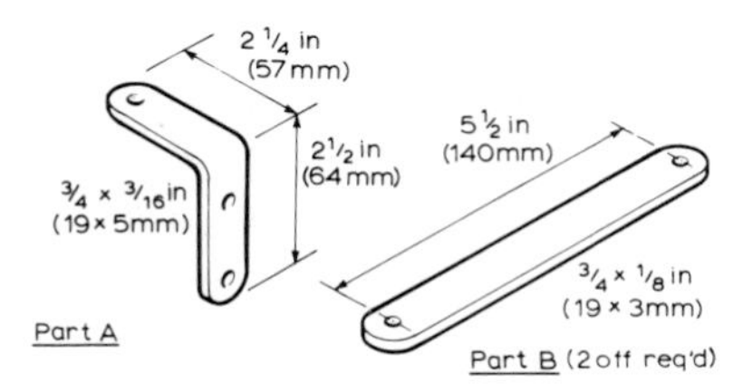

Fig. 2.13. Details of parts A and B for lever-operated tailstock

Start by preparing part (A) in *Figure 2.13*. This is marked out and drilled before shaping. The two lower holes are drilled at ¼in (6mm) clearance and the upper one at 3⁄16in (5mm) clearance. The part can be shaped by holding one end in a vice and bending the metal cold. It should be bent to such an extent that the upper portion will be horizontal when fixed. The two holes have to be positioned in this bracket to give the best fixing to the tailstock by means of bolts and nuts. The tailstock is drilled through for bolts. The bracket must also be fixed so that the projecting portion is accurately in line with the centre of the tailstock barrel. This is best done by centre-punching for one hole only and fixing the bracket with a single nut and bolt. The second hole is now drilled through the bracket just fixed so that, in effect, it is used as a templet. It may be possible to drill and tap the tailstock so that the bolts screw directly into the casting.

Two pieces are needed for part (A). They are cut to length and held together for marking out and rounding of the ends. They must be drilled while clamped together, the holes being 3⁄16 in clearance.

A piece of steel bar about 3 in by 3⁄4 in by 3⁄8 in (76 mm by 19 mm by 10 mm) is used for part (C) in *Figure 2.14*. After

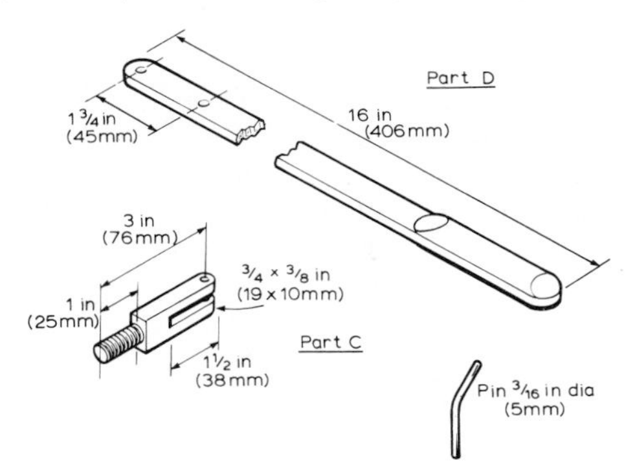

Fig. 2.14. Details of parts C and D for lever-operated tailstock

marking it to shape, the hole at the end is drilled to 3⁄16 in (5 mm) clearance. It is helpful if a hole is drilled at the base of the slot; waste can then be sawn out more easily. This slot is smoothed with a file so as to provide a slight clearance for the main lever.

The right-hand end of the bore on the tailstock barrel must now be threaded according to the diameter of the hole itself. The opposite end to the slot on part (C) is cut down to a width of 7⁄16in. Using a file, this is now prepared to approximately circular shape, allowing for the fact that the metal is 7⁄16in thick. This spigot is then threaded to 7⁄16in Whitworth to suit the thread cut in the barrel end. There will be 'thin' areas of thread down the sides because of the suggested metal thickness, but there will be adequate thread for secure anchorage. Check the size and type of threads on the machine being adapted, and use taps and dies to conform.

The overall length of the main lever is not important, but the suggested size has been found to be very satisfactory in use. Holes are drilled to 3⁄16in clearance, and the ends rounded. A comfortable handle needs to be made at the end of the lever. One way of achieving this is to Araldite a piece of wood to both sides of the metal and, when the adhesive has set, round over the ends and smooth with glasspaper.

Next, parts (A), (B), and (D) are assembled. For this either rivets or 3⁄16in bolts with washers and locknuts are used. Rivetting gives a rather neater job. Assembly must leave the parts free to move. The pin is a piece of 3⁄16in (5mm) rod, bent as shown in the drawing.

Before mounting the device on the lathe, it wil be necessary to remove the handwheel from the tailstock, probably by taking out one or two setscrews.

Foot clutch

Even more useful than the lever-operated tailstock is a foot-operated clutch (*Figure 2.15*). Frequently, when turning, it is necessary to stop the work to inspect the surface of the wood. This especially so in faceplate work, where it is difficult to produce a clean surface free of torn grain. A foot-clutch is also very useful on repetition turning, as it is possible to keep the motor running while work is being mounted and removed from the lathe and, if a screw-chuck is in use, the power of the motor –

controlled by the clutch – can be used to screw the wood on to the chuck. A clutch of the type illustrated was fitted to a lathe and used for about thirty years. Despite heavy use, only one new belt has been needed during that time.

To bring the work to a complete standstill it is necessary to have a faceplate on the left-hand side of the headstock. This faceplate is also used for rotating the work by hand so that any part of it can be inspected.

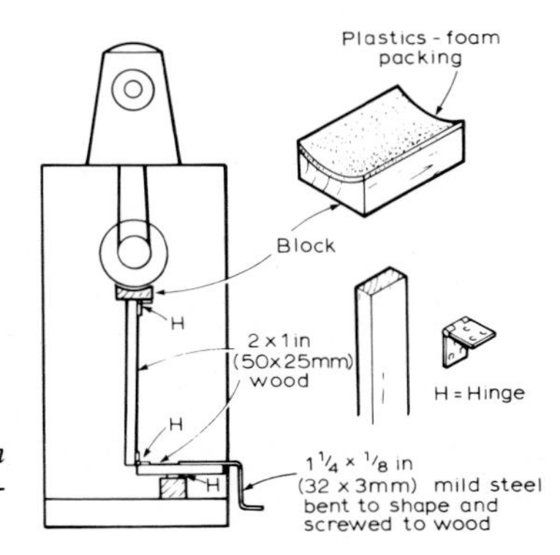

Fig. 2.15. Diagrammatic section and details of home-made foot-operated clutch

The drawing shows the general arrangement of this pattern of clutch, which is for a lathe where the motor is fitted below the machine. The motor is, as is usual, mounted on a hinged platform. When the clutch pedal is depressed, the motor and platform are swung up slightly, thus slackening the belt.

The cradle is a block of wood shaped to an approximate fit against the motor, and with foamed plastic cushioning added as shown. An excellent way of securing the cradle to the motor is by the use of two lengths of 'Flexiband', a continuous metal strip from which, with clamps and housing screws, any length of fastening can be made.

As a rear-mounted motor is always on a pivoted platform, it should not be difficult to devise a similar clutch where the upright member of the assembly passes through the top of the cabinet or bench and so to the underside of the motor.

3 Setting up work in the lathe

Before methods of holding work in the lathe are described, it is necessary to consider the preparation of the timber stock before it is mounted. With spindle-work, some allowance is usually needed in excess of the finished length. This depends on the nature of the job and the method of mounting, but an allowance of about 1 in (25 mm) is suitable if the work is to be held between centres.

Preparing the wood

It is normal to start with a block of wood which has been sawn to square section then, by removing the arrises, reduced to an octagonal shape. While it does not have to be an exact octagon, the nearer it is, the better for working. This is achieved fairly easily by gauging (*Figure 3.1*): first draw the diagonals across the ends, then mark out with the gauge and plane away the arrises by hand or machine.

There are two reasons for this preparation: it is quicker to remove the arris waste by plane and, more important, turning is safer because the toolrest can be placed closer to the wood. The larger the original square of wood to be turned, the more is it advisable to prepare the work as described. The reason for this is shown diagrammatically in *Figure 3.2*.

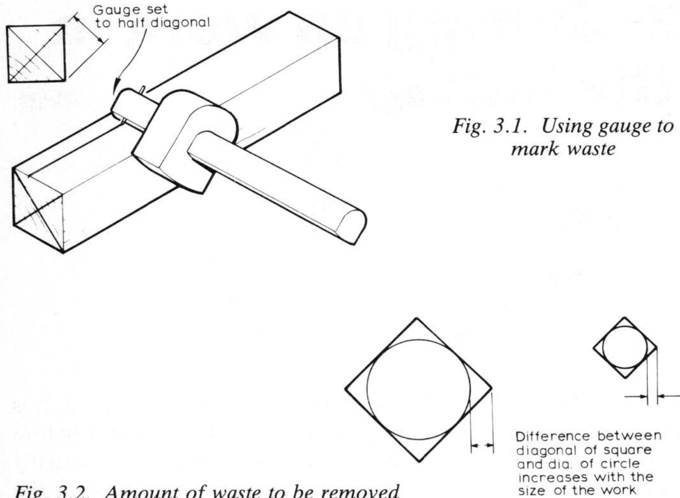

Fig. 3.1. Using gauge to mark waste

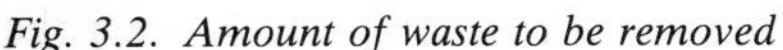

Fig. 3.2. Amount of waste to be removed

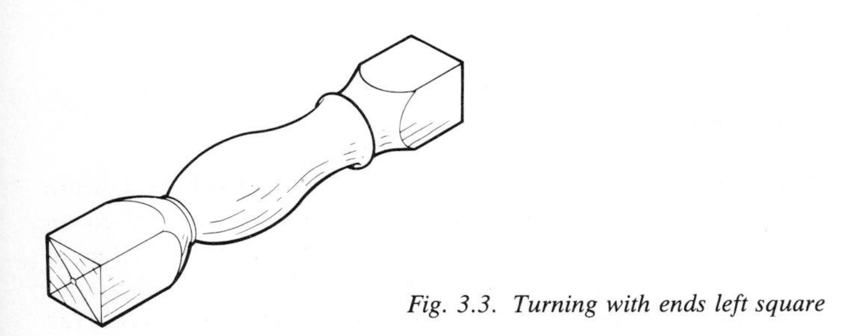

Fig. 3.3. Turning with ends left square

It is not unusual for turning to be restricted to the middle of the wood, with one or both ends left square, as in the chair or stool leg shown in *Figure 3.3*. For such jobs, the wood should be properly planed to the size required for the non-turned part, which is almost always square in section. As initial preparation to octagonal shape cannot be done, extra care is needed during the early stages of turning.

Fitting live centres

When preparing work for mounting between centres, it is well worth while to make a diagonal sawcut for the live-centre prongs, as shown in *Figure 3.4.* The harder the wood and the

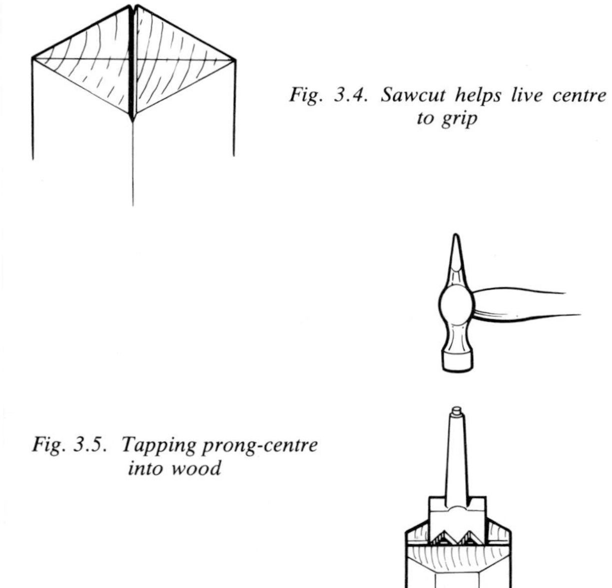

Fig. 3.4. Sawcut helps live centre to grip

Fig. 3.5. Tapping prong-centre into wood

greater the diameter, the more need there is for this sawcut. Its purpose is to give a positive anchorage for the live centre. If it is not made, the resistance the wood offers to the cutting tool is greater than the grip between live centre and wood, with the result that the centre revolves but the wood does not. Centres must be sharpened from time to time with a file.

Another method of fixing the live centre securely is to tap the centre gently into the end of the wood, as shown in *Figure 3.5.*

The centre should be struck with a hammer only if the end of the taper has a little step machined in it, as in *Figure 3.6*: if the end of the taper is plain, as in *Figure 3.7,* it must not be struck with a hammer as this will burr it over slightly, which will spoil the fit of the centre in the mandrel.

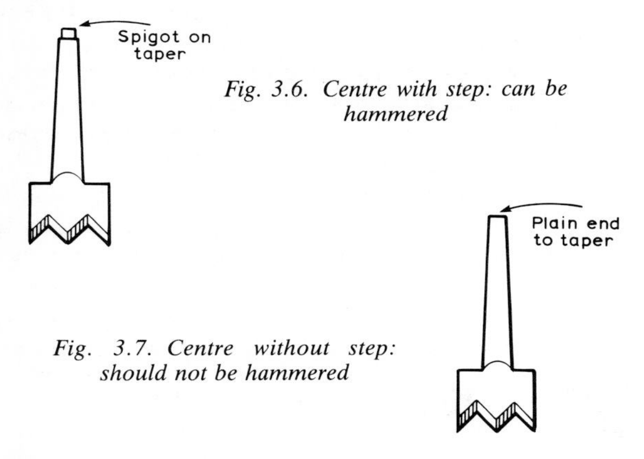

Fig. 3.6. Centre with step: can be hammered

Fig. 3.7. Centre without step: should not be hammered

The right-hand end of the wood does not need much preparation, but it helps if the middle of the wood is pricked with a bradawl to ensure that the centre locates itself properly.

With both cone- and ring-centres, there is the problem of friction created between a moving and a stationary surface. It is quite possible for this friction to become so great that the heat generated causes burning of the wood, so the support provided by the centre is reduced as the wood becomes charred. Although it is often suggested that a spot or two of oil should be applied to the end of the wood to act as a lubricant, oil can penetrate fairly easily into end-grain and cause discolouring, as well as leading to possible difficulties with the finishing process. A far better lubricant is paraffin wax, applied by rubbing a candle across the wood so that some of the wax is forced into the bradawl hole.

In spindle-turning, in which the grain is parallel to the bed of the lathe, the work is not always held between centres. Preparation of wood where some form of chuck or special holding device is being used is described next.

Faceplate turning

Preparation for faceplate turning is just as important as for spindle work. If a bowl is to be turned, then the wood for the job may have been bought as a turning disc. These bowl blanks are bandsawn circular and sold for the purpose. Their edges are often coated with paraffin wax in an attempt to seal them against absorption of moisture and so keep the moisture content of the block stable after it has been seasoned, probably in a kiln. Bowl blanks of this type need no particular preparation before turning and are ready for mounting.

When a commercially prepared disc is not being used, the wood should be cut to a circular shape, preferably with a bandsaw. Otherwise, thinnish material can be cut with a bow- or coping-saw, and thicker wood will have to be cut to octagonal shape with a handsaw. Assuming that the wood is initially cut to a square, then the largest possible circle should be marked in,

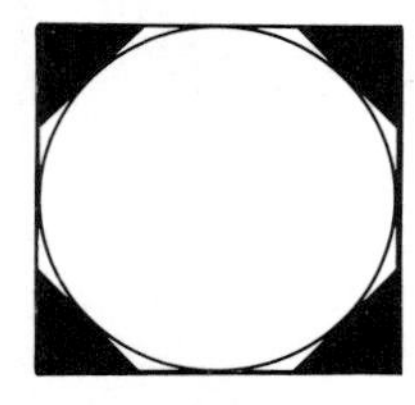

Fig. 3.8. Waste to be removed for faceplate turning

with the point of the compasses on the intersection of the diagonals (*Figure 3.8*). Where the turning is very large, say above 9 in (228 mm), then the method of sawing shown in *Figure 3.9* is advisable.

Bowls are usually turned in two distinct stages: the outside is turned first, then, after remounting on the faceplate or chuck, the inside is completed. When the work is mounted on a faceplate and not in any form of special chuck, there are two methods of fixing it. The first one is to screw the faceplate directly to the wood. As the screws go into what will be the hollow side of the bowl, relatively long ones can be used to be sure of a good hold. If four screws are used, then a length which gives about 1 in penetration is normally adequate.

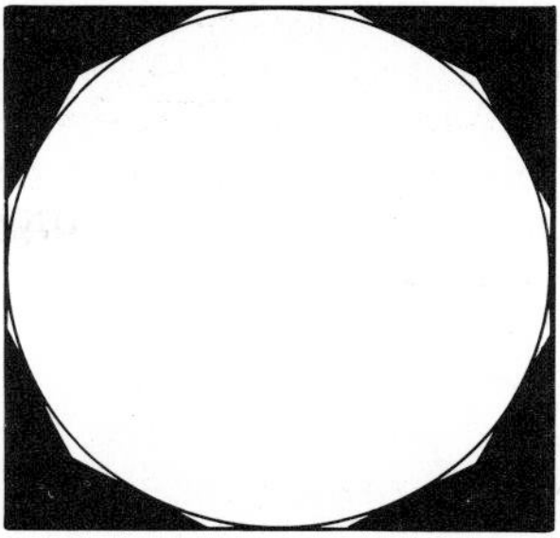

Fig. 3.9. Method of removing waste on work of large diameter

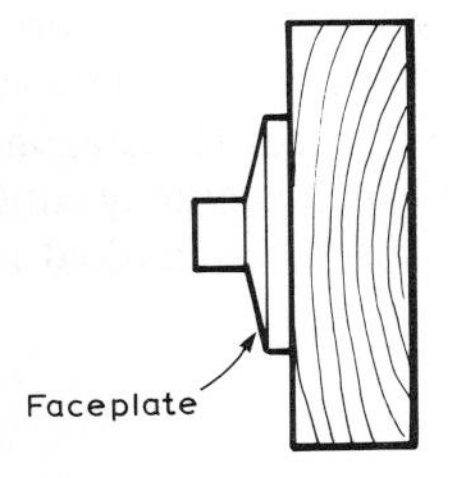

Fig. 3.10. Work fixed directly to faceplate

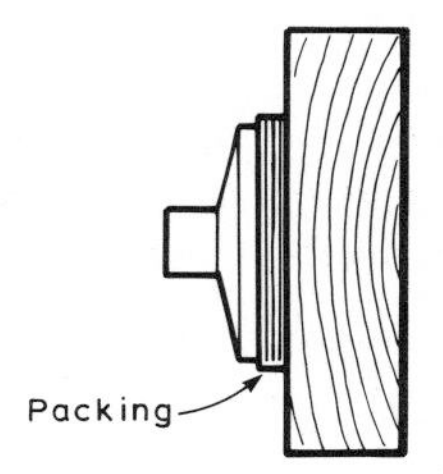

Fig. 3.11. Packing between faceplate and work

The second method is first to screw a packing-piece to the wood block. This may be anything from ½in to 1in thick; plywood is frequently used. The faceplate is then screwed to the packing-piece. These methods are illustrated in *Figures 3.10* and *3.11*.

Remounting

It is when the work is reversed that complications can arise with faceplate mounting. The inside must be concentric with the outside, or the bowl will finish up with its walls of unequal thicknesses, as shown on plan in *Figure 3.12*. The other main concern when mounting the work for hollowing is the length of the screws used. If they are too short, they will have insufficient holding power; if too long, then the thickness of wood left in the base of the bowl will be excessive, restricting its capacity and probably making it look rather clumsy. Long screws also increase the risk that the tool will strike them during turning.

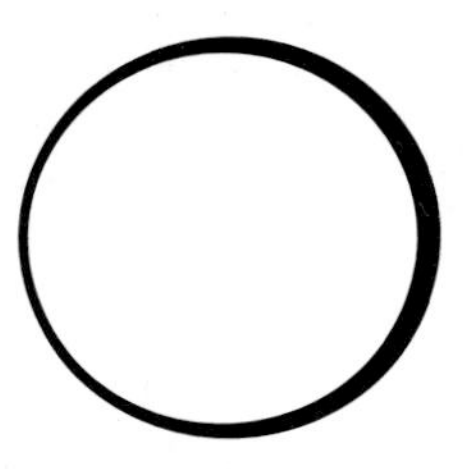

Fig. 3.12. Eccentric mounting results in walls of unequal thickness

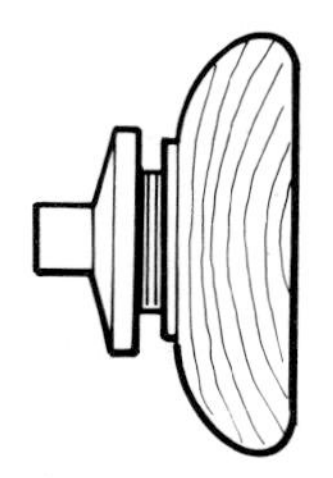

Fig. 3.13. Packing used is smaller than faceplate

As a rule, the screws used to fix the bowl base to the faceplate should be of such a length that they do not penetrate the wood more than ½in. (Check all screws used in case there is an odd one of excess length.) The pilot-holes for the screws also need to be made with care, as oversize holes reduce the grip of the screws, and excessively long holes may penetrate the surface. It is common practice to use, between plate and bowl, a piece of packing smaller in diameter than the faceplate (*Figure 3.13*). This is to enable the outside of the bowl to be glasspapered, and the finish to be applied, without the faceplate getting in the way.

An alternative to screwing the work to the faceplate for the hollowing stage is to glue the wood to the packing piece. In fact, they are not glued directly to each other but to a sheet of brown wrapping-paper between them. On completion of turning, a chisel is gently forced into the glue line to separate the paper and free the bowl. This is a technique best reserved until some competence has been gained, but it is a good one, and it enables quite thin bottoms to be made without risk of hitting screws or exposing screw holes.

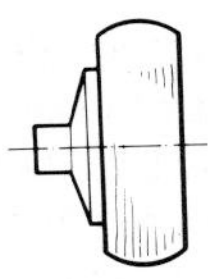

Fig. 3.14. Some shapes can be turned entirely from one side

A bowl of the shape shown in *Figure 3.14* can be turned from one side after it has been fixed to the faceplate. Because it does not have to be remounted, the base of the block must planed flat before mounting, especially if it is fairly thin, such as a top for a small table.

Distortion of bowls

Even when a bowl is to be turned from a well-seasoned block, there is often one way of forming the bowl, relative to the grain, which is better than the other. If the end-grain on the edge of the block is found to be like *Figure 3.15,* then it matters little which

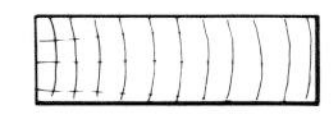

Fig. 3.15. Annual rings seen with radial sawing

way round the bowl is formed. Such a block would have been cut from a plank which had been 'radially sawn'. This method of conversion produces stock which is reasonably stable – that is, not likely to warp and distort. But when the annual rings on a turning blank are examined, they will often be found to be as shown in *Figure 3.16.* If any further or drying out takes place, even before turning, such a piece will tend to take up the cupped shape shown in *Figure 3.17.* Cupping is usually away from the heart-side of the wood, because shrinkage takes place in different directions relative to the annual rings.

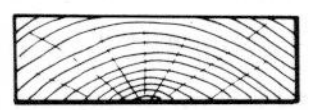

Fig. 3.16. Annual rings seen with tangential or slash sawing

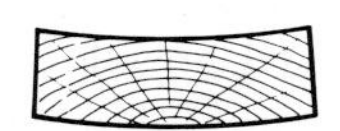

Fig. 3.17. Tangential-sawn stock will tend to 'cup'

When a block is hollowed on one side, with solid wood across the opposite side, as in a bowl, then a particular problem can arise. If any further drying out takes place, its effects will be more pronounced on the hollow side than on the solid side. This is because on the hollow side there is only the thin wall of the bowl to resist the shrinkage which accompanies loss of moisture, whereas on the base, there is some wood across the whole width. Because of this, the bowl can take on the shape shown in *Figure 3.18*.

If the faults shown in *Figures 3.17* and *3.18* are combined, the result may be a bowl which will distort so much that it can

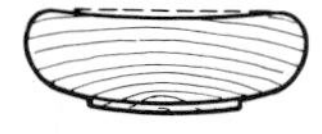

Fig. 3.18. Warped effect of turning tangential stock with heart-side down

become noticeably oval. On the other hand, if the block is arranged so that the effects illustrated react against each other, the resulting bowl is more likely to be reasonably free from distortion. The rule, therefore, is to have the annual rings as shown in *Figure 3.19,* where the heart-side, on top, is the side to

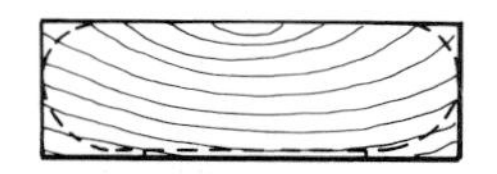

Fig. 3.19. Preferred way to turn bowl relative to the annual rings

be hollowed and the lower side, which is away from the heart, is to be the base.

So the following rules emerge for faceplate-work and bowl-turning in particular. First, use timber which is well seasoned. If the timber may not be as dry as it should be, then store it indoors for several weeks before using it – preferably where there is gentle heat. Second, examine the annual rings and follow the procedures shown by *Figure 3.19*.

Screw-chuck

Probably the most common way of holding work in the lathe, other than on the faceplate or between centres, is by the screw-chuck. Various patterns are available, but all are based on a standard woodscrew. As only a single screw is used, the screw-chuck is limited to fairly small and light work. This is particularly true where the screw is in end-grain, as screws never hold so well in end- as they do in side-grain. The screw-chuck is especially useful where the whole of the right-hand end of the work has to be shaped, as for a doorknob, or where the end has to be hollowed, as for an egg cup. The screw-chuck can be used whatever the direction of the grain.

A sectional drawing of a simple pattern of screw-chuck is shown in *Figure 3.20.* Although an ordinary woodscrew is used, it is necessary to saw off its head. The gauge of the screw must match the hole in the chuck – the hole normally is made to suit a

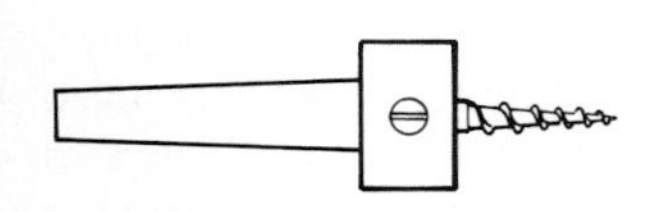

Fig. 3.20. Simple screw-chuck

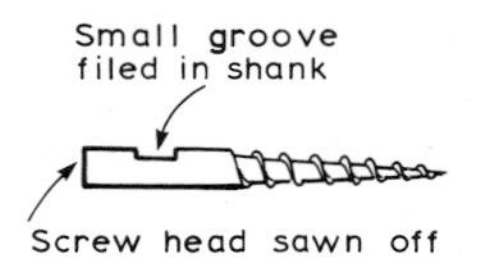

Fig. 3.21. Preparing screw for screw-chuck

No. 12 or 14 screw. As the screw is held in place by a grubscrew, it helps to prevent it from working loose and withdrawing if a small flat slot is filed in it as shown in *Figure 3.21*: the grubscrew bears on this flat. The disadvantage of this simple variety of screw-chuck is that it can tend to work loose in the headstock.

Depending on the nature and size of the work, it is often possible to use a screw-chuck of any pattern in conjunction with support from the tailstock centre. It will probably be possible to use such support only while turning the bulk of the external surface, leaving the extreme right-hand end to be completed after the tailstock has been withdrawn. The same technique can be adopted if the work is to be hollowed, like an egg cup: support can then be given by the tailstock up to the hollowing-out stage.

An excellent type of screw-chuck is shown in *Figure 3.22.* It is based on the use of a No. 14 woodscrew, of which various lengths can be used. It is also possible to adjust the amount by which the screw projects from the chuck body (A). The slotted and threaded plug (B) is screwed into the body from the back or taper end. The screw is next slipped through the collet (C) and this is screwed into the front of the body until the shank of the

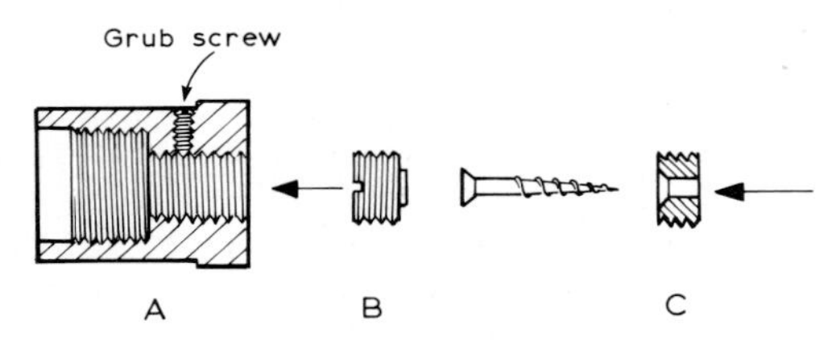

Fig. 3.22. Exploded sectional sketch of adjustable screw-chuck

woodscrew is under the grubscrew. The plug is then tightened down on the screw shank, and finally the grubscrew is tightened down. The chuck is then fitted to the mandrel nose. This chuck is available in diameters of 1½in (38mm) and 2½in (63mm). Produced by one of the leading British lathe manufacturers, it is available with threads to suit those to be found on most popular lathes.

Another variation of the screw-chuck is shown in *Figure 3.23.* This has a diameter of about 3in (76mm). The screw is brazed on, which may be a disadvantage but, on the other hand, gives the chuck a dual function. The part holding the woodscrew is secured in place by three setscrews. Once these are removed and the outer portion freed, the rear half of this combination becomes a small faceplate. The makers produce this chuck for their own lathe, for both right- and left-hand ends of the mandrel nose.

When mounting end-grain on a screw chuck, it is very important that the end of the wood is both square and flat. If it is not square, the wood will tend to oscillate. Not only will this cause vibration, it will reduce the maximum diameter which can be turned. If the end is not flat, the single screw will not hold it firm, which means that the block will tend to wobble when the turning tools are applied.

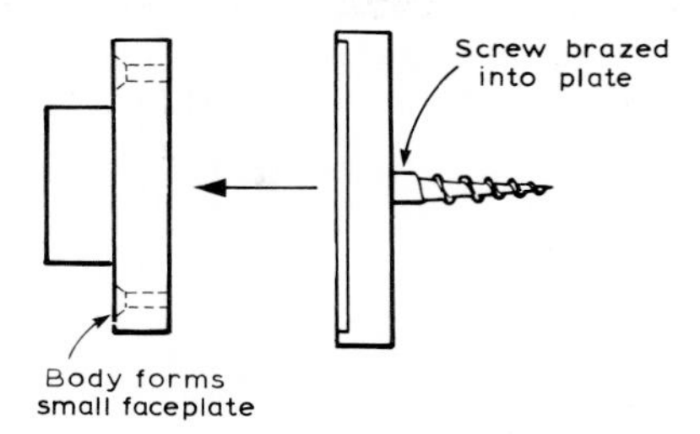

Fig. 3.23. Combined screw chuck and small faceplate

The screw in the chuck grips the wood more positively if the threads are filed slightly. A small file is used so that the ridge, or crown, of the thread is sharpened slightly and also made thinner. This is carried out with one hand holding the file and the other rotating the mandrel. The sharper, finer thread cuts more cleanly into the wood fibres, instead of partly compressing and partly forcing them out of position.

Ring-chuck

A device which gives a very positive grip to the workpiece is the ring-chuck, made by many lathe manufacturers as an 'extra' for their machines. A sectional drawing of this chuck is shown in *Figure 3.24.* Before the work can be mounted, preliminary turning between centres is needed. The object of this is not just to make the wood cylindrical, but to form the lip which is required at one end. It is this lip that the ring part of the chuck grips, and so the diameter of the lip – and its thickness and bevelled edge – have to be formed fairly accurately if the full holding power of the chuck is to be obtained. The advantage of this chuck lies in the strength of its grip on the wood, which allows work which projects a considerable way to be firmly held at only one end. On the other hand, it has two disadvantages: first it tends to be a little wasteful of wood, because of the initial

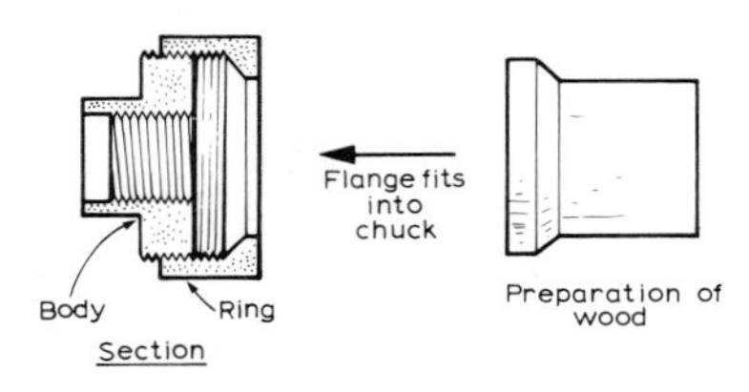

Fig. 3.24. Ring-chuck

turning needed to produce the lip, which is of larger diameter than any part of the completed turning. Secondly, only work of a diameter which will pass through the ring can be tackled.

Cup-chuck

Although cup-chucks have been an accepted method of holding certain types of work for many years, only one size was available for any given make of lathe. Now, a maker has produced a wide range of sizes and variations of the cup-chuck, designed to fit almost any make of lathe.

The basis of this chuck is its tapering hollow, or bore, into which the wood is placed. For maximum benefit from the system, it is advisable to use a pair of them, one designed to be held in the headstock, the other in the tailstock. The headstock fitting screws on to the mandrel of the lathe of the same maker, or on to an arbor which has a Morse taper to fit the mandrel of any lathe with a Morse taper socket. The tailstock end is held in what is in effect a revolving centre (*Figure 3.25*).

Sizes available give a holding capacity from as little as ¼ in (6 mm) square to 4 in (101 mm) square or from ⅜ in (9 mm) diameter to 2⅜ in (35 mm) diameter. Six pairs make up the set, each pair except the largest accommodating a limited range of

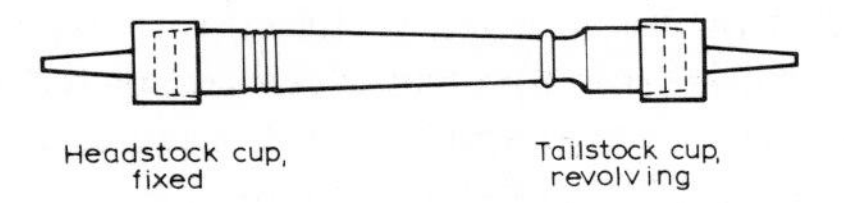

Fig. 3.25. Cup-chucks

Fig. 3.26. Symmetrical sections which can be held in cup-chuck

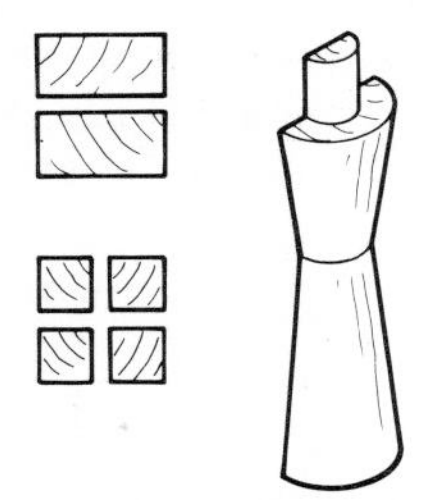

Fig. 3.27. Split turning which can be held in cup-chuck

sizes. The largest has three steps within the cup and is specially intended to take square stock of 2 in, 3 in and 4 in.

These chucks, which rely entirely on friction for gripping, have the following advantages. The workpiece can be instantly removed and, when replaced, will always run true. They accept work which is other than square or round in section, provided it is symmetrical, as in *Figure 3.26.* They accept work of a composite nature. This method of chucking is therefore ideal for 'split' turnings, the two most common of which are shown in *Figure 3.27.* Their use minimises waste at ends and eliminates the need for 'parting off'.

Universal chuck

One of the outstanding innovations of recent years is a universal chuck, known as the 'six-in-one'. It is as an internal expanding dovetail chuck that it has made its mark as a revolutionary method of holding and revolving the workpiece.

Traditional methods of holding the wood when bowl-turning have changed little in many years, and their problems and limitations have already been described: the initial stage of turning is fairly straightforward; it is when the work is reversed for the hollowing stage that difficulties arise. The six-in-one chuck offers a strong, sound, and reliable way of holding work for faceplate turning without the use of screws or additional waste to the work. Furthermore, the wood remains accurately concentric when mounted in the chuck, even if the work is removed and remounted several times.

Principles of the six-in-one chuck are shown in *Figure 3.28.* It can be likened to a collet-chuck working in reverse – that is,

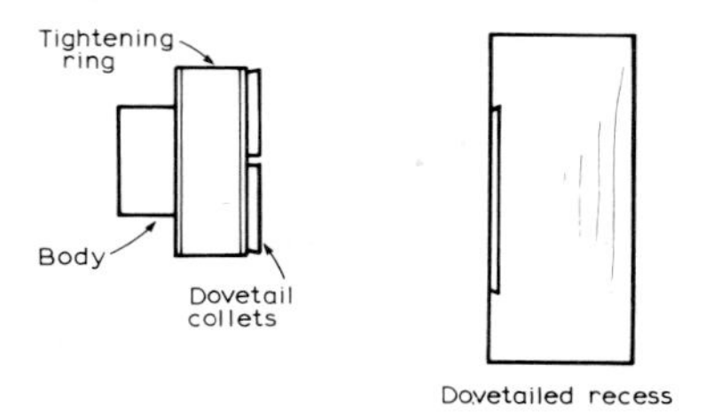

Fig. 3.28. Expanding dovetail chuck

expanding rather than contracting. As the outer ring of the assembly is tightened, the four dovetail segments are forced outwards and internally grip a shallow recess already prepared in the workpiece. This recess usually need not be more than ⅛ in deep and is made with an undercut edge to enable the edge of the segments to exert a dovetail effect. The wood is initially held on a faceplate to enable the outside and base to be prepared and the essential recess to be turned.

With the dovetail segments removed, the chuck can be used as a ring-chuck. The advantages and disadvantages of the ring-chuck have already been discussed; some of the limitations of the ring-chuck are overcome by the variation known as the 'split ring', another feature of the six-in-one. This is a two-part ring as shown in *Figure 3.29.* One advantage of the split ring is that the maximum diameter of the work is not restricted by the ring; work up to 4 in (102 mm) diameter – or even more – can be securely held. It is also less wasteful of material; the preparation needed is a groove cut as shown in *Figure 3.30* to the dimensions

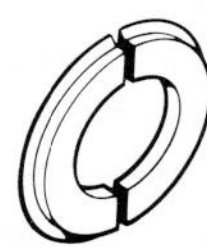

Fig. 3.29. Split ring

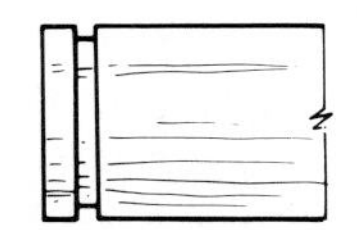

Fig. 3.30. Preparing wood for split-ring mounting

given in the instructions provided with the chuck. If *Figure 3.30* is compared with *Figure 3.24,* it will be seen that when preparing the wood it is not necessary to start with a diameter in excess of that required for the actual turning, as is necessary with a standard ring-centre.

The six-in-one can also be used as a screw-chuck. A centre boss is drilled and countersunk at the rear for a No. 14 woodscrew. This is held in place by a grubscrew through the side of the boss, which is held in place by the split ring and outer ring. *Figure 3.31* shows this central boss.

Another use of the universal chuck is as an internal screw-chuck. There only the body is used. Work is prepared to a

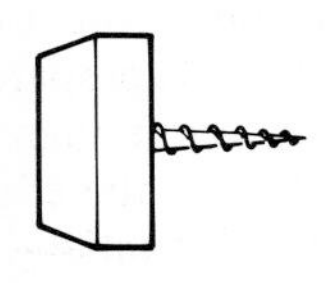

Fig. 3.31. Centre boss of six-in-one chuck

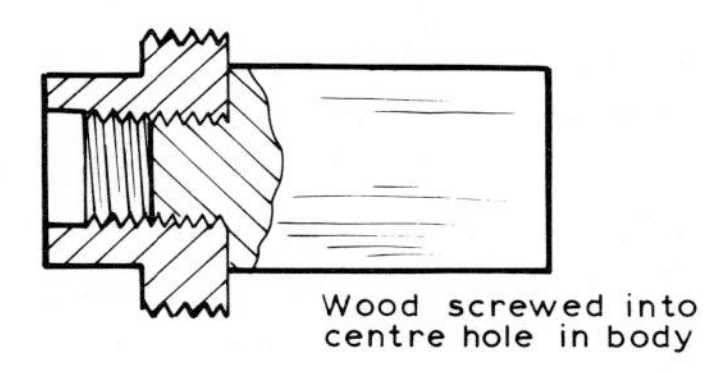

Fig. 3.32. Internal screw-chuck

cylindrical shape between centres, and a spigot is 'threaded' into the hole (see *Figure 3.32*). The tailstock is used to help centralise the work, and also to apply pressure as the wood is screwed into the chuck as far as it will go. The grip will remain at its strongest if turning is completed without removing the wood – removal and remounting tends to result in a slightly less positive hold.

Finally, and again using the body only, the chuck can be used as a small faceplate, with provision for three fixing screws.

The six-in-one chuck fully lives up to the claims made by the firm that markets it. It solves most of the problems of holding the workpiece in the lathe, the expanding collet being the big breakthrough, especially for bowl-turning. It is made to fit more than 20 different makes of lathe at the right-hand side of the mandrel, and for many a model is made with a thread which fits the outside, or left-hand side, of the lathe.

Coil-spring chuck

A chuck which has appeared on the market during recent years is known as the coil-spring chuck. The principle of this device is illustrated in section in *Figure 3.33*. The spring is a continuous coil, held in place under its own tension, but capable of being compressed and so reduced in diameter by tightening the outer ring.

This chuck is mainly intended for gripping end-grain work of fairly large diameter, particularly for work which has to be hollowed, such as vases and boxes. Initially, the wood is mounted between centres and the end prepared as shown in *Figure 3.34*. At this end a groove, in which the coil is located, has

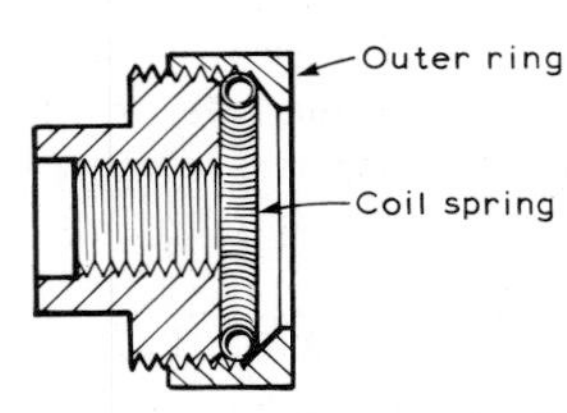

Fig. 3.33. Coil-spring chuck

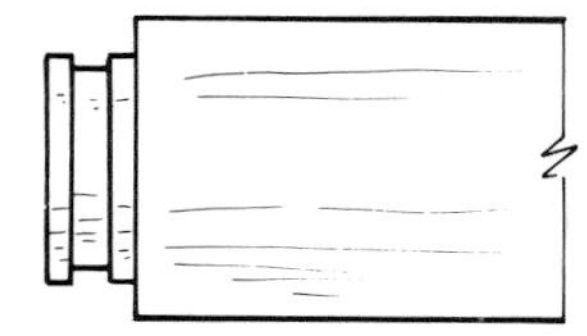

Fig. 3.34. Preparing wood for coil-spring chuck

to be formed. To mount the work in the chuck, the end is inserted as far as it will go and the outer ring is tightened with a special spanner. The coil is thus compressed and forced into the groove, thereby holding the wood.

Although the coil is the main feature of this chuck, it can be used in other ways. With outer ring and spring removed, the main body can be used on its own as a faceplate. It is also provided with a split ring, it has a woodscrew adapter, and it can be used as an internal-threaded chuck.

Collet-chuck

Another chuck of fairly recent introduction is the collet-chuck, a method of holding work which has long been in use on metal-turning lathes. The principles of the collet-chuck are shown in *Figure 3.35*. As the outer ring is tightened, the conical shape of

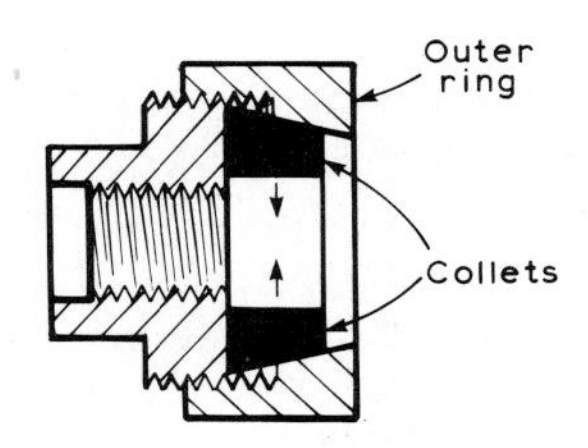

Fig. 3.35. Collet-chuck

the interior faces forces the collets together, thus gripping the wood externally. A set of collets will hold work over a limited range of diameters as the adjustability of a set of collets of any given size is restricted to ¼ in or so. The chuck is purchased with a set of three collets, enabling wood from ⅜ in diameter to be held. For work of larger diameter, it is first necessary to turn a spigot of about 1 in diameter and 1 in long so that this can be held in the chuck.

All chucks which screw on to the nose of the mandrel of the headstock should, like faceplates, be used only with a fibre washer behind them.

Mandrels

Woodturning mandrels are another new idea and one is shown in *Figure 3.36.* They are precision-ground from carbon steel, with a Morse taper shank at one end. The opposite end is 'centred' with a small dimple, enabling it to be supported on a revolving centre. Such mandrels are made in five diameters from ¼in (6mm) to 1in (25mm), lengths increasing with the diameters from 3in (76mm) to 15in (381mm). Clamping washers and nuts are included.

These mandrels provide a convenient way of holding work which has a hole in its centre and are particularly useful when a small batch of identical pieces has to be turned, such as a set of four toy-wheels. These mandrels, like the collet-chuck, are products of the firm which makes the six-in-one universal chuck.

Home-made devices

Most experienced turners devise many ways of their own for holding work, especially if it is unusual. An example is the simple wooden mandrel shown in *Figure 3.38* holding a napkin ring. The mandrel is turned with a slight taper and is normally used as it was turned – between centres. Such mandrels can also be held in a ring or similar chuck, thus leaving the right-hand end free. Alternatively, the wooden mandrel can be mounted, turned, and used on steel mandrels as shown in *Figure 3.36.*

A similar wooden mandrel is shown in *Figure 3.39.* Here the mandrel is held in a ring-chuck or on a screw-chuck. It is used for holding small boxes and similar hollow items while the outside and underside are completed, and during polishing. If there is a tendency for the workpiece to slip on the mandrel, a couple of small pins are driven into the end of the mandrel. The projecting heads are then snipped off and a small file is used to form points, which grip the bottom of the box and prevent it from slipping.

Sooner or later the turner will have to tackle a very small piece of work for which a collet-chuck is not available. Often such small items are made from dowelling, in which case the simple home-made chuck shown in *Figure 3.40* can solve the problem of holding the dowel. Assuming the dowel is ⅜in or ½in in

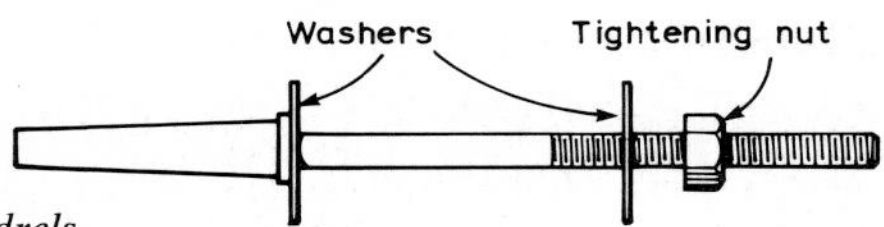

Fig. 3.36. Turning-mandrels

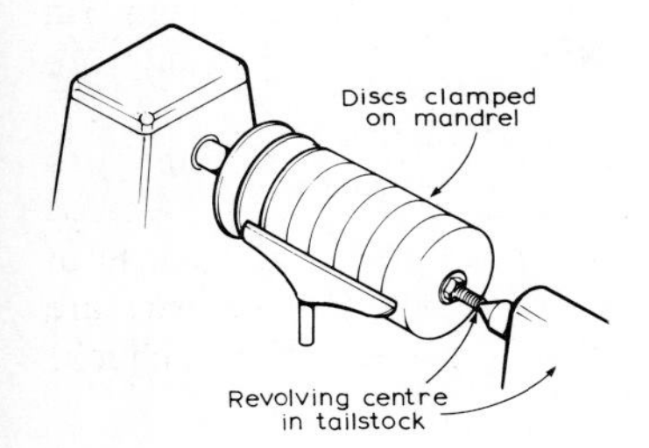

Fig. 3.37. Turning-mandrel in use

Fig. 3.38. Wooden mandrel in use holding napkin ring

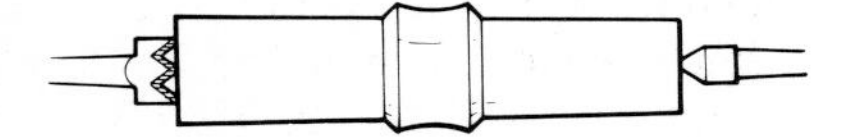

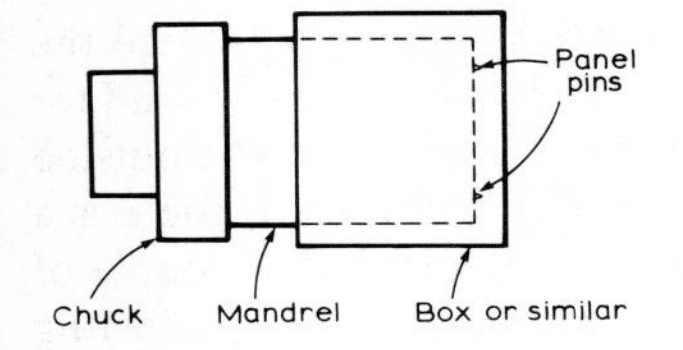

Fig. 3.39. Wooden mandrel fixed to chuck

Fig. 3.40. Simple collet-chuck

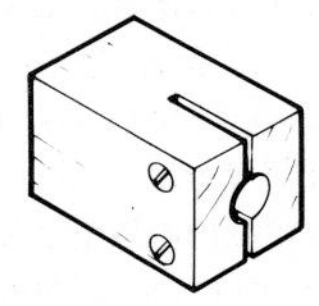

diameter, the block from which the chuck is to be made needs to be about 2 in by 1¼ in by 1¼ in (50 mm by 31 mm 31 mm). The block is mounted on a screw-chuck and the central hole to take the dowel is bored on the lathe. The block is then sawn as shown and pilot-holes for screws are bored in one side. When the dowel is inserted, the screws are tightened. This is, in effect, a simple collet-chuck.

Sometimes the turner is called upon to form a hole of special section in a piece of wood, where the work is entirely internal and screw-holes are not wanted in the finished job; such a problem is shown in *Figure 3.41*. While it is possible to mount

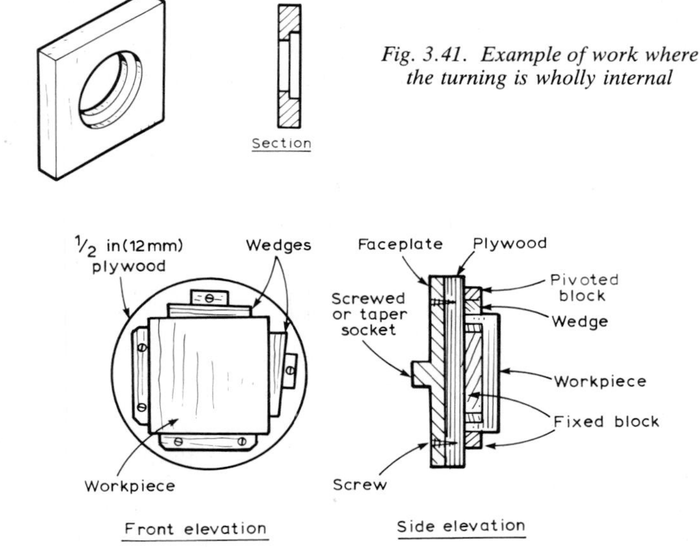

Fig. 3.41. Example of work where the turning is wholly internal

Fig. 3.42. Jig for holding work while turning shaped central hole

the work on a screw-chuck for one side of the turning, difficulties arise when reversing the wood. A faceplate jig can be used, as shown in *Figure 3.42*.

To make a jig of this type, a plywood base is first screwed to the faceplate and turned to a true fit. Next, the corner blocks are screwed in place on setting-out lines scribed on the plywood. Blocks behind the wedges are fixed by a single screw, which allows them to take up the exact angle of the wedges as they are tapped home. A jig of this type must be accurately made, or the hole in the block will be off-centre. If possible, the block is cut oversize and mounted as described, and then the revolving centre can be used to 'centre-pop' the hole. True size can then be set out from the centre-mark and turning carried out. Later, the block can be trimmed to the true size.

As the last four examples of simple, home-made holding devices illustrate, a large range of expensive accessories is not really required. Many such jigs and fixtures are used by turners. They have the advantage of being made-to-measure for the job in hand, and they usually cost next to nothing to produce. The only limitation is the ingenuity of the turner.

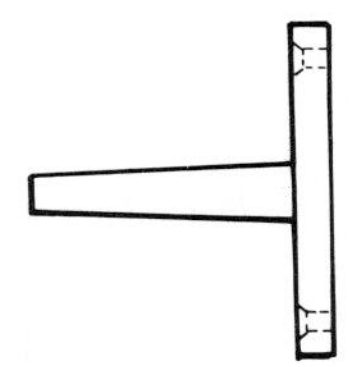

Fig. 3.43. Small faceplate on Morse-taper arbor

Finally, it is even possible to turn in hardwood a small faceplate (*Figure 3.43*) on a Morse taper arbor. It is suitable only for light work because of the possibility that the taper may work loose during turning, but, with a suitable pad glued to the surface, it is a useful drilling pad when boring on the lathe.

4 Tools and their use

Most of the tools employed in woodturning are used for the actual shaping of the wood. They fall into two broad groups, depending on the way in which they remove unwanted wood. The first consists of those which remove the wood by scraping; the other are those which are intended to do their work by actually cutting wood in the form of shavings. The word 'intended' is used deliberately, as cutting tools can be used in a scraping manner, but only by novices in desperation or in ignorance.

Cutting tools can be subdivided into those which have flat blades, which are chisels, and those with blades of curved section, which are gouges. The parting tool does not quite fit into either of the above groups, as it has a cutting action peculiar to itself, best described as part cutting and part scraping. Examples of the four tools are illustrated in *Figure 4.1*.

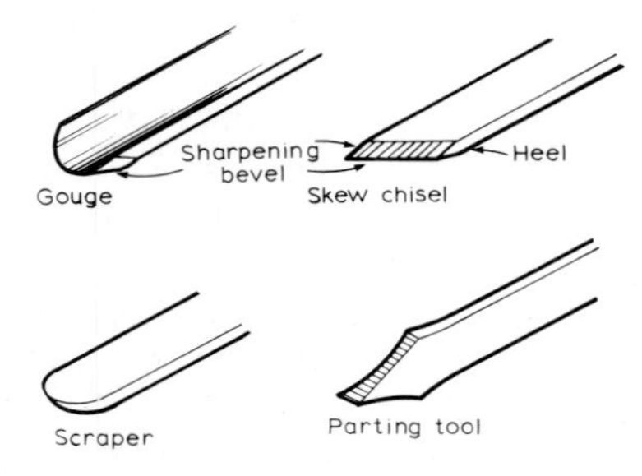

Fig. 4.1. Principal tools

Sizes of tools

Turning-tools are made in three broad ranges of sizes or weights. At the bottom end of the scale are the lightweight tools. These are about 13 in (330 mm) long and – although made as scrapers, gouges, chisels, and parting tools – they are available in only a very restricted range of widths up to a maximum of about ½ in (12 mm). These lightweight tools are really intended for the type of work which can be done in drill-powered lathes or similar small lathes used by modelmakers. They can be useful for small work on a bigger lathe (and standard-size tools can be used on small work and small lathes).

The popular weight for turning-tools is that known as 'standard pattern' or 'standard strength'. They are around 18 in (457 mm) in length, including the handle, and are available in all the accepted shapes, with a maximum width for both gouge and chisel about 1¼ in (32 mm). The thickness of metal is up to ¼ in (6 mm). These tools will deal with the bulk of work an amateur is likely to tackle, as the size of the tool is roughly in proportion to the diameter of the work, and this is usually restricted by the size of the lathe.

Even on a lathe of modest size, as likely to be used by the home turner, many keen craftsmen prefer tools at the heavyweight end of the range. These are known as 'long-and-strong' and are usually over 22 in (560 mm) in overall length, with chisels available up to 2 in (50 mm) in width and gouges up to 1½ in (37 mm). The metal for the chisels and scrapers is up to ⅜ in (9 mm) thick. Long- and strong-gouges are also available with particularly deep fluting, specially intended for bowl and faceplate work.

Buying tools

Tools can be bought in sets or singly. There is little advantage in buying tools in a set, other than an attractive cardboard box and maybe a very slight price-saving. The better arrangement is for the beginner to buy the basic tools and to add to these as the need arises and as experience is gained. Experience is important, because often the same turning operations can be carried out with tools of different sizes. For example, one man may prefer to smooth a cylindrical piece of work with a skew chisel of one size, while another might choose one either larger or smaller. Such personal preference can only be based on experience.

Different turners will advocate slightly different basic kits of tools, either in size or type. Fairly small skew chisels are often included in basic kits, both as boxed sets and as suggested lists. However, a lot of skill is needed to use a skew chisel properly, particularly a small one, and this comes only after practice. The reasons for this will become apparent when their uses are described later, and even more apparent when the theory is put into practice on a revolving piece of wood.

The following five tools are suggested as an absolutely minimum basic kit: 1 in square-end gouge, 1 in skew chisel, 3⁄16 in or 1⁄4 in parting tool, 3⁄8 in fingernail gouge, and 1⁄2 in square- or round-end scraper.

The blade and handle of a turning tool are fitted together by means of a tang formed on the end of the blade, which is driven into a hole of suitable size bored in the handle. Because turning-tools, unlike woodworking tools, are never struck on the

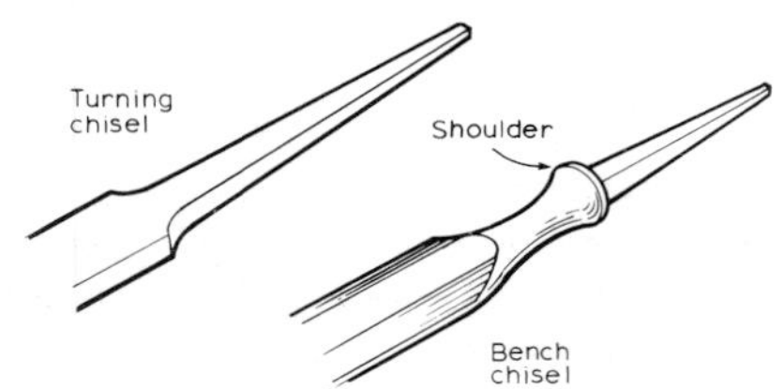

Fig. 4.2. Tangs of tools

handle, there is no need for the tang to have shoulders formed on it, but a ferrule – usually of brass – is fitted over the neck of the handle to resist side-thrust and prevent splitting. The difference between tangs is shown in *Figure 4.2*. Turning tools, apart from some exceptions mentioned later, are made from cast steel, but the tangs are left 'soft' during hardening and tempering.

Tools can be purchased with or without handles, but an initial set must be obtained with them. With the basic set, and after a little experience, making handles for additional tools can provide useful practice, so additions to the kit can be bought without handles, at an average saving of approximately 20 per cent. Bought tools usually have handles of beech and, although this is a quite suitable wood, other hardwoods – such as ash and sycamore – can be used. Ferrules for the handles can be obtained from turnery suppliers or suitable scrap tube can be used. Guidance on projects such as handles is given in Chapter 9.

Parting tools

The traditional parting tool has remained little changed until recently, when a new variation appeared on the market (*Figure 4.3*). It is used with the hollow side down and gives a much

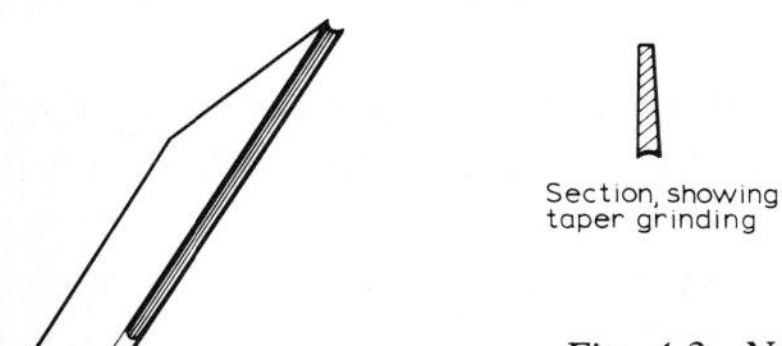

Fig. 4.3. New-pattern parting tool

cleaner cut than the conventional pattern. This is because it is taper-ground – and thinner on the 'heel' edge – along its blade, thus providing clearance in the groove it makes when cutting. This tool is manufactured from 'high-speed' steel for longer life between sharpening. A similar tool is made by another manufacturer, but it is not taper ground.

Scrapers

Although scraping tools never work as efficiently as cutting tools, there has been a significant increase in patterns manufactured, and numbers sold, of such tools. One reason for this is that much of the re-awakened interest in woodturning has been focussed on the use of those woods known as 'exotics', such as box, ebony, and rosewood. Because these are among the hardest and densest woods in use, scraping is a suitable method of working, for the harder the wood, the more satisfactorily it can usually be scraped. Softwoods (with the notable exception of yew) and some of the soft hardwoods are difficult to scrape to a good surface.

Because scraping is so often used for these scarce and expensive woods, such work is often small – chessmen, small boxes, knobs, and handles, for example. This has led to the production of small scraping tools with blades around ⅜ in (10 mm) wide and 3/16 in (5 mm) thick. Typical shapes which are available are shown in *Figure 4.4.* Although the shapes sold cover a wide variety of

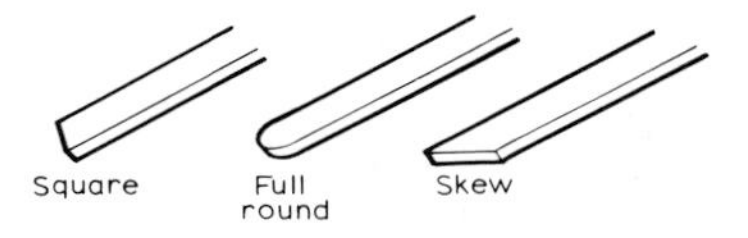

Fig. 4.4. Miniature scrapers

situations, one great advantage of scraping tools is that their ends can fairly readily be modified by grinding to suit the nature of the work. (That is another reason why a grindstone is such a useful accessory to the lathe.)

Grinding and sharpening of tools are dealt with in Chapter 5, so it is sufficient to say here that scraping tools tend to lose their sharpness fairly quickly. This is mainly because they are presented to the wood in such a manner that the wood tends to abrade the edge, and because sometimes a lot of heat, which draws the temper, can be generated. This has prompted one supplier to produce a small range of scrapers which are tipped with high-speed steel; these are shown in *Figure 4.5.* This steel, much used in the engineering industry, is capable of taking a keen cutting edge but – even more important – it will retain it for longer than ordinary tool-steels.

Another innovation, not long on the market, is the high-speed steel scraper-bar. It is simply a length of steel as shown in *Figure*

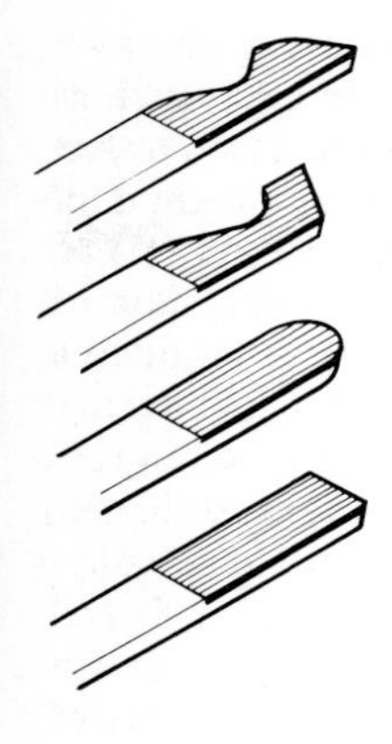

Fig. 4.5. Long-and-strong scrapers with high-speed steel inserts

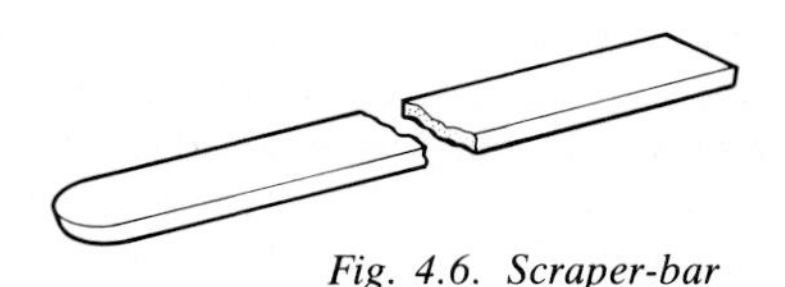

Fig. 4.6. Scraper-bar

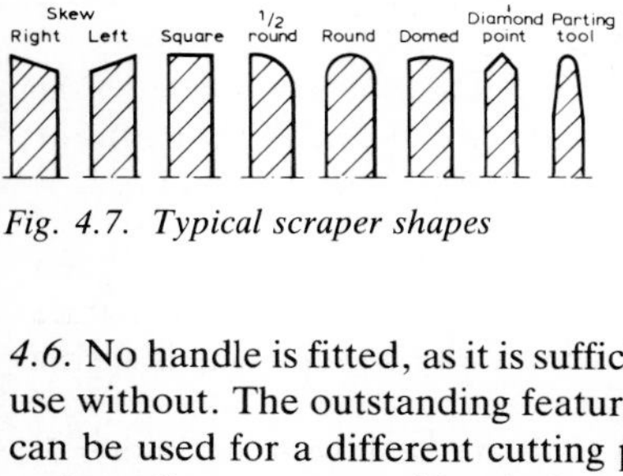

Fig. 4.7. Typical scraper shapes

4.6. No handle is fitted, as it is sufficiently long to be quite safe in use without. The outstanding feature of this tool is that each end can be used for a different cutting profile or shape.

As well as scrapers with relatively small blades, there is now a range of scrapers classed as extra heavy. They have blades which are 1½in (38mm) by ⅜in (10mm) in section; a selection of blade shapes is shown in *Figure 4.7.* The particular advantage of these solid and heavy scrapers is that they have a damping effect on any vibration of the wood or the lathe, enabling full control and a fine cut to be achieved.

We will now take a closer look at gouges, chisels, and scrapers to examine the principles on which they work and the type of cutting operation for which each one is best suited. Only the manner in which the tool shapes the wood will be discussed; more detailed guidance on their manipulation is given later.

We have to accept that the lathe, the wood being used, and particularly the shape and nature of the job being turned, all impose certain limitations on the selection of tool and of method of working, and that tools cannot always be used to their maximum efficiency because of these limitations. Moreover, for many turning operations there is a choice of tool, although this is often only a matter of size. Experience plays a part in the selection of the tool to use, as one man's method of working may not be quite the same as another's, although both may be experts. Many experienced turners, even though they are likely to have a number of gouges in regular use, usually have a favourite which they use at every opportunity.

Gouges

More wood is removed by gouges of one sort or another than by all the other tools put together.

For work between centres, gouges can be sharpened so that their ends are either square or rounded, the later being referred to as 'fingernail' sharpened. The two types are shown in *Figure 4.8*. Gouges may be shaped either way whether they are

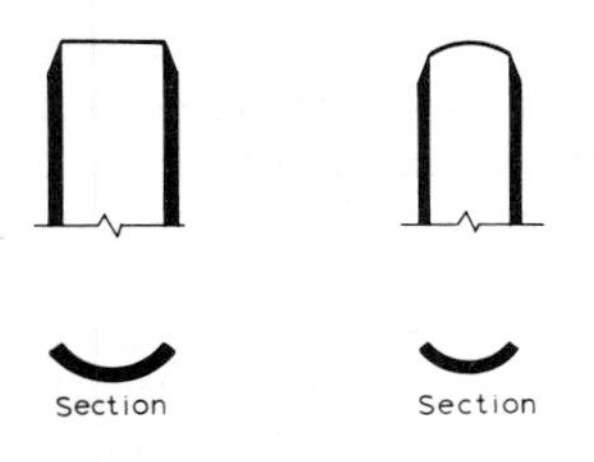

Fig. 4.8. Square-end and finger-nail gouges

lightweight, standard, or long-and-strong. The method of sharpening depends on how the turner will put them to use.

When a piece of wood is mounted in the lathe, the first operation is usually to make it into a cylinder which is slightly larger than the maximum diameter of the final job. This stage is often called 'roughing' and so the gouge to use is a roughing gouge. Roughing is the main job of the gouge which is sharpened with its end square, and a popular size is 1 in or 1¼ in wide.

In use, the roughing gouge is rolled from side to side so that all parts of its cutting edge are brought into contact with the wood while it is being shaped. This provides maximum benefit from the time and trouble spent in sharpening, as not all the wear, and thus the dulling, takes place at any one point on the cutting edge. It is also one way in which the shape shown in *Figure 4.9* can be

Fig. 4.9. Concave shape with square side

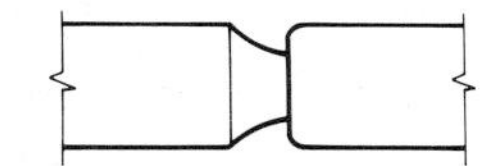

produced, a hollow where the concave shape is on either the left or the right. This tool, properly sharpened and correctly used, can remove wood quite quickly. Although it has been strongly suggested that the wood should be prepared to octagonal shape before it is mounted in the lathe, many experts rely entirely on their roughing gouge to reduce wood from square to cylinder.

One well-known supplier of tools lists a '1¼in roughing gouge'. It is of deep section, as shown in *Figure 4.10*. The

Fig. 4.10. Deep-fluted gouge

amount of curvature of the blade of a gouge used for roughing purposes does not affect its cutting action nor its use to any great extent; it is very much a matter of personal preference.

The first principle which must be mastered is the angle at which the gouge must be presented to the work, when viewed from the side. The gouge will cut most efficiently when it is at the highest point on the wood at which cutting can take place, which is also the position at which the sharpening bevel has maximum contact with the wood. This is a rarely broken rule for cutting with both gouges and chisels.

If the beginner needs a general rule, a very suitable one is 'Keep the bevel rubbing on the work'. When a tool is at its most efficient, there is all-round gain: the waste is removed quickly, control of the tool is easy, and – most important of all – the surfaces produced are cleanly cut, requiring little subsequent sanding.

Another way of considering this cutting action is to examine the angle between the bottom of the curve of the gouge and the cylindrical – or near-cylindrical – shape of the wood. In geometrical terms, the gouge should form a tangent to the cylinder, as illustrated in *Figure 4.11*. One way of establishing this position is to initially place the gouge obviously too high on the wood, as shown in *Figure 4.12*. If the gouge is now allowed to slide slowly

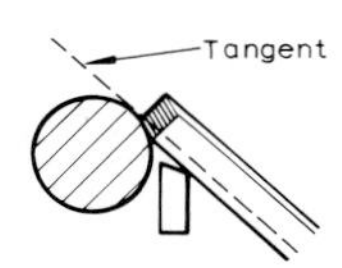

Fig. 4.11. Gouge should cut high on the wood

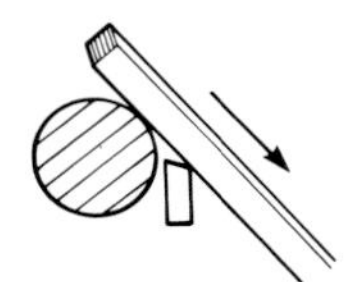

Fig. 4.12. Establishing highest cutting position

down the toolrest until the cutting edge just begins to cut and at the same time the handle is lifted very slightly, then this tangent line will have been established. Incidentally, placing a gouge in the position shown in *Figure 4.12* during turning is a safe way of checking that the wood is truly cylindrical; if any flats remain, the gouge will vibrate.

Vibration can also result from the wood being slightly loose between the centres. This sometimes happens during turning, usually because the tailstock centre is bedding into the wood. This slackness must be taken up; at the same time, check that the tailstock body and the tailstock barrel are locked tight.

While the relatively high position of the gouge and the tangential angle are important, the ideal position cannot always be exactly achieved. Two other factors are involved: the diameter of the work, and the angle at which the gouge is sharpened. The latter can be controlled within limits, but the diameter of the work cannot be changed simply to suit the optimum cutting action of the tool. The way that diameter dictates the position of the gouge is shown in *Figure 4.13*. The two basic rules remain: to cut as high up on the wood as possible, and to keep the bevel rubbing on the work – you cannot follow one without following the other.

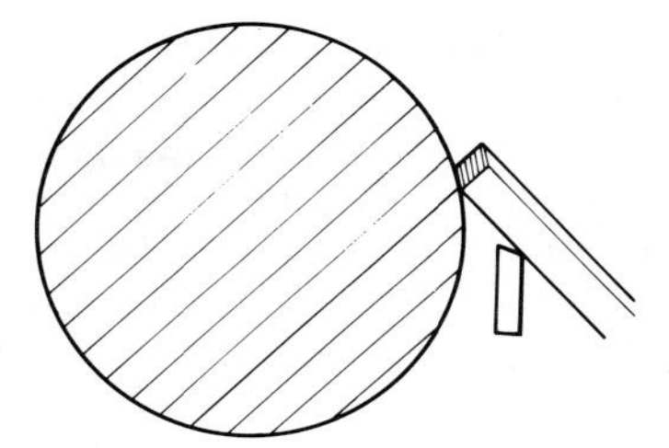

Fig. 4.13. Effect of large diameter on position of gouge

There is a common but incorrect way of presenting the gouge to the wood. Because of lack of instruction or of understanding of how the tool works, beginners tend to hold it more or less horizontally, as shown in *Figure 4.14,* and pointing approximately to the centre of the wood. This reduces the gouge to a scraper, and its cutting action on the wood can be likened to that of a

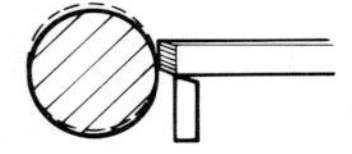

Fig. 4.14. Gouge only scrapes if held horizontally

bench-plane with the blade at a right angle to the sole and so also to the wood. Little cutting would take place with such a plane.

A gouge held in this way tends to 'tear' the surface of the work because, although it is performing as a scraper, it is an inefficient one. Dust, rather than shavings, would be removed, and the tool would become dull quickly. Moreover, because the gouge is not really cutting the wood properly, it is in fact offering resistance to it, so the wood tends to 'ride up' on to it, as indicated by the dotted line in *Figure 4.14*. This can lead to chatter or vibration, which will be all the more pronounced if the wood is long relative to its diameter.

The nature of the waste as it is removed is usually a very good guide to the sharpness of the tool and, even more important, to whether it is being correctly used. When a gouge or skew chisel is being used properly, the shavings flow from the cutting edge in long, continuous ribbons (though this also depends on the species of wood). If a tool removes little more than dust instead of shavings, this a sure sign that something is wrong.

The roughing gouge has, of course, to be moved along the toolrest during the cutting operation, and it will be found to cut rather better if it is pointed a little in the direction of movement. This movement may be towards the headstock or towards the tailstock. As it is moved, the gouge should be rotated slightly on to its side. Both of these points are illustrated in *Figure 4.15*. The

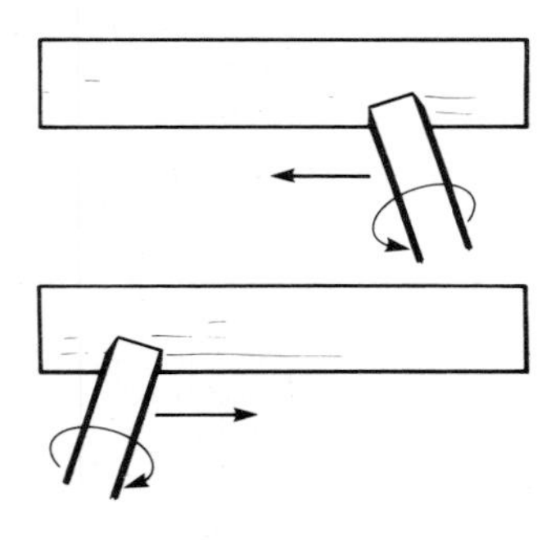

Fig. 4.15. Movement of gouge when roughing

rotation of the gouge on its axis is often made as a continuous movement while the gouge traverses the wood so that, by the end of the cut, the gouge is almost on its side, having rotated through nearly 90 deg. This technique has the advantage of using the whole of the gouge's cutting edge.

Sometimes the initial roughing of the wood is not meant to achieve a cylindrical form but a more conical one, this depending on the final shape of the project. The correct procedure is to move from the larger diameter to the smaller, as shown in *Figure 4.16,* where the arrow indicates the direction in which the gouge

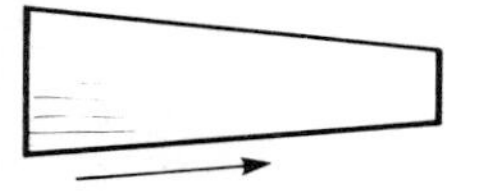

Fig. 4.16. Preferred direction of movement when work tapers

must move to give the better cut. To work from small diameter to large would result in the gouge cutting against the grain and possibly tearing out chunks of wood. The correct action can be likened to sharpening a pencil with a penknife: the cutting takes place towards the thinner end.

Skew chisel

When a piece of wood has been roughed out to cylindrical form, it is often desirable next to make the surface smooth. The shape to be produced will affect to some extent the sequence of working as, if the shape is to be fairly intricate, there is little point in making the initial cylinder as smooth as possible. However, a cylindrical or conical shape often forms part of a more elaborate profile, and this will need to have a smoother surface than can usually be achieved by the roughing gouge. This smoothing action is one of the main functions of the skew chisel.

The skew chisel is the tool which takes more mastering than any other lathe tool, and the skill involved in using it with complete control is of a fairly high order. But, like most skills, it is within reach of all who go the right way about acquiring it.

The skew chisel has a slanting blade bevelled on both sides. The acute-angled corner (less than 90 deg) is sometimes called the 'point' or 'toe', and the obtuse-angled corner (more than 90 deg) is sometimes called the 'heel'. The typical position of the chisel for a smoothing cut is shown in *Figure 4.17,* which also

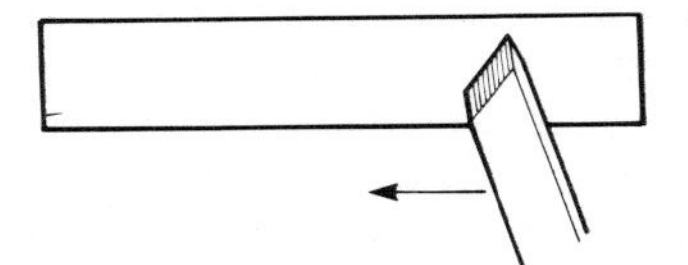

Fig. 4.17. Position of chisel when smoothing

shows the position of the chisel at the start of the cut – that is, a little way in from the end of the workpiece. It is possible to start a skew chisel cut from the end of the wood, but this should not be done until proficiency has been attained. So the skew chisel is worked towards the ends of the work, not from them.

As with the gouge, the chisel should be positioned as high on the wood as is possible, and with the bevel rubbing on the wood. Only half the width of a chisel-blade can be used for smoothing cuts. This is the heel end, as illustrated in *Figure 4.18*. The chisel is shown in *Figure 4.19* in its cutting position on the wood. While a competent turner can use rather more than half of the blade, the nearer the point of the blade comes to the work, the nearer the turner is to trouble. If the point comes too close to the wood,

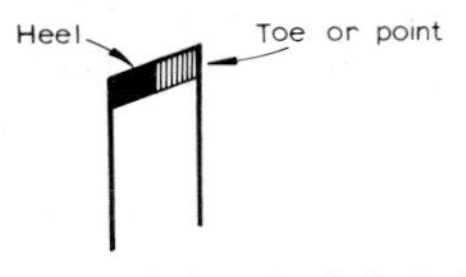

Fig. 4.18. Only shaded half of blade can be safely used when smoothing with chisel

Fig. 4.19. Point of chisel kept well clear of wood

it will instantly 'dig in', the result being a piece of wood split off from the surface and a hole in is place. No amount of attempted control of the tool, or firm gripping of the handle, is likely to prevent this digging-in once the point of the blade has reached the danger zone, when the lathe takes over from the turner.

Basic spindle cuts

The two basic cuts for spindle work are the concave cut, or hollow, and the convex cut, or bead (see *Figure 4.20.*) Variations of these two shapes are almost endless and, when used in combination, give boundless scope for creating profiles.

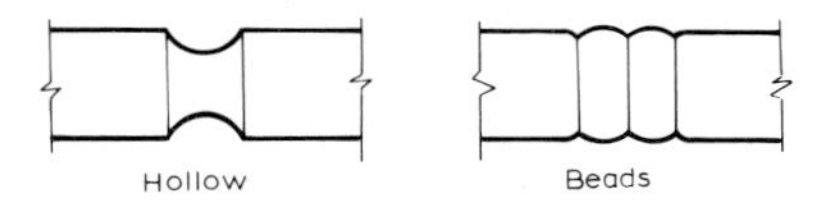

Fig. 4.20. Basic spindle cuts

The hollow

The hollow must be cut with a gouge of the fingernail type, the size of which depends to some extent on the size of the hollow.

The tool must be smaller than the width of the hollow: if this is to be 1 in or more, most turners would use a ¾ in or a ½ in gouge. The wider gouge is preferred for a shallow hollow and the narrower one for a deeper hollow.

The gouge in its position at the start of the cut is shown in *Figure 4.21*. Notice that it is almost right over on its side and is initially pointing more or less to the centre of the wood. The gouge at the end of this first cut is shown in *Figure 4.22*. While

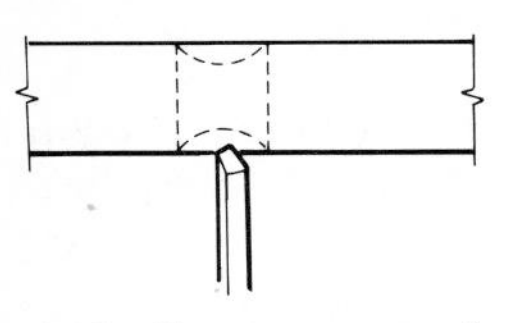

Fig. 4.21. Gouge at start of hollowing cut

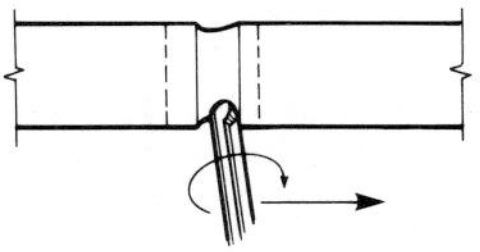

Fig. 4.22. Movement of gouge when forming hollow

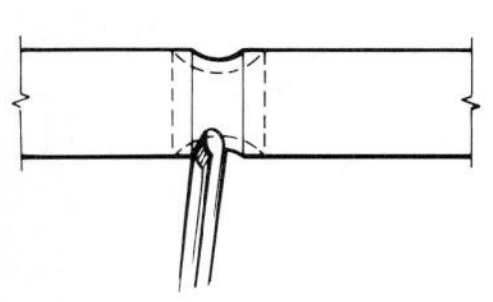

Fig. 4.23. Gouge reversed for second cut

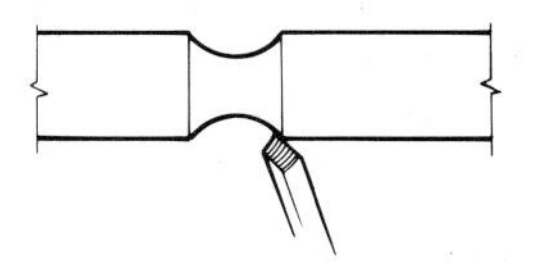

Fig. 4.24. Start of finishing cut

the movement of the gouge during this cutting is continuous, there are in fact three elements to it. First, the handle is moved to the right. Second, the handle is lowered to enable the blade to cut higher on the wood as the hollow begins to take shape. Third, the handle is rotated a little in a clockwise direction, so that the bulk of the cutting is being carried out with the centre part of the blade. Careful comparison of the positions of the gouges in *Figure 4.21* and *4.22* will reveal how these three movements combine into a single one.

The second cut in forming a hollow is similar to the first, but working in the opposite direction. This should result in a reasonably well formed hollow, but much smaller than the one required. This sequence of cutting from one side to another is repeated until the desired size of hollow is reached. Note that in the cutting operations, the gouge always starts well over on its side and pointing to the centre of the wood. In this way, the bevel of the gouge is rubbing on the wood, as seen in *Figure 4.24*. Notice that again the cutting is from large diameter to small, or 'downhill'.

The bead

The beads shown in *Figure 4.20* call for very different techniques, mainly because they are formed with the skew chisel. For work of average size, say 1½ in to 3 in in diameter, a 1 in chisel is about right. The first cut is made with the point of the chisel, as shown in *Figure 4.25*. This cut can be made to only a limited

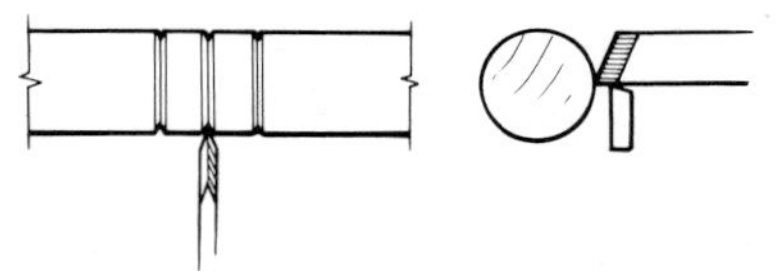

Fig. 4.25. First cut in forming beads

depth, as wood is not removed. The incision is then enlarged to from a more pronounced vee-cut, the depth of which depends on whether the bead is to be fully semicircular or with a flatter curve. Depth, in any case, is normally judged by eye, and one of the turner's skills is to make these cuts, and eventually the beads, of uniform size.

How the initial incisions are made vee-shaped by cutting in from both sides, again with the point of the chisel, is shown in *Figure 4.26*. It is possible to form a vee, after the initial incision,

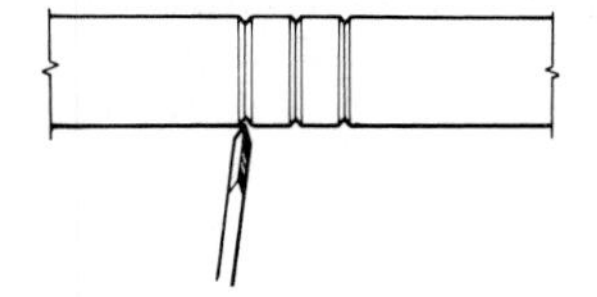

Fig. 4.26. Cutting shallow vees before forming beads

by having the point of the chisel uppermost, and then using the lower part of the blade to do the cutting, the chisel being advanced into the wood by raising the handle.

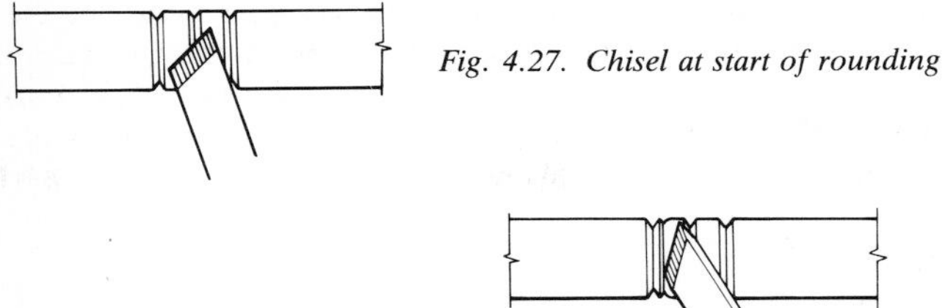

Fig. 4.27. Chisel at start of rounding

Fig. 4.28. Movement of chisel when forming bead

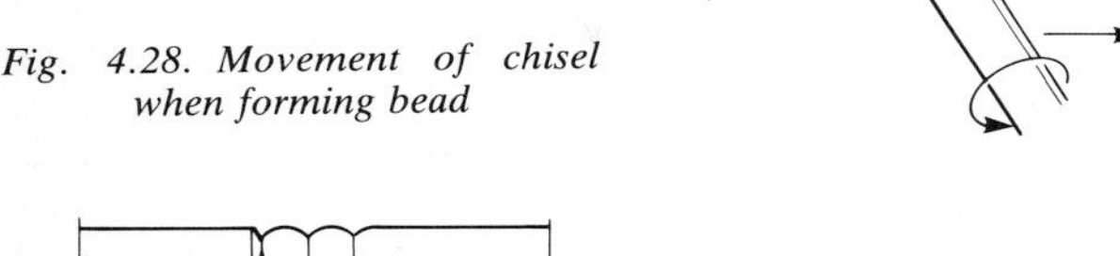

Fig. 4.29. Chisel at end of cut

The actual rounding starts with the chisel high on the wood, with the centre of the blade on the mid-point of the bead and with the sharpening bevel rubbing, as shown in *Figure 4.27.* The movement of the chisel in forming the bead is again really a combination of three separate movements carried out as one. The chisel handle is moved to the right – to form the left-hand side of the bead – and also rotated in an anticlockwise direction. In order to bring about the rolling action needed to form the curve, the handle is raised slightly, the chisel finishing the cut completely on its edge. The chisel part-way through this action is shown in *Figure 4.28* and at the end of the cut in *Figure 4.29.* If the beginner can form beads which are uniform in size, of regular curvature, and with wood cut so as to leave a clean surface, then he has acquired a fair degree of skill.

Using the parting tool

When a fairly broad incision has to be made in the wood, the parting tool is used. A common application of this technique is squaring up the ends of the work and in so doing indicating its finished length and the waste at the ends, as shown in *Figure 4.30.* Often in turnery work, a pin, or circular tenon, is formed at one end of the wood, and using the parting tool is one way of cutting in the shoulder and at the same time establishing the diameter of the pin (see *Figure 4.31*).

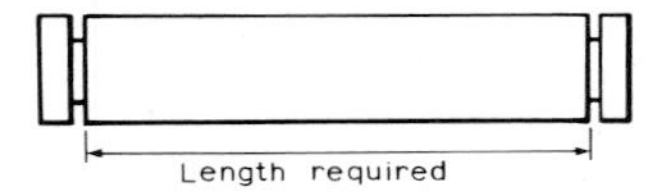

Fig. 4.30. Using parting tool to mark length

Fig. 4.31. Starting to form pin or circular tenon

The parting tool is fairly easy to use, but even so, there is a right and a wrong way of making it cut the wood. It is initially placed high on the wood, as shown in *Figure 4.32.* Two earlier rules apply: the parting tool forms a tangent to the work, and so the bevel rubs on the wood. Cutting takes place as the handle is raised. When the tool is operated in this tangential position, there is normally no need to move the handle forward in order to maintain the cutting action. This is shown in *Figure 4.33,* where

Fig. 4.32. Position of parting tool at start of cut

Fig. 4.33. Parting tool remains tangential to cut surface

Fig. 4.34. Incorrect use of parting tool

the tool is well advanced into the wood. It should never be used by pointing it towards the centre of the wood and then simply pushing it directly in, as shown in *Figure 4.34.*

Although the parting tool cuts the wood very quickly, it works in a most inefficient manner – indeed, it breaks one of the basic rules of cutting wood. If an ordinary wood-chisel were to be placed at the edge of a piece of wood as shown in *Figure 4.35* and then struck on the handle, the corner of the timber would be split, not cut. Timber cannot be properly cut in this way unless the fibres of the grain are first severed, which prevents splitting. (It is this characteristic or wood which necessitates different shapes of teeth on saws, depending on whether they are intended primarily for cutting along, or across, the grain.)

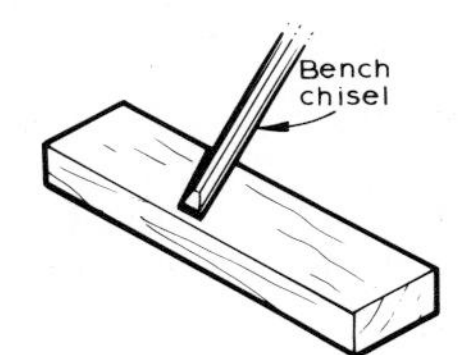

Fig. 4.35. Corner of wood would split if chisel were struck

Because of the way in which the parting tool tears, rather than cuts, the grain, the quality of the surface which the tool leaves is usually very poor. As the parting tool is often used only for preliminary cutting, this is of little consequence. An example of the use of the parting tool for preliminary cutting, partly to establish the location of certain features on the work and partly to determine the essential dimensional limits of these features, is shown in *Figure 4.36*. The sketches show how the parting tool is

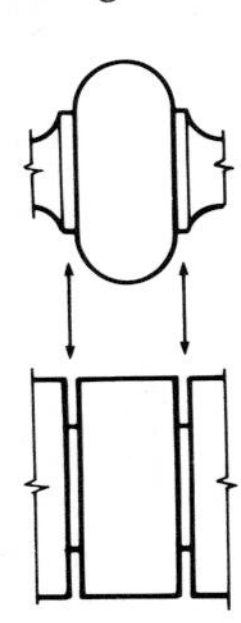

Fig. 4.36. Use of parting tool to establish limits of features

used to form the grooves on either side of the bead, thus fixing its size and also the diameter of the work immediately alongside it. In practice, the grooves would be formed so as to allow a fraction for final trimming.

It is a common design trick to introduce a small flat surface between a bead and a hollow, as shown in *Figure 4.36,* particularly in traditional turning where the work tends to be fairly ornate; much modern turning is comparatively restrained, with more flat surfaces or gentle curves. This small flat surface between two curves is known as a 'quirk', and it helps to define the start and end of a feature.

Scraping

In normal circumstances, scrapers are not used for spindle turning, for which gouges and chisels will cut the wood in an efficient manner which leaves the surface clean and smooth. The exception is where the wood is particularly hard, and such wood is almost certain to be used only on fairly small work, such as knobs, handles, and chessmen. The decision for or against using scrapers for spindle-turning rests with the profile being turned: the more intricate the work, the greater the justification for using scrapers.

One advantage of scrapers over gouges and chisels is that they can be ground to suit the shape of the work. An example is illustrated in *Figure 4.37,* where the scraper has been ground to

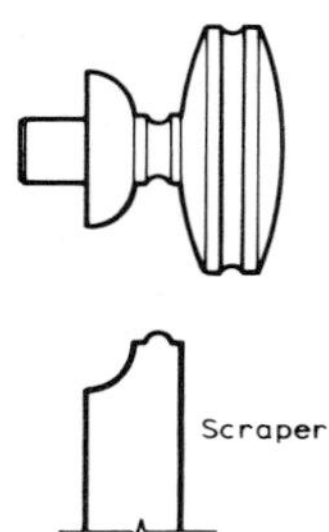

Fig. 4.37. Scraper specially ground for shaping base of handle

suit the base part of the knob. Usually, it is worthwhile to make such a tool for a special profile only if several items of identical and intricate shape are needed, but it is for purposes such as this that scraper blanks are available.

Some years ago, an order was received for 200 wooden toy soldiers to the shape shown in *Figure 4.38.* As the overall height was only 1¼in (32mm), the detail involved was quite intricate, especially around the head. Also shown is the profile of the

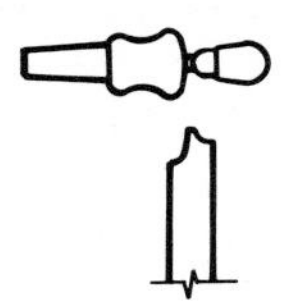

Fig. 4.38. Scraper made from ¼in (6mm) bench-chisel to form neck and head of soldier

scraper tool which was ground and used to form the shoulders, neck, and head. This particular scraper was produced from an ordinary ¼in (6mm) firmer chisel, and it was used for making the whole battalion of soldiers without having to be re-sharpened. Some time later, an antique was being restored, which called for a new turned part with beads only about ⅛in (3mm) apart. The same chisel was re-ground; it is shown, with the turned profile, in *Figure 4.39.*

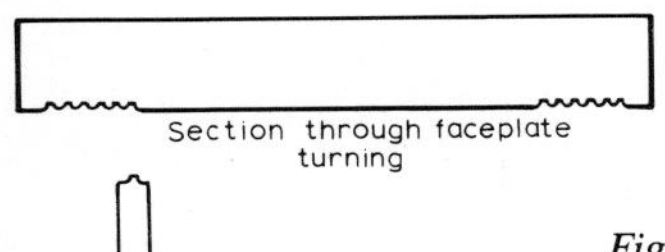

Fig. 4.39. Same chisel ground to turn beads

Scrapers are the easiest of all lathe tools to use, as the movements involved in making the cut – or scrape – are much more simple than with the gouge or chisel. With the latter, constantly changing compound angles are involved, with quite complex movements of the hands needed to maintain these angles during the cutting action.

The first point to understand about scrapers is that they remove wood not directly by the sharpness of the cutting edge but by the burr which is produced during sharpening. In this respect they can be compared to a cabinet scraper and, like a cabinet scraper, they will remove fine shavings when properly sharpened and used. When a cabinet scraper is used, it is made to lean in the direction of working at an angle of 70 to 80 deg with the work, as shown in *Figure 4.40,* to enable the burr to bite into the wood. The technique is very much the same when scraping on the lathe.

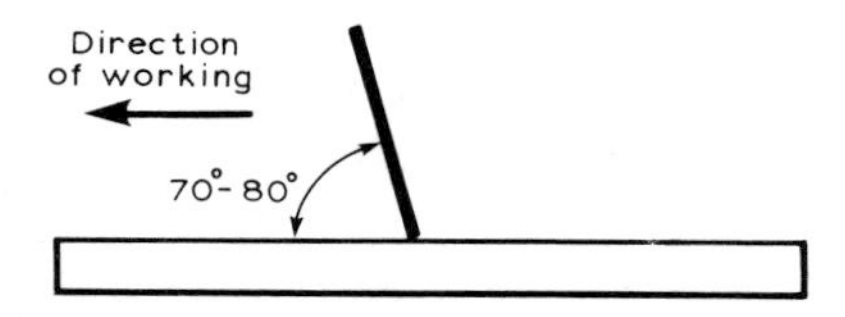

Fig. 4.40. Angle for cabinet scraper

The theoretically correct cutting position of a scraper is shown in *Figure 4.41:* it is level with the centre of the wood. In order to make it cut properly, the handle is lifted until the blade forms an angle of 70 to 80 deg. In practice, the turner adjusts this angle until he feels that the scraper is biting and working properly, as

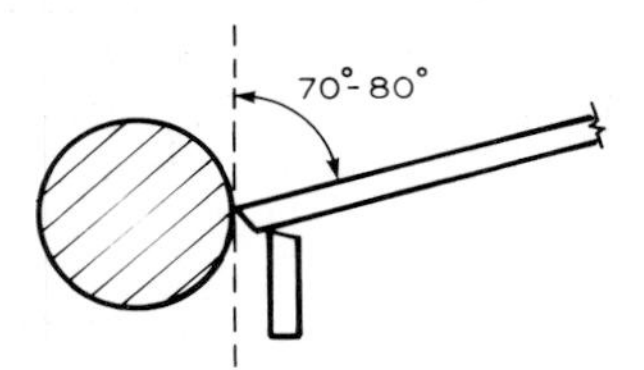

Fig. 4.41. Scraper is pointed downwards slightly

the precise angle varies according to factors such as the density of the wood, the height of the toolrest, and the angle at which the scraper has been sharpened.

An example where scraping methods are essential is shown in *Figure 4.42,* where a lid for a small box is being prepared. A good fit is desirable, and scraping the inside of the lid is the only satisfactory way of achieving this. Another example is in *Figure 4.43,* where there are small raised beads on a sloping surface. The corners (S) must be scraped. If the beads are fairly close together, say ¼in (6mm) or less, then the whole of the spaces between them would have to be scraped.

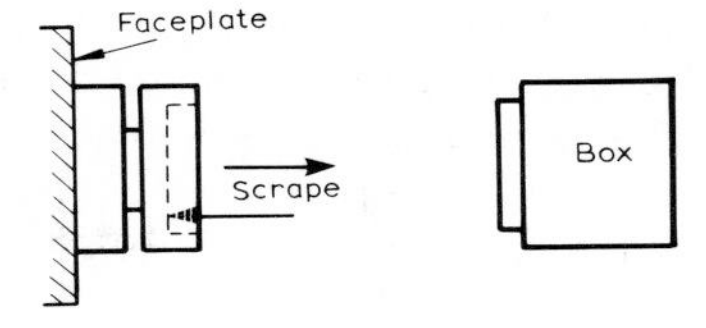

Fig. 4.42. Scraping inside of lid of small box to obtain good fit

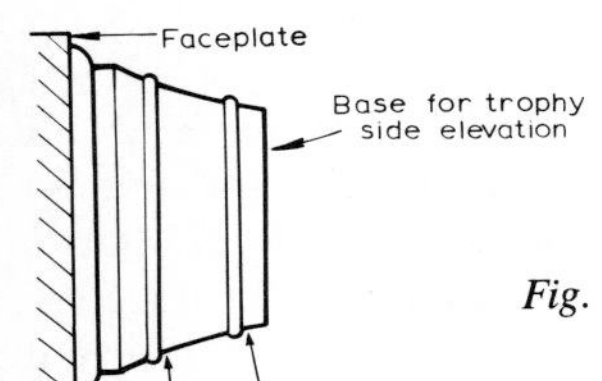

Fig. 4.43. Corners marked S must be scraped

Scrapers are used more for faceplate turning, and especially for hollowing. Gouges can be used only to a limited extent when hollowing faceplate work, although a bowl can be turned entirely with one if the hollow is rounded; otherwise scrapers are preferable. Turned boxes need to have the wall fairly straight and the bottom flat; this calls for scraping.

Gouges for faceplate-work

Gouges which are used for faceplate-work differ from those for work between centres in the way they are sharpened. The difference lies in the angle of sharpening, gouges used for faceplate-work having much steeper angles. Fuller information on sharpening is given in Chapter 5.

For faceplate-work, and bowls in particular, only gouges up to ½ in (12 mm) wide are used; in fact, the ⅜ in (9 mm) size is the popular choice of most turners. A larger gouge would absorb so much power that it would either stop the motor or would tend to be snatched from the hand and so be difficult to control. It is really a matter of what experience has proved to be the most successful and the most suitable size for the task in hand.

The long-and-strong pattern with deep fluting is the ideal gouge for bowls, as shown in section in *Figure 4.44.* The extra length and rigidity of this pattern are desirable for two reasons.

Fig. 4.44. Section through long-and-strong gouge as used for face-plate work

First, with work of large diameter there is a greater tendency for the wood to influence the tool movement. Second, the amount of gouge which overhangs the toolrest is often considerably more than in spindle work. The leverage imposed on the gouge is considerable, hence the need for extra strength and for sufficient length to counteract the leverage effect. A gouge for bowl-turning can be either square-ended or of the fingernail pattern; while the former is the one normally adopted, the choice is to a large extent a matter of personal preference.

The basic procedures for using the gouge for faceplate-work are essentially the same as for between-centres turning. The same two golden rules apply: the gouge should be used as high on the wood as it will cut, and the bevel should rub on the surface. This is illustrated in *Figure 4.45,* where the gouge is

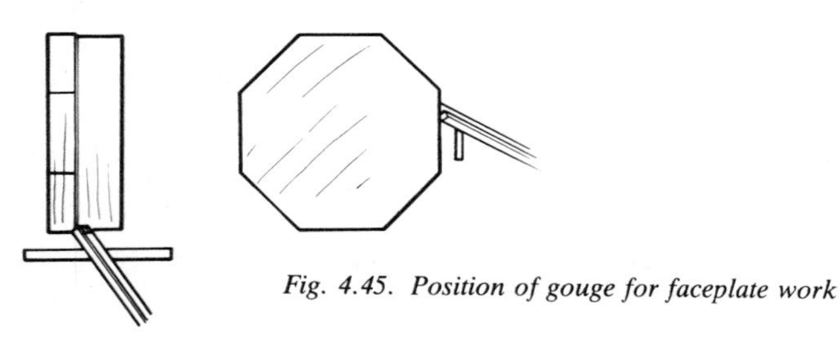

Fig. 4.45. Position of gouge for faceplate work

shown carrying out the roughing cut. Note that the gouge tends to be used rather more at an angle to the work in faceplate turning than when working between centres. This helps to minimise the difficulty of obtaining a clean-cut surface on work where the cutting is inevitably with, then against, the grain; this is explained more fully in Chapter 7.

5 Sharpening the tools

However wood is cut or shaped by hand or machine, and whether it is hardwood or softwood or the operation is on a large or small scale, sharp tools and cutters are essential. This is just as true for lathework as it is for bench work. However, the methods of obtaining an effective cutting edge on a lathe tool are in many respects peculiar to this branch of woodworking. This is because lathe tools cut the wood in a way somewhat different from most other methods of woodworking.

The equipment used for sharpening is standard and not extensive. A grinding wheel is essential for the serious turner because lathe-tools must be of the correct shape in order to perform properly and only a grinding wheel can ensure this. As well as correct shape, correct sharpening angles are very important for lathe work, and many tools are used straight from the grindstone, the honing, or oilstone, stage being omitted.

Because of the necessity to have provision for grinding, many lathes – but not all – are designed so that they can be fitted with a grindstone arbor, as explained in Chapter 2, normally as an optional extra. This facility can be properly provided only by the manufacturer and is a point to be borne in mind when a lathe is being purchased.

Grinding wheels

Generally, the larger the diameter of the grinding wheel, the better, since the effective curvature of the periphery will be less. This results in a ground surface which is relatively flat rather than excessively concave. A popular size of grinding wheel fitted as a lathe attachment has a diameter of 6in (152mm) and a thickness of 1in (25mm). This is for a lathe with the standard capacity of 30in (762mm) between centres, and powered by a motor of ½ h.p. or more. Small lathes, including the power-drill attachment types, will probably have a maximum wheel-size of 4in (101mm) or 5in (127mm), and a thickness of ½in (12mm). There is inevitably a fair amount of friction between wheel and tool; this can absorb a lot of the power imparted by the motor to the attachment.

When one buys a new wheel, the diameter of the hole or bore in the centre needs to be specified as the last dimension; thus a 6in by 1in by ¾in wheel has a diameter of 6in (152mm), a thickness of 1in (25mm), and a bore of ¾in (19mm) diameter.

There are quite a number of independent bench-grinders on the market. They do not have their own pedestals and so require some form of mounting. Often they can be lightly screwed to a workbench and then dismounted and stored when not in use; the screwholes can be used repeatedly as the grinder is required. Many such machines are of the heavy, industrial type, used mainly for engineering work, but there are some mainly for lighter use by woodworkers. These have wheels of 6in (150mm) by 1in (25mm) or 5in (125mm) by ½in; the choice is an economic one.

The grit-size, or degree of coarseness, of the wheel is important, and this is where an independent machine scores over an attachment. Independent machines are usually double-ended so that wheels of different grit size can be mounted and are thus available at the same time. With such machines, the original wheels are generally medium grit and fine (coarse wheels are really for industrial use). Where a single wheel has to be used for an attachment, medium grit should be chosen.

The turner needs a general-purpose wheel suitable for tool and cutter grinding. The hardness or grade should be such that, as the particles of grit become worn or smoothed, they are loosened from the wheel, thus exposing fresh, sharp particles.

Grinding wheels should not be used for soft metals, such as copper or aluminium, which rapidly clog them. If the rim of the wheel becomes unevenly worn or the surface is clogged with metal particles, it is possible to skim it so as to true it up again and rid the surface of contaminants; but a special wheel dresser is required.

There is a danger when grinding that particles of grit or metal will be thrown from the wheel into the operator's eyes. Modern grinding machines are fitted with transparent visors which allow the grinding operation to be seen but deflect flying debris. A grinding attachment is not likely to be equipped with such a visor, so goggles should always be worn when the wheel is in use.

Modern grinding wheels are designed to run dry and at a fairly high speed, especially when compared with the large, old hand-driven natural sandstone wheels, which ran in a trough of water at only a few revolutions a minute. The modern power-driven wheel is very efficient at removing metal quickly, but there is an ever-present danger to the tools at this speed. Too much pressure of the tool on the wheel, or a wheel which is in poor condition and so abrading the steel very slowly, causes friction. This can generate enough heat to reduce the hardness of the steel, leaving the tip of the tool softened and so less able to be sharpened or to hold its edge. Extreme overheating makes the end of the tool change colour to a bluish grey, when it is said to be 'burnt'.

Because of this danger, a container of water should always be on hand when grinding; indeed, some grinders have water troughs attached to them. The tool should be dipped into the water frequently while grinding. The purpose of the water is to keep the tool cool, not to lower the temperature should it be raised to danger level. Prevention is very much easier than cure, which is to grind away all the softened steel – a lengthy and wasteful process – or to re-temper the tool, which is beyond the abilities of most woodturners.

The smaller the tool being ground, the greater is the risk of overheating – sometimes referred to as 'drawing the temper'. This is because the less metal there is, the quicker will it heat up, and the heat being generated cannot be dissipated. But over-heating can be quite localised, as in the tip of even a quite large skew chisel. Remember that changes can take place in the steel before any visible signs appear; hence the need for frequent dipping in cold water.

Oilstones

An oilstone is essential. Stones vary in composition, size, and grit, and are either natural or artificial. Natural stones are very expensive nowadays and, because of the improved quality of the artificial types, have negligible advantages. The stone generally favoured by turners is the India artificial stone of medium grit.

Rectangular oilstones vary in size up to 8 in (203 mm) by 2 in (51 mm) by 1 in (25 mm), and this is the size recommended. If the stone is also to be used for sharpening other than lathe-tools, it will need to be housed in a box, as shown in *Figure 5.1.* The

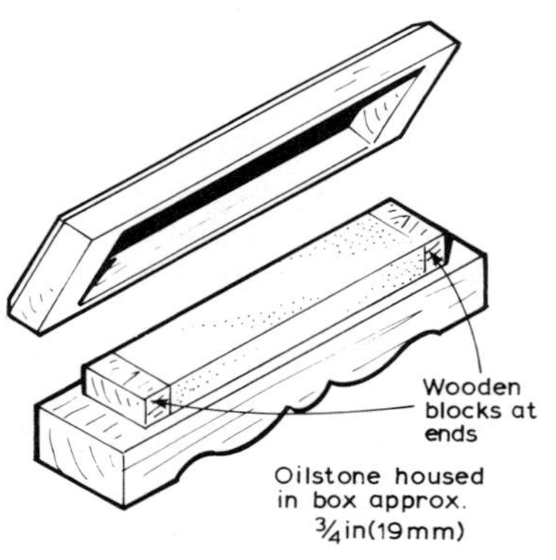

Fig. 5.1. Oilstone in box

blocks of wood at the ends enable the tool to over-run the stone, so that the whole of the surface is used, thus helping to even out wear and keep the stone flat. A lid is essential to keep out dust.

Oilstones are made in three grades: coarse, medium, and fine. The two largest sizes are also available as combination stones, either coarse on one side and medium on the other, or medium and fine. These combination stones are not as advantageous as they first appear, especially when the stone is properly housed in a box. The medium stone, used correctly, will impart an edge keen enough for lathework.

As a complement to the rectangular oilstone, a slip-stone is important. There are many sizes and shapes, but a handy size for the turner is 4½in (114 mm) by 1¾in (44 mm) by ½in (12 mm) to 3⁄16in (5 mm) and of the shape illustrated in *Figure 5.2*. A medium grit will prove satisfactory.

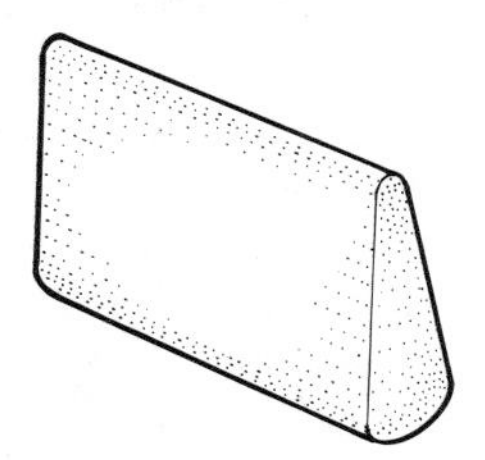

Fig. 5.2. Slip-stone

For oil- and slipstones, oil is needed, so an oilcan is also required. For honing purposes, a light machine oil is suitable. It can be purchased in small injector cans from cycle and other shops. Do not use waste car-sump oil, but clean oil of a low viscosity (20 or less); it can be diluted with a little white spirit or paraffin to produce more 'bite'. The main function of the oil is to swill the minute particles of steel from the surface of the stone. Lack of oil will result in the surface of the stone becoming choked and ceasing to cut. An occasional wash with paraffin is good for stones, and new ones should be soaked in oil and paraffin mixture for some time before use.

A leather strop – a strip of leather fixed rough-side down on a wooden board – is not essential but many craftsmen use one as an aid to sharpening chisels. One is illustrated in *Figure 5.3;* its main purpose is to remove the 'wire edge' left after honing.

A ticketer should be included in the sharpening kit. This need be no more than a piece of steel rod – preferably silver steel – about ¼in (6 mm) in diameter and 6 in (152 mm) long. It is used to produce a burr on a scraper, although the back of a small

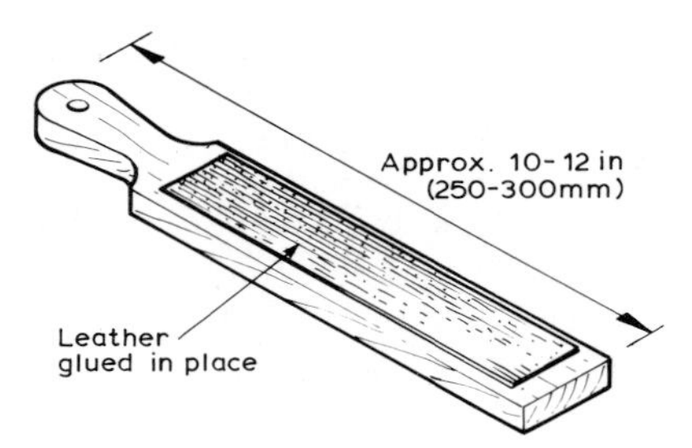

Fig. 5.3. Leather strop

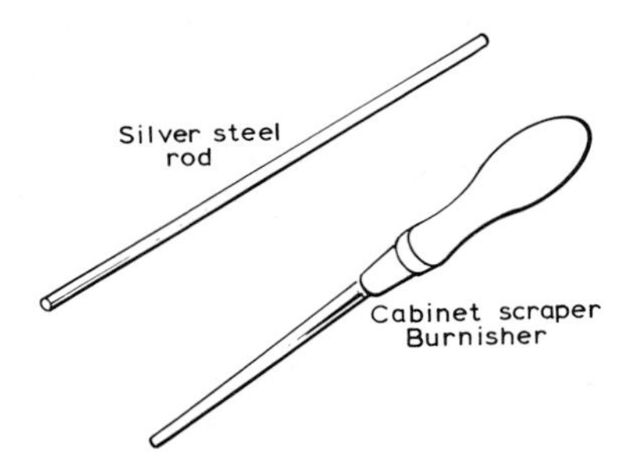

Fig. 5.4. Ticketers

scribing gouge can be used, as it often is for burring a cabinet scraper. There is, however, a tool for such purposes called a burnisher (*Figure 5.4*).

Grinding and honing

Even brand-new tools may not be ground to suit their particular use or the personal choice of the turner. Gouges used for spindle-turning and those for faceplate work are sharpened in quite different ways. Indeed, the manner of sharpening is a distinctive difference between the two groups, irrespective of whether the ends are sharpened square across or fingernail style. The difference is in the angle of grinding and in subsequent treatment.

For spindle turning, the angle of grinding needs to be around 30 deg, very much as it is for bench-chisels and planes. This is the angle shown in *Figure 5.5* and it is established by eye rather than

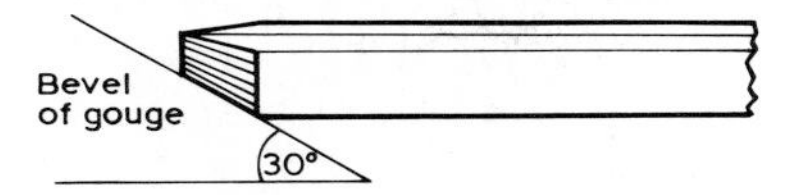

Fig. 5.5. Angle of sharpening for spindle-gouges

by an instrument. Gouges for spindle-work must be honed with the oilstone. Two methods are employed by turners, the choice being a matter of adopting the one which suits the individual.

The first method, shown in *Figure 5.6,* is where the tool is moved over the stone. It is essential to combine a rocking movement with the to-and-fro one in order that the whole of the

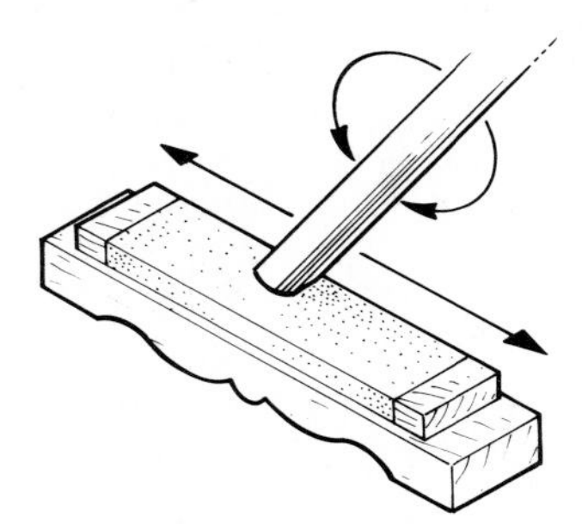

Fig. 5.6. Movement of gouge on oilstone

cutting edge is brought into contact with the stone – and as smoothly and evenly as possible. It is imperative that the angle the tool makes with the stone is not changed; that is, the handle must be maintained at the same height. Failure to maintain a constant angle creates a multitude of angles on the bevel, which results in the tool cutting less efficiently.

Lathe-tools which are honed after grinding are honed at the same angle as they are ground – that is, 30 deg. To put it another way, they have a single sharpening bevel, not the double one associated with most woodworking tools. This means that when the gouge is placed on the stone, as in the end view shown in *Figure 5.7,* the handle is moved up or down until it is established

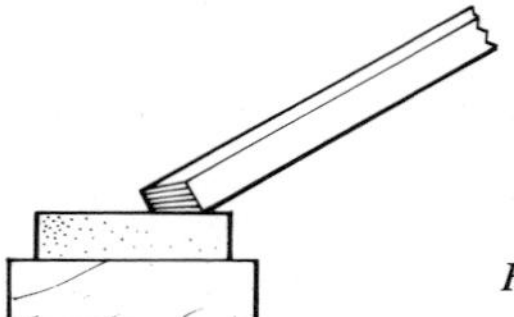

Fig. 5.7. End view of gouge on oilstone

that the grinding bevel is making full contact with the stone. In practice, slightly more pressure is applied at the cutting edge, just to ensure that metal is being removed from there, but not so much as to create a second bevel.

Rubbing on the stone is continued until a small burr develops at the cutting edge. The burr can be detected by drawing a finger off the edge of the gouge (*Figure 5.8.*). For spindle-work this burr must be completely removed with the slipstone, as shown in *Figure 5.9.* If the gouge curve is larger than that of the stone, the

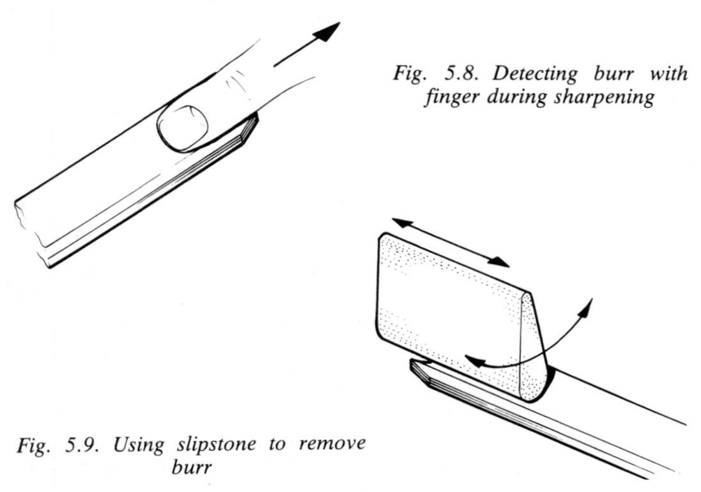

Fig. 5.8. Detecting burr with finger during sharpening

Fig. 5.9. Using slipstone to remove burr

slipstone must follow the dual movement shown by arrows in order to cover the whole of the cutting edge. The slipstone must run flat in the gouge; on no account must a bevel be formed inside the hollow of the tool. A pronounced burr is often removed as a sliver of steel – frequently called a 'wire edge'. If the slipstone does not detach the burr, then a few more gentle rubs are given to the sharpening bevel on the oilstone, followed by more use of the slipstone on the inside.

In turning, very small hollows are often needed, and these may be smaller than the smallest gouge available. Because of this, the ¼in (6mm) gouge – the smallest at present manufactured – is often sharpened so that the rounded end is elongated and made more narrow (*Figure 5.10*).

Fig. 5.10. Sharpening very small gouge

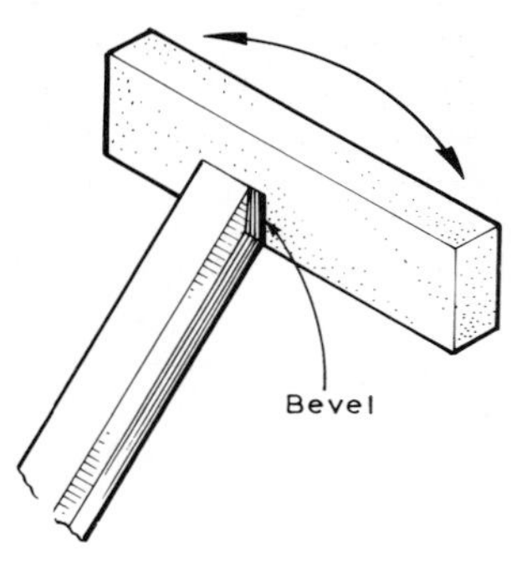

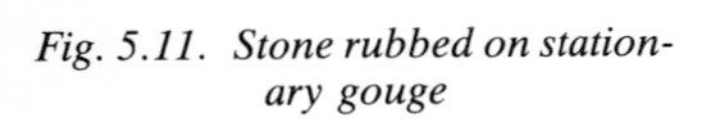

Fig. 5.11. Stone rubbed on stationary gouge

The alternative method of honing a gouge is to hold the tool still and move the oilstone over it. With this technique, the stone is usually used without being boxed, so that the weight and size which the user's hand has to hold are those of the stone only. In order that the gouge remains steady, it has to be supported, so it is best to hold it against the edge of your bench or, as many professionals do, against the toolrest. The tip of the gouge is pointed upwards at an angle and the stone is rubbed against, and around, the bevel as in *Figure 5.11*. Rubbing is continued until a

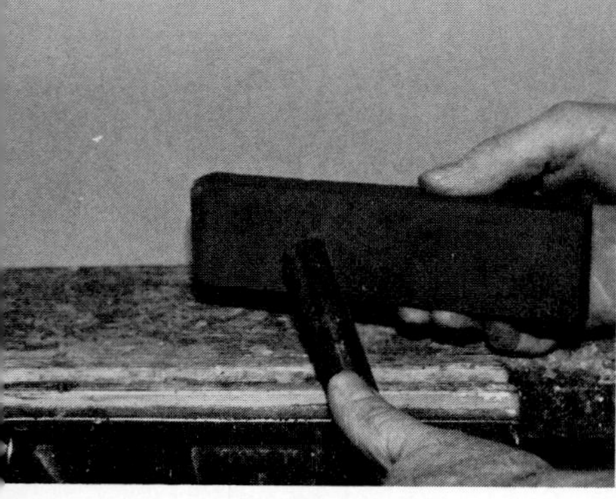

Fig. 5.12. Rubbing oilstone on gouge, which is supported on side of vice

Fig. 5.14. Sharpening gouge on oilst[illegible] Gouge is rocked from side to side [illegible] bevel remains flat on stone

Fig. 5.13. Rubbing oilstone on gouge, which is supported on side of vice

burr can be detected. The burr is then removed in the manner already described (see also *Figures 5.13* and *5.14*).

Every time a gouge is sharpened on an oilstone, the angle of sharpening is likely to become a little steeper. This is because rather more pressure is applied at the cutting edge. After many honings, the angle will have changed enough for the gouge to require re-grinding.

Skew chisels

Skew chisels are still to be seen in toolshops with the grinding bevels formed with curves, as shown in *Figure 5.15*. This has always puzzled turners, as a skew chisel is never used like this.

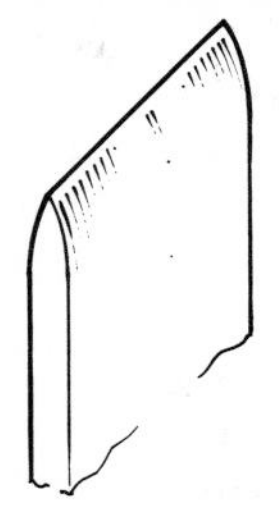

Fig. 5.15. Chisel as often supplied

Indeed, the lack of a consistent angle would make the tool far more difficult to handle, as its controlled use is dependent on a satisfactory sharpening bevel. Fortunately, most tool manufacturers now supply their skews sharpened as shown in *Figure 5.16*. Bevels on each side are equal and should be at approximately 30 degrees to one another, as illustrated in *Figure 5.17*.

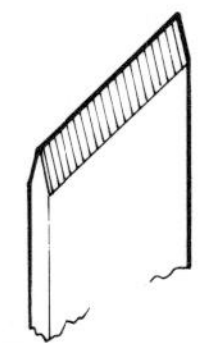

Fig. 5.16. Skew chisel with standard flat bevels

Fig. 5.17. Angles for sharpening skew chisel

With skew chisels, the angle which the cutting edge makes to the end of the blade also has to be considered. For convenience, this is expressed as the angle X in *Figure 5.17*. This can be anything from zero to 40°, but an angle of 25 to 30° is usually preferred. The greater the angle, the finer the point, and as a fine point is useful for incision work, it is helpful to have one skew sharpened to a fairly slender point.

Former generations of turners favoured skew chisels which were sharpened more or less 'square across'. This method of grinding was particularly to be seen on their broader chisels, primarily used for smoothing cylindrical work of large diameter. Old references to turnery mention chisels up to 4in wide, twice the width of the broadest ones available today. The explanation for this is probably that the old-timers often did turned work of very large proportions – ornamental wooden columns for architectural purposes, for example, and wooden patterns used in the production of cast-iron columns.

Strictly, grinding should be carried out only on the face, or rim, of the wheel no matter what is being ground. But with skew chisels, a common practice is to carry out the initial grinding in this way, then to finish off on the side of the wheel. Because the cutting edge of the chisel is skewed, it is not easy to grind both sides to a uniform and well balanced double bevel. This problem is sometimes compounded by restrictions on approaching the wheel at an angle, especially if the wheel is an attachment to a lathe. The side of a wheel should be used as little as possible, and never for heavy grinding. The side of a grinding wheel cannot be dressed or re-faced, so little can be done once the side has lost its cutting ability.

As when sharpening a spindle-gouge, honing follows the grinding of a skew chisel. The chisel is placed on the oilstone, lubricated with a few drops of oil. The blade is held, a few inches from the cutting end, by the right hand, which is raised or lowered until it can be felt that the bevel is making full contact with the stone surface. This feeling is done mainly by the fingers of the left hand, which are placed low down on the blade to apply pressure when honing. Getting the chisel to sit correctly on the stone requires a lot of practice by the inexperienced turner, and a lot of care even from the expert. Too low an angle means that steel is being removed well away from the cutting edge, so a great deal of rubbing would be needed before the cutting edge came in contact with the stone. If the handle of the chisel is raised too much, all the rubbing is concentrated at or near the cutting edge, so a second, steeper bevel is created.

As the chisel is moved to and fro along the stone, the left hand applies most of the downward pressure, while the right hand controls the angle of the chisel. It is essential that a constant angle is maintained throughout honing, otherwise rounding of the bevel is likely to occur, which will impair the cutting quality of the chisel even if the edge is really sharp. Some workers move the arms from the shoulders and manage to control the angle, others move mainly from the hips. How it is done is not important, but controlling the angle is – most of the skill in sharpening woodworking edge-tools is in keeping the angle constant.

Figure 5.18 shows the skew chisel at the start and end of the honing stroke. To maintain the constant angle, the chisel, as it moves forward, should remain parallel to the starting position. The knack comes with experience, but an essential requirement is to lock the right-hand wrist. If the wrist is allowed to flex, the result is more than likely to be rocking of the chisel and unwanted rounding of the bevel, as shown in *Figure 5.19*. Such

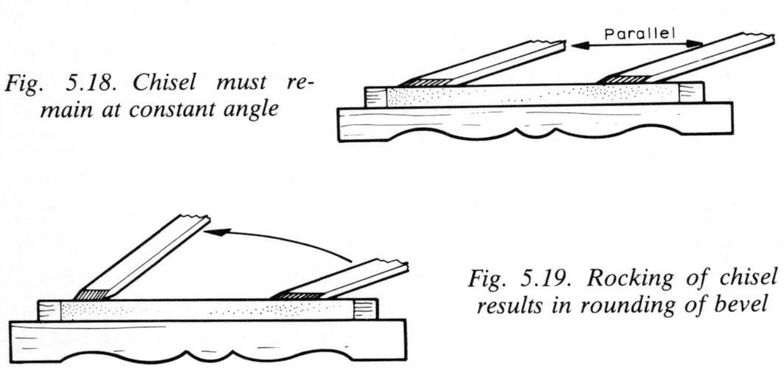

Fig. 5.18. Chisel must remain at constant angle

Fig. 5.19. Rocking of chisel results in rounding of bevel

rocking is a very common fault; the natural movement of the hand when sharpening tends to raise it on the forward stroke and lower it on the return. This rocking movement seems to be less pronounced when the right hand is well down on the blade, so that the fingers are almost touching those of the left hand. We are assuming that the turner is naturally right-handed: left-handers need only reverse the 'handing'.

Rubbing continues on one side until a light burr can be felt by drawing the finger lightly off the chisel, as for the gouge. The rubbing is then repeated on the reverse side for several strokes. To ensure that the burr is completely removed from the blade, two or three more strokes on both sides usually do the trick.

To remove any traces of the burr, a leather strop can be used. A fair amount of pressure is required but the chisel is moved only in the direction shown in *Figure 5.20.* The tool is lifted clear

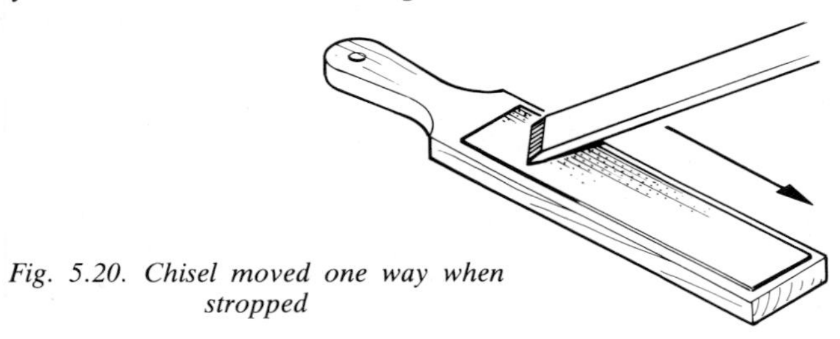

Fig. 5.20. Chisel moved one way when stropped

of the leather on the return. Somtimes strop enthusiasts will start the stroke of the chisel by smacking it down on to the leather.

Some workers like to use the strop to assist in sharpening. If a strop is treated with a mixture of oil and fine carborundum powder, it acts like a very fine oilstone and, while removing the burr, also improves the cutting edge. This is a popular technique amongst woodcarvers, whose tools have to be exceptionally sharp in order to tackle fine detail in all directions of the grain.

It helps a little with skews if the first side to be rubbed on the stone can be alternated each time the tool is honed. This is because the first side tends to need more rubbing to establish the burr than the reverse side does to remove it. In practice, frequent touching-up of a turning tool is preferable to allowing it to become quite blunt before re-honing. This means that the expert will give both sides of the skew chisel a small number of rubs on the stone, without really creating a burr which must then be removed. The burr acts as proof that effective rubbing has taken place but, with practice, the effectiveness of honing can usually be checked visually. What matters is whether the chisel cuts the wood after sharpening and leaves a smooth surface.

Bowl gouges

It has already been mentioned that gouges are known as 'spindle' gouges and 'faceplate' (or 'bowl') gouges, and that a fundamental difference between the two lies in the methods of sharpening.

Bowl gouges are ground with a much steeper angle than that used for spindle-work, this being from 45 to 60 deg, as shown in *Figure 5.21.* Some turners prefer an angle at one end of this

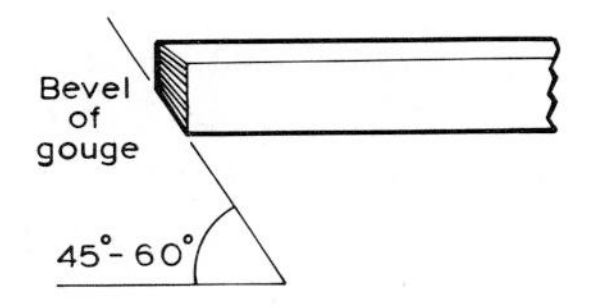

Fig. 5.21. Angle of sharpening for faceplate, or bowl-turning, gouge

range, some at the other, a steeper angle being advantageous for truing up the periphery of work of particularly large diameter.

A bowl gouge can be used straight from the grindstone – that is, without honing it to a keen edge. When so used, it is the burr which does the cutting although the gouge is not used as a scraper. The approach angle of the gouge to the work is quite different from that of the scraper, and a gouge used straight from the grinder can be made to remove quite substantial shavings very rapidly.

The alternative to using the gouge directly after grinding is to hone it so that the fairly heavy burr resulting from grinding is removed and a more normal cutting edge prepared in its place – but without using a slipstone. In this case the oilstone can be used as previously described, although most experienced turners probably rub the stone over the stationary gouge, which is supported on the edge of the bench or toolrest.

These two ways of sharpening bowl gouges are each worthy of consideration. Where the wood is of a particularly grainy nature, such as elm and African mahoganies, the preference is for the gouge used straight from the grinder. The reason is that the burr is better able to cope with the strong fibres of these woods, and is less likely to have its cutting action affected by the interlocking and irregular grain often associated with them. On the other hand, timbers with a particularly uniform texture – sycamore and beech, for example – respond well to a gouge which has been honed to give a distinct cutting edge.

Scrapers

Scrapers are used primarily for faceplate work and occasionally for spindle work in special conditions. Methods of sharpening, however, are the same, and scrapers are not divided into those used for faceplate work and those used for spindle turning.

The grinding angle of the scraper end is shown in *Figure 5.22*. It is approximately 60 deg, although there is a fair amount of

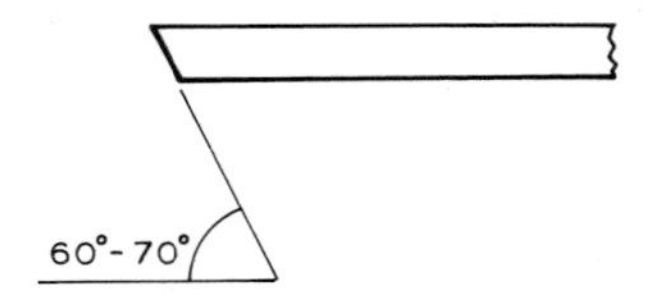

Fig. 5.22. Angle of sharpening for scrapers

tolerance. As when sharpening a gouge, grinding the end of a tool right up to its edge produces a burr. It is this burr which gives the scraper its cutting ability. Not only is the scraper a fairly simple tool to use, it is also the easiest to sharpen – provided that a good grinding wheel is available.

Some turners prefer to produce the cutting burr in a rather different way, especially when touching-up between one grinding and the next. After initial grinding, the burr produced by the grinder is removed by rubbing the top surface of the scraper flat on an oilstone, as shown in *Figure 5.23*. If this does not remove the burr, the oilstone is rubbed across the grinding bevel, as illustrated in *Figure 5.24*; again rubbing the scraper, flat, across the stone should remove all traces of the burr.

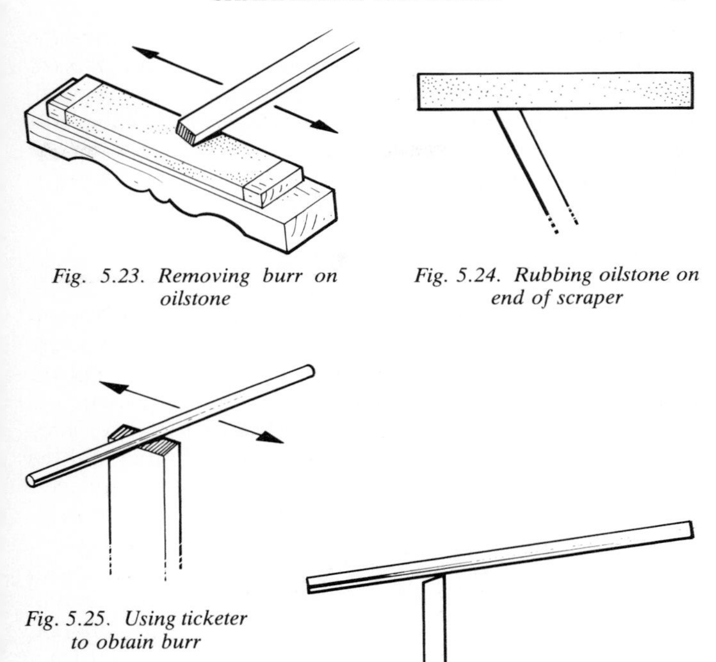

Fig. 5.23. Removing burr on oilstone

Fig. 5.24. Rubbing oilstone on end of scraper

Fig. 5.25. Using ticketer to obtain burr

Fig. 5.26. Angle of ticketer slightly steeper than angle of grinding

Now the cutting burr has to be produced: this is when the ticketer is employed. The scraper is firmly held upright, and the ticketer is stroked sideways along the edge of the sharpening bevel, as shown in *Figure 5.25*. Fairly considerable pressure is needed, as the extreme tip of the bevel has to be pushed out of place and turned over to form a burr. The angle that the ticketer makes with the scraper edge should be only sufficiently steeper than the grinding bevel to create this burr: this is illustrated in *Figure 5.26*.

The choice between these alternative ways of producing the burr on the scraper is a matter of personal preference. Experienced turners generally use the scraper straight from the grinding wheel: maybe the grinder used has just the right characteristics to produce an effective burr, or the right grinding technique has been developed after much practice.

Sharpening problems

A large number of factors affect sharpness. Modern tool-steel is usually consistent in quality, hardness, and temper; but there are variations. Slight differences in steels affect their sharpening or, more especially, their ability to retain a good cutting edge for a reasonable length of time. Other points which affect sharpening are the grinding wheel, the pressure of the tool on it, and the angles adopted. Even experts will admit that they can produce a superb cutting edge 19 times out of 20, but the twentieth time, for reasons not obvious, the result is an edge below its best.

One undoubted reason why tools appear to perform with slightly varying efficiency is that wood is a very variable material. Not only are the characteristics of one species very different from those of another, they can often be quite dissimilar from one sample to another of the same species. For example, English oak is usually very hard and dense, while some imported varieties are remarkably mild.

While it is true that sharp tools are always needed when woodturning, this is, paradoxically, even more true when turning soft woods (which are not necessarily softwoods – see Chapter 12). Blunt tools on soft wood are likely to produce a rough and ragged surface. This is because a blunt tool has to be forced in order to remove any wood at all, the result being that the fibres are prised out, rather than cut. While blunt tools will not cut hard wood any more easily than they will cut soft wood, they do not tear out the grain in the same way.

The wood being turned can have a marked effect on the results of sharpening, however well this has been carried out. Some timbers are so abrasive that even a well-sharpened lathe-tool will cut for only a few minutes before re-sharpening is required (see Chapter 12). Broadly, the harder the wood, the more quickly it will dull the tool, and when turning soft woods, the tools will need less frequent sharpening. The rule is, though, to keep tools sharp at all times.

A final word on sharpening: some experienced turners who have lathes with facilities for rear turning keep on the left-hand side of the headstock a faceplate on which is stuck a disc of fine emery or similar paper. This is used to touch-up tools between normal grinding and honing. It is quite effective if not overused.

6 Supplementary tools and equipment

In addition to tools used for shaping the wood, certain other tools are required by the woodturner. Many are likely to be found in any workshop where wood is used, others are more specific to the craft of the turner.

Among the workshop tools, a tenon saw will be needed for sawing the vee-cut at the end of a piece of wood when a positive grip is required for the driving centre. Size of saw is not critical; the popular 10 in (254 mm) blade is ideal. A hammer, also of average size, will be needed from time to time. Do not use bench-chisels or gouges on the lathe: they are too light for such work and in most cases the bevels will be wrong.

Bradawls and screwdrivers will be in fairly frequent use for mounting work on the faceplate, so a range of sizes of both tools is desirable. A couple of rules, at least, will be needed. Either a folding rule opening to 36 in (or 1 m) or a flexible steel tape is required when marking stock at the preparatory stage and for measuring larger items while being turned. A 12 in (300 mm) steel rule is essential for the more precise measurements which are often needed. The steel rule is particularly useful in conjunction with callipers.

Callipers and compasses

Callipers are probably the most used of all supplementary tools employed in lathework. There are two classes, the 'inside' and the 'outside'. Ou[illegible]e callipers, as the name suggests, are used for establishing and checking the outside diameters of a work-piece; a typical pair is shown in *Figure 6.1*. This particular type is known as 'firm-joint', the legs being held by friction, which can be controlled by adjusting the screw which holds them together.

The callipers have two main purposes. First, they are used to establish an existing diameter by closing the legs on to the work and then measuring the gap between them. The second use is when the work is being turned to a set diameter: the callipers are set to the required diameter, and the work is checked as turning proceeds until its diameter has been reduced to the size required.

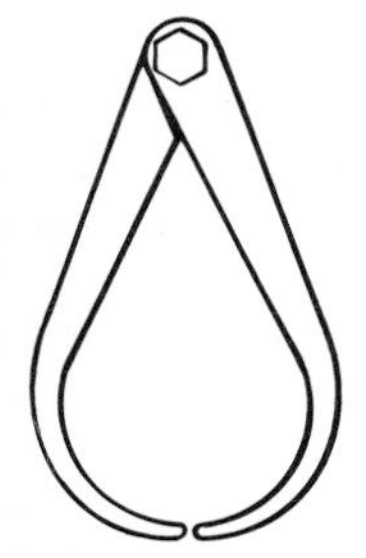

Fig. 6.1. Firm-joint outside callipers

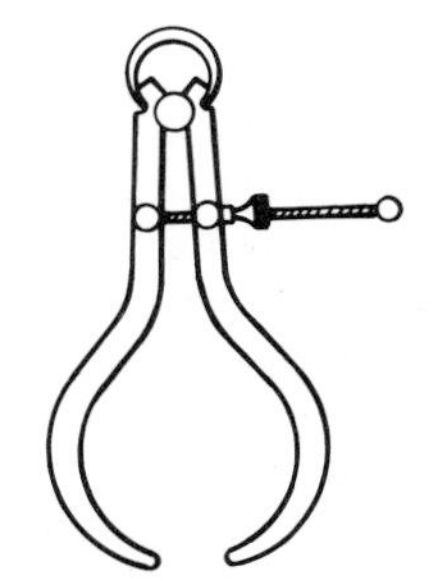

Fig. 6.2. Fine-adjustment callipers

At all times, callipers must be used gently, because forcing them into the work can have the effect of opening the legs. Re-checking of the callipers with a rule as work proceeds is always a wise precaution. For the complete beginner, it is safer to stop the lathe before using callipers but, with experience and when the feel of the tool has been acquired, outside callipers can be used with care while the work is revolving.

A variation of firm-joint callipers is shown in *Figure 6.2*. Here the legs are held by the bow spring at the top, and setting is controlled by the adjusting screw at the side. They are called 'fine-adjustment' callipers.

A pair of inside callipers is illustrated in *Figure 6.3*. They are used when work is being hollowed and are similar in principle to outside callipers. Inside callipers should never be used while the work is revolving. The risk of their being gripped by the work is very high if the lathe is running, which could easily result in the callipers being snatched from the hand of the user and his fingers being twisted or injured. Inside callipers are also available in the fine-adjustment version.

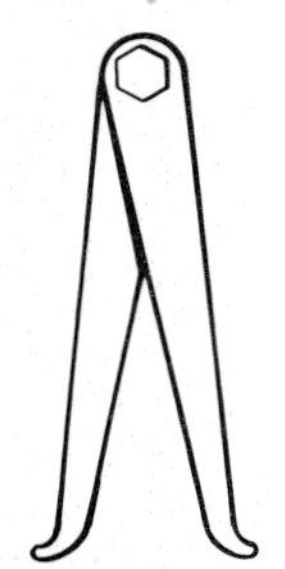

Fig. 6.3. Firm-joint inside callipers

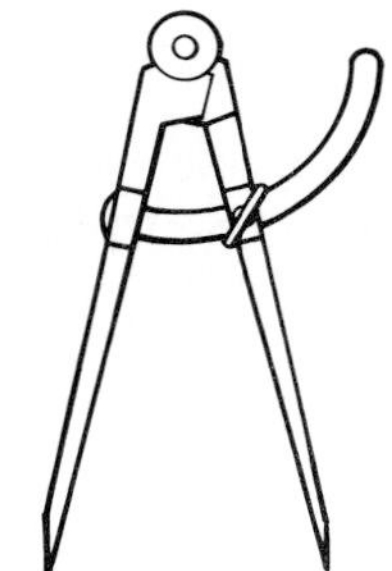

Fig. 6.4. Wing-compasses

The wing-compasses shown in *Figure 6.4* can be useful, especially in faceplate work, as shown in *Figure 6.5*. The line scribed may be needed because the wood on the outside has to be removed or, more likely, because the area within the scribed circle has to be removed. To have a positive line accurately and

Fig. 6.5. Using compasses on revolving work

clearly marked on the wood is especially useful if the work is being hollowed in order that a piece can be fitted on completion, such as a brass insert for an ashtray or a glass insert for a butter-dish. Compasses are used while the work revolves, when it is a simple matter to establish the centre of the work visually: lightly insert one leg of the compasses into this centre and scribe the line with the other leg (see *Figure 7.10*).

A circle on a revolving piece of wood can also be marked with a rule and pencil, measuring the radius from the centre. It is advisable to check the diameter, as work marked out like this tends to finish slightly bigger than intended, unless extreme care is taken.

Using wing-compasses is, of course, a very good way of marking a block of wood with its circular shape when preparing it for a piece of faceplate turnery. Ordinary pencil compasses can be used, but wing-compasses are rather more robust, with a point which is not likely to break off, and they can be locked to a set diameter.

Peg gauge

A fairly common operation in woodturning is to form what can be called circular mortice and tenon joints. The mortice is no more than a hole, usually bored on the lathe, and the tenon is a circular peg formed at one end of the other piece of work. An example of this method is the joint between the stem and base of a reading-lamp (*Figure 6.6*). It is also used between the legs and

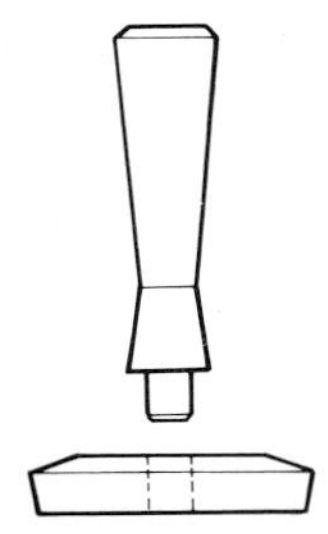

Fig. 6.6. Typical use of circular tenon on reading lamp

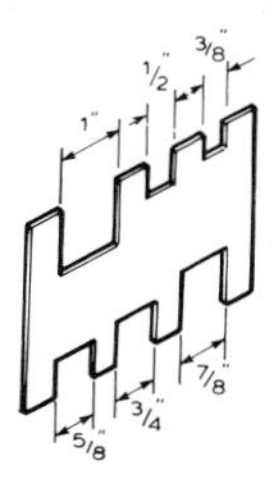

Fig. 6.7. Home-made gauge for pins

seat of a simple stool. Since the hole is bored out by a drill-bit, its diameter is restricted to a standard drill size, so the peg or tenon must be turned to make a good fit in the hole. While outside callipers can be used to check the diameters of such pegs, the simple gauge shown in *Figure 6.7* is well worth making. A piece of 16 gauge (about 1/16 in thick) brass or aluminium sheet, about 4 in by 3 in, is shaped as shown, the slots corresponding to the sizes likely to be used for making joints. The edges of the slots can be filed to fine limits so as to give just the right degree of tightness when used in conjunction with a particular bit. A gauge such as this not only saves time in the long run but enables very accurate joints to be made.

Centre square

For a variety of reasons, the turner sometimes finds himself with a piece of wood turned to circular shape but cut in such a way that the location of the centre of the work has been lost. For re-establishing the centre fairly accurately, usually for the purpose of re-mounting in the lathe, the centre square is a useful device which can be either bought or made at home from wood or metal. The square is shown in *Figure 6.8*; *Figure 6.9* shows

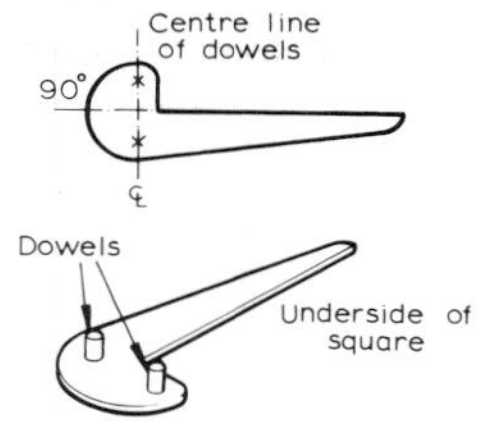

Fig. 6.8. Centre square

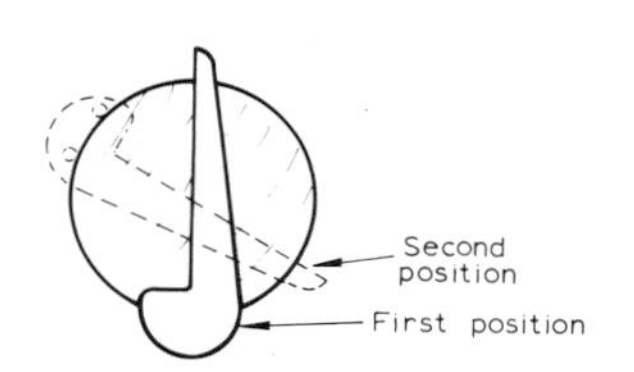

Fig. 6.9. Using the centre square

how it is used. Two lines drawn in any position of the square, held with its pegs touching the periphery of the workpiece, will intersect at the centre.

Sizing tool

One most interesting and useful new tool is known as a 'sizing tool' (*Figure 6.10*). Its purpose is to produce a turning to an accurate, pre-determined diameter. It is designed to take either a ¼in or a ⅜in parting tool, which can be locked in the barrel part of the tool by means of the two thumbscrews. How the tool

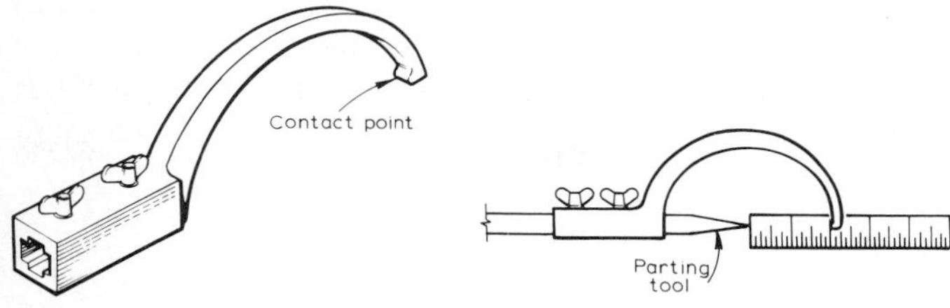

Fig. 6.10. Sizing tool

Fig. 6.11. Setting the sizing tool

is set to the required size is illustrated in *Figure 6.11*. The diameter is measured between the point of the parting tool (which is, of course, movable) and the nodule on the inside end of the sizing tool. In use, the sizing tool or the parting tool (depending on what diameter is set) is supported on the toolrest with the parting tool as high on the wood as is practicable. The combined tools are then lowered on to the wood until close to the required diameter, then used with backwards and downwards pressure to produce an accurately finished diameter.

It is important for the rounded projection at the rear part of the tool to be kept in close contact with the wood, as a gap here would result in an undersize diameter (*Figure 6.12*).

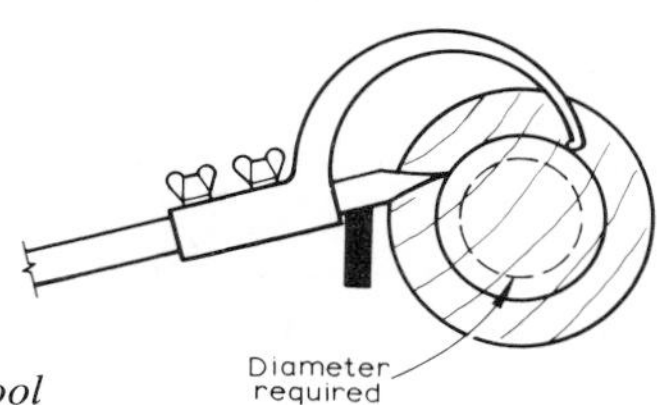

Fig. 6.12. Using the sizing tool

Because the parting tool is locked in place in the sizing tool, it is not possible to cut the wood in what is the best way when using the parting tool freehand. Loss of maximum efficiency, however, is more then compensated for by the ability to produce an accurately controlled diameter. The tool is particularly useful when tenons are being formed.

Copying devices

Any turner will be involved sooner or later in repetition work, if only a set of identical legs for a chair or stool. For this, some form of adjustable templet is both a timesaver and an aid to accuracy. Such a device is the 'Mimic' shape tracer, which is shown set to a typical profile in *Figure 6.13*. It consists of a series

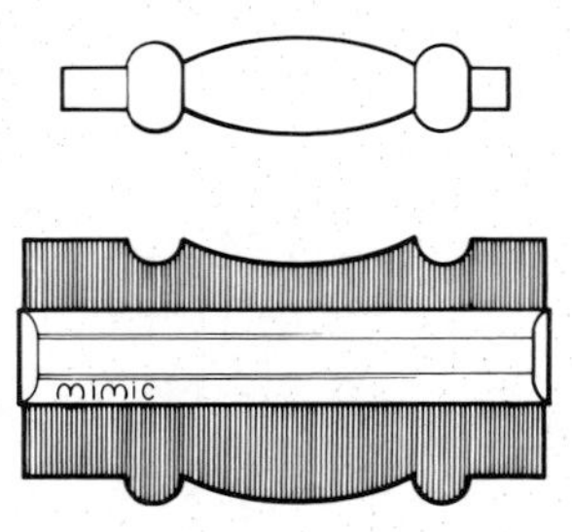

Fig. 6.13. Mimic tracer

of fine steel rods held between rubber pads in the centre section, with an overall length around 6in. The friction between rubber and rods is low enough to allow movement, when required, between the two, but sufficient to hold the rods against light pressure or normal handling. In use, the first turning is produced to the profile required, then the tracer is set to this profile, which, in effect, acts as a pattern. Subsequent turnings are then made, using the tracer as a templet. It is essential to have the work stationary when the tracer is first set, because the needles must be pressed against the pattern firmly in order to make them slide through the rubber pads. Because of the limited size of the Mimic, it may be usable for only the most intricate part of a piece of work. Some types of this templet can be joined together, thus increasing the length as required.

Another fairly new device introduced as an aid for the woodturner and designed specially to facilitate repetition work is known as the 'Craft Copying Attachment'. It consists of a series of carriers and fingers, mounted on a tubular metal bar which, in turn, is mounted to the rear of the lathe. Carriers can be moved laterally along the bar, and also pivoted forward or backward so as to control the projection of the fingers. The bar has to be mounted on the lathe cabinet or bench by the turner, for which purpose a block at each end of the bar will almost certainly be required as packing. These blocks can be fixed permanently to the cabinet or arranged so that they can be held by bolts and wing-nuts, or G-cramps. Six carriers and fingers are supplied with the tool, with additional ones available as extras. Fewer than six can be used (*Figure 6.14*).

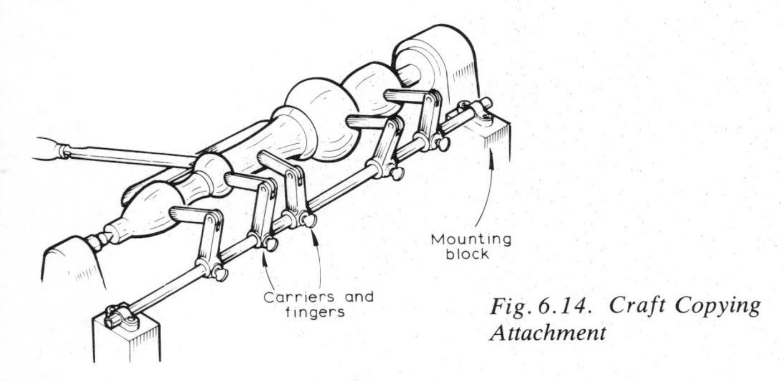

Fig. 6.14. Craft Copying Attachment

If an old turning has to be copied, as when carrying out restoration work on an antique, then the procedure is as follows. Mount the original leg, or whatever part is being copied, between the lathe centres. Considerable care will almost certainly be needed here, as the original points of mounting will more than likely have been removed. It is essential to re-establish accurately the centres at each end of the work, or the piece will revolve with a wobble, making precise copying well-nigh impossible, so use a centre square, previously described.

The next step is to move the carriers laterally along the rod to coincide with the main features of the original turning; these are likely to be the maximum and minimum diameters and the small flats or quirks which are often introduced between a concave curve and convex one.

Next, the carriers are pivoted on the bar so that the fingers only just touch the features selected, but in such a manner that by their own weight they will drop down past the wood. The fingers are then pivoted upwards and clear of the wood so that they are pointing backwards, and the original turning is removed from the lathe.

Wood for the new component is next mounted on the lathe and roughed out. The lateral limits of all the features are then marked in. One method of doing this is with rule and pencil, the pencil-point being applied to the work while it is revolving to give an instantaneous circular line. The fingers are next lifted forward so that they are resting on the wood. Shaping is now carried out by gouge and chisel, and as soon as the required diameter is reached at any point where there is a finger, the finger will drop clear of the work into the downward positon.

The device must not be regarded as automatic, as the fingers in no way control the amount of wood being removed: a moment's carelessness could easily result in too much being removed. Moreover, the shaping between one finger and the next has to be established by the turner.

As well as for copying an existing piece of turnery, the Craft Copying Attachment can be used when making a set of indentical components, such as a set of four legs. The procedure is to turn the first leg with the fingers of the attachment clear of the wood in the backward position. The completed leg is then treated as the pattern from which the remaining legs are turned.

Home-made templets and marking devices

Though one of the joys of woodturning is the limitless variety of shapes that can be produced, even the expert is rarely successful if he is thinking out the profile he requires as he proceeds with the actual turning of the wood. The shape required should be decided beforehand, at least in its essential form. This stage usually involves sketches.

The sketches, or drawings taken from books, still have to be translated into three-dimensional form in solid wood. One way of doing this is to prepare a templet in the negative form of the shape to be produced.

A typical outline for a turning is shown in templet form in *Figure 6.15*. Templets of this type are usually made in stiff card. They enable two or more turnings to be checked as work is proceeding to ensure that the final shapes are all the same. A

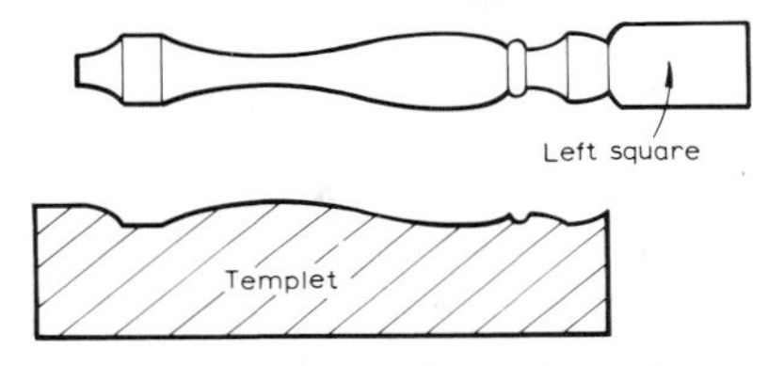

Fig. 6.15. Card or plywood templet

more permanent form of templet can be made from thin plywood, but this entails more work than making a templet from card.

Another home-made device which can be used for repetition work as an aid to both speed and accuracy is the pricker stick (*Figure 6.16*). It consists of a lath about ¾in by ¾in in section and of a length to suit the work in hand. The lath is marked out

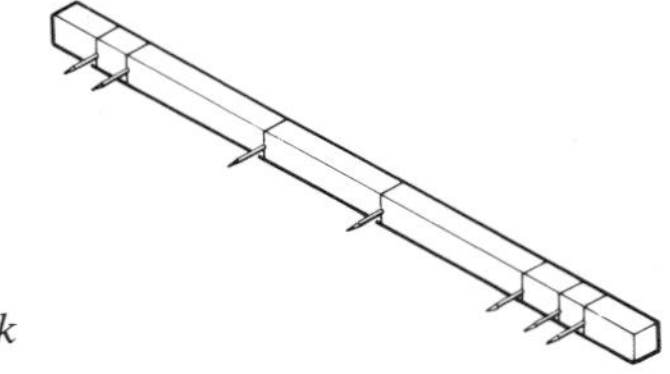

Fig. 6.16. Pricker stick

to indicate the limits of all main features of the profile, then fine nails are driven right through where the marks are made. In use, the work is first turned to cylindrical form, then the pricker stick, resting on the toolrest, is gently pressed against the revolving wood so that the nails score the surface. The marks will be clearer if a pencil-point is used to emphasise the nail scribings.

A variation of the pricker stick is a strip of wood with pencil-lines marked on as for a pricker stick. In use, the strip, which can be plywood or solid wood about 1½in by ¼in, is

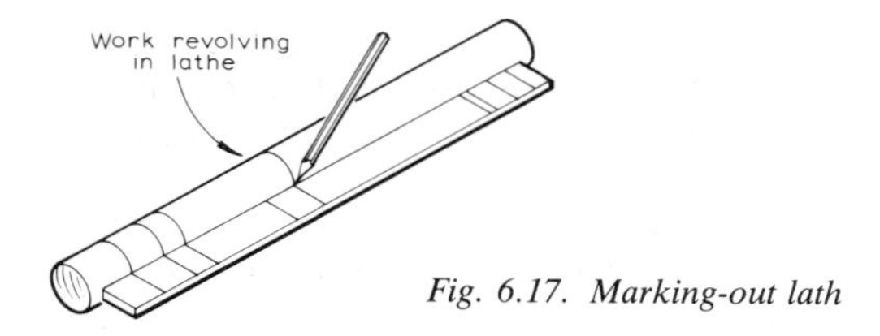

Fig. 6.17. Marking-out lath

lightly held against the revolving cylinder of wood while supported on the toolrest. A pencil is then used as shown in *Figure 6.17* to transfer marks from strip to workpiece.

Spindle-steady

Problems arise in spindle-turning when the work is both relatively long and fairly thin. Although some timbers are more resilient than others, all tend to bend if the cross-section is small compared with the length. When such a long, slender piece of wood is mounted between centres for turning, the natural springiness of the wood is compounded by two further factors. No matter how gently the wood is held between the centres, some pressure is exerted on the ends, and this causes the middle to move sideways. The second difficulty is an effect of the cutting tool on the wood. Even with tools which are perfectly sharp, the wood resists the cutting to some extent, and this resistance makes the wood move away from the tool, if it can. Slender wood is not sufficiently rigid for the tool to cut efficiently, and the wood will flex and 'whip' as a result. This problem can be overcome by supporting the wood near its mid-point, which in effect reduces the length of the wood from centre to centre by half. Such a support is known as a 'steady'.

Steadies are available as extras for metal-turning lathes, but none seems to be commercially made for woodturning lathes. Over the years, woodturners have designed and made their own, so there are many variations of this home-made accessory.

To some extent, the design depends on the type of bed which the lathe has, because it is usual to fix a steady to the bed.

Steadies also need to be devised in such a way that they can be quickly fixed and removed and are fairly easy to move sideways, as they are not always wanted exactly at the half-way position of the wood.

The essential features of a typical steady are shown in *Figure 6.18*. The complete assembly is held in place on the bed by a wedge driven between the bottom of the bed and the dowel or bolt fixed through the upright legs. The horizontal arm can be adjusted so as just to support the work. It is essential that the

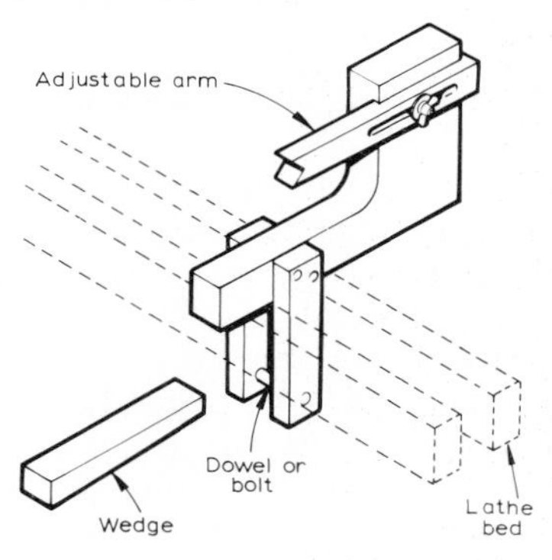

Fig. 6.18. Steady

centre of the vee-cut at the end of the arm is at exactly the same height as the centre of the lathe. If not, the steady will have the effect of deflecting the wood – the very opposite to its purpose.

These items are most of the accessories needed from time to time by serious turners. One other is an ordinary hacksaw blade. With it a fine groove can be cut on a spindle or hollow vessel. The blade is rested on the toolrest and held there firmly, then gently lowered on to the work until a shallow groove is cut. Then with the blade turned over, friction will char a very conspicuous brown ring in the wood. Hold the blade in a protecting pad of cloth until the technique is mastered.

7 Bowl turning

As a rule, it is easier for the woodturning beginner to produce an acceptable item on the faceplate than between centres. This is partly because scraping methods are soon understood and mastered, and scraping is a technique used far more in faceplate work than in spindle-turning. It is also because the skew chisel is the tool that is likely to pose the most problems to the tyro, and skews are never used on faceplate work.

There is a false idea that bowls are almost always made to hold fruit and that they therefore need to be at least 8 in (200 mm) in diameter and made from a blank cut from 3 in (76 mm) stock. In fact, very acceptable and useful bowls (for sweets and nuts, for example) can be made from much smaller blocks. Diameters of 5 in (125 mm) made from 1½ in (38 mm) stock will be found to hold far more than expected.

Tools and methods are the same whether the bowl be large or small, although bigger bowls are a little more demanding of skill. Some reference has already been made to bowl-turning in general, so the following guidelines must be read in conjunction with what has previously been said about methods of mounting the work and the principles of using turning-tools.

Truing-up

When mounting the work on the faceplate, remember what has been said about the annual rings, and follow the instructions given for screwing the faceplate on to (normally) the side of the block which will eventually be hollowed. Mount the faceplate as centrally on the block as possible, then screw it on to the lathe mandrel.

Even with a block which has been sawn to a circular shape, the first stage in faceplate work is to trim the periphery so as to make the block truly circular. A bowl is rarely turned to a specific diameter, the aim usually being to make it as large as possible from the available block. This is why the faceplate needs to be central in the first place, and why only the minimum should be taken off when truing up. Truing-up is best carried out with a

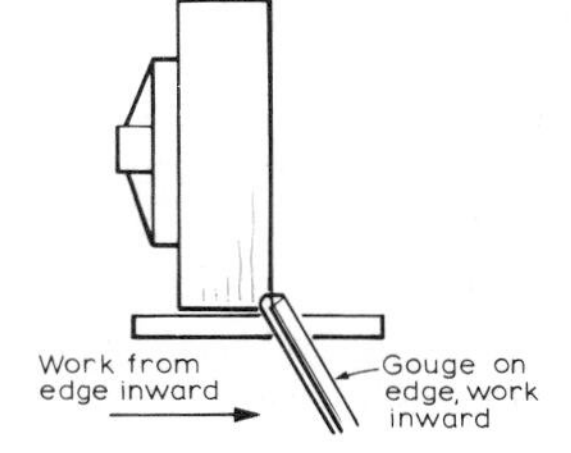

Fig. 7.1. Trimming the periphery of the bowl

gouge, either ⅜ or ½ in (9 mm or 12 mm) wide. It can be of standard weight, although ideally it should be a long-and-strong type. Refer to what has already been said about the shape of the end and methods of sharpening. Remember the golden rule for using a gouge to get the best out of the tool – the sharpening bevel must rub on the surface of the wood. This is shown in *Figure 7.1*. It is better to work from the edge inwards, thus avoiding any tendency to split at the corners (see also *Figures 7.11* and *7.12*).

The preference for holding turning tools for most operations is to have the left hand on top of the blade, with the fingers wrapped around it. The tool is then held in a controlled way by having the fleshy part which lies below the little finger of the left hand firmly on the toolrest. This holds the tool in a very positive way so that it cannot easily move laterally along the rest unless deliberately made to do so (see also *Figure 7.13*). This applies equally to chisels, gouges, and scrapers – but there are many exceptions to this general rule.

If a scraper is being used for the initial truing-up, either a square-end or a round-end tool is suitable. The preferred shape is one which is slightly rounded. A small size, say ½ in, is easier to control and use than a larger one. Only very light cuts should be taken, and especially if the block has been sawn to octagonal, rather than circular, shape.

Grain effect

Once the edge has been trimmed, whether by gouge or scraper, the newly-cut surface should be examined carefully as the work is revolved by hand. It is likely to show two areas which are slightly darker than the other two. Closer examination will reveal that the lighter areas have a somewhat smoother finish than the darker ones, where there may even be some tearing of the grain.

The light and dark effect depends to some extent on the colour of the wood, and also on the way light is reflected from the surface. The degree of roughness of the grain in these two darker areas depends on the species of wood, the sharpness of tools, the angle of cutting, and whether a gouge or scraper has been used: a gouge, correctly used, is likely to cut more cleanly than a scraper.

The reason for these alternating areas is the fact that, for part of the periphery, cutting is with the grain and for part of it against the grain. Reference to *Figure 7.2* should make this clear.

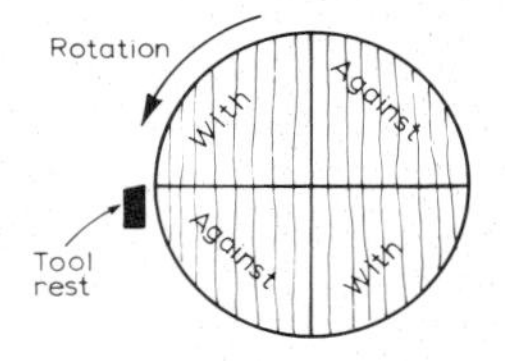

Fig. 7.2. Areas 'with' and 'against' the grain

Here the block is viewed from the tailstock end, the arrow indicating the direction of rotation. As the edge of the wood passes the tool, supported on the toolrest, the 'with' area will be relatively smooth. However, as the 'against' areas are cut, the tool is moving against the grain. Cutting wood against the grain is always likely to leave the surface somewhat rough, and even to tear the grain. In faceplate work, these two areas of against-the-grain cutting cannot be directly avoided, but steps can be taken to lessen the consequences.

Forming the base

Bowls are usually made with a rim or base about ⅛in to 3⁄16in high. This is the part to be formed after trimming the edge. The first cut at this stage is a groove or recess around the base, made with a square-end scraper. This groove is shown in elevation and section in *Figure 7.3*, and the square-end scraper used is shown in *Figure 7.4*. The sketch shows the scraper from below, showing

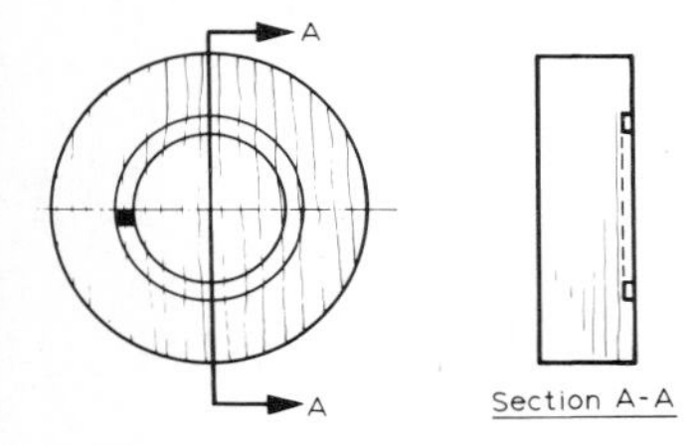

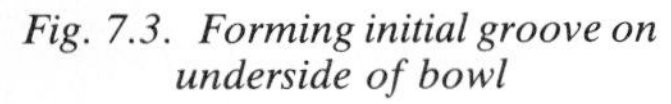

Fig. 7.3. Forming initial groove on underside of bowl

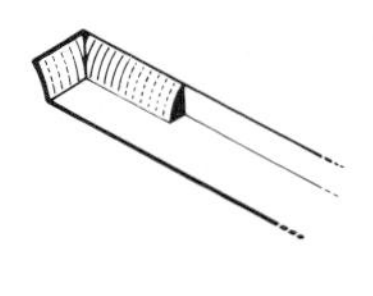

Fig. 7.4. Scraper ground at end and side

how the grinding takes place at the end and for a short distance along the edge. The need for this will be apparent by referring back to *Figure 7.3* (see also *Figure 7.14*). The black square in the groove represents the end of the tool which is cutting the groove and so penetrating part-way into it. Because the cut being made is circular, clearance is required on the lower left-hand corner, which is why the scraper is ground as shown. This is a small point, and the groove could be formed without too much difficulty by a scraper ground on the end only, but the side grinding has advantages for the next stage. (In turning, one stage merges into the next, so a series of small stages becomes a more continuous, longer one. However, the beginner is likely to make better progress in mastering the lathe if he tackles the work in the step-by-step way being described.)

Wood on the outer part of the groove is next to be removed, *Figure 7.5* showing this part of the work when nearing completion. The wood can be removed either making a series of cuts directly into it with the scraper, or by moving the scraper sideways from the initial groove. The latter method will work only if the scraper has been ground as shown in *Figure 7.4*, which allows side-cutting to be carried out. *Figure 7.6* shows the bowl when this stage has been completed.

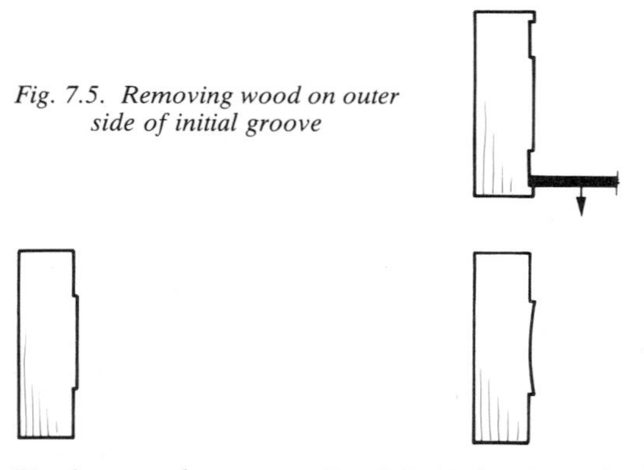

Fig. 7.5. Removing wood on outer side of initial groove

Fig. 7.6. Wood removed to form base

Fig. 7.7. Underside made slightly concave

Assuming that the bowl is being made from a block of wood which has sawn surfaces all over, the part which forms the underside of the bowl will next need attention. As well as skimming the wood to provide a smoother surface, it helps a great deal if this part of the bowl is made very slightly concave. This ensures freedom from rocking after the bowl is complete, but, even more important, it will eliminate any tendency for the bowl to rock when mounted on its base in readiness for hollowing. The amount of dishing needs to be only about $\frac{1}{16}$ in (1.5 mm) when a straightedge is placed across the surface (*Figure 7.7*).

Shaping the outside

The outer, lower edge can now be rounded. The scraper is moved around the curve to produce the required shape, as shown in *Figure 7.8*. Although a fairly narrow scraper is best for removing the bulk of the waste, a wider scraper, say 1 in, will be useful for the final trimming of this part. (See also *Figure 7.15*.)

After the first forming of the groove (*Figure 7.5*), all the remaining shaping can be completed with a gouge. The gouge is used well over on its side, starting off in the groove and pointing to the edge of the block, also slightly upwards. The gouge is shown as it is moved to the edge in *Figure 7.9*. Rounding is

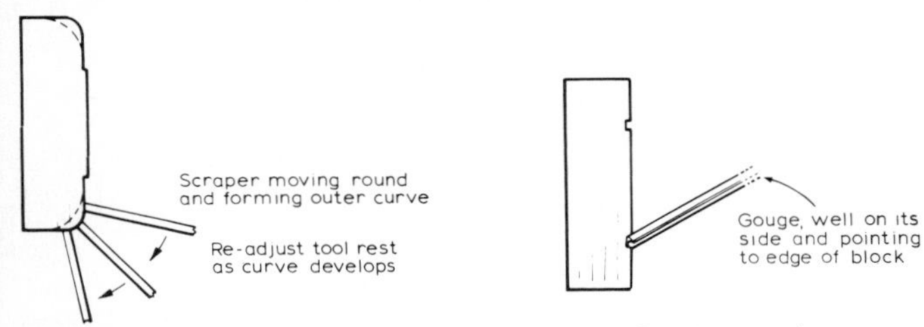

Fig. 7.8. Forming outer curve with scraper

Fig. 7.9. Starting to form outer curve with gouge

carried out in a manner basically similar to the scraping method. The gouge is shown in *Figure 7.22* as it traverses from the base towards the outer edge. Note that it must move in the direction shown to get the best advantage of grain direction to mimimise the against-the-grain effect. (See also *Figure 7.16*.)

Even the slight dishing of the centre part can be accomplished with a small faceplate gouge. Because the amount of hollowing at this part is very slight, the direction of working can be either from the centre or towards it, but the gouge is still used well on its side so that the bevel rubs on the wood.

If the chuck is of the pattern which incorporates a small faceplate, it is ideal for the stage when the bowl is reversed, as it is helpful for the faceplate to be smaller than the diameter of the bowl-base. If a small faceplate is being used, then its diameter should be marked on the underside of the bowl. This is to enable the faceplate to be screwed on in an exactly central position.

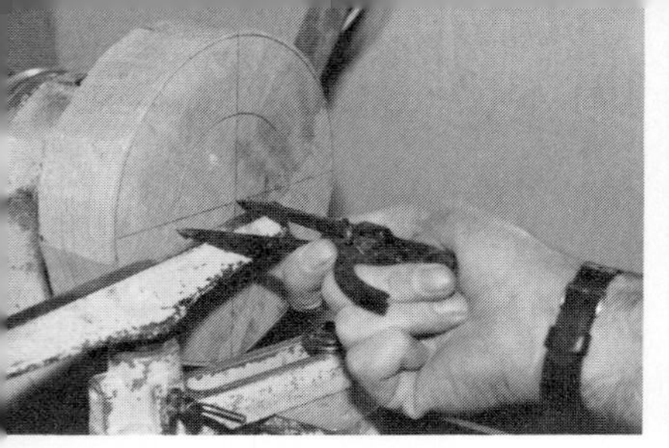

Fig. 7.10. Using wing-compasses to mark out base of bowl

Fig. 7.11. Using gouge on its side when starting to trim periphery

Fig. 7.12. Using gouge on its side when starting to trim periphery

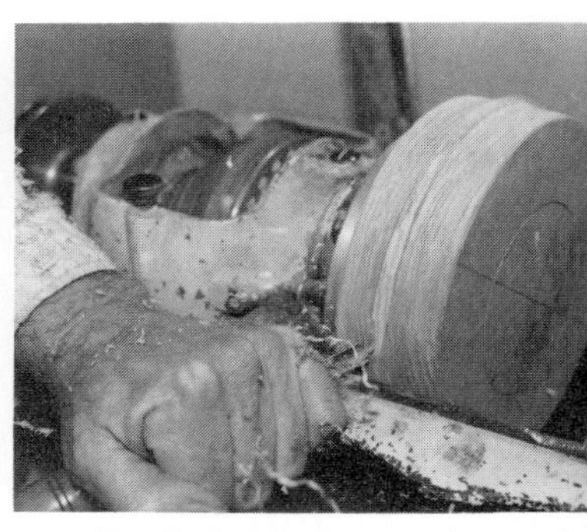

Fig. 7.13. Nearing completion of trimming

Fig. 7.14. First cut on underside of bowl

Fig. 7.15. Forming lower curve on underside of bowl, early stages

Fig. 7.16. *Completion of underside*

Fig. 7.17. *Start of hollowing, using a gouge*

Fig. 7.18. *Hollowing procedure, using a scraper*

Fig. 7.19. *Hollowing with a gouge*

7.20. *Hollowing at advanced stage*

Fig. 7.21. *Checking depth of bowl*

Reversing the work

One of the problems encountered in faceplate turning where the wood is worked partly from one side and partly from the other is maintaining concentricity. If, when the work is reversed, it is very slightly off centre, then the error can often be disguised. But if the degree of eccentricity is large, this can lead to problems, and it is better to correct it by re-mounting.

One way of ensuring that the second side is concentric with the first is to recess the faceplate very slightly into the wood. This is shown in *Figure 7.23*, the recess being formed with a square-end

Fig. 7.22. Movement of gouge when rounding

Fig. 7.23. Recessing base for small faceplate

scraper and to a depth of 1⁄16 in. It is essential that the diameter of the recess is such as to allow the faceplate to fit exactly, otherwise its purpose is lost.

When screwing the faceplate, or any other mounting device, on to the underside of a bowl, extreme care needs to be taken with the length of screws used, and also with the pilot-holes made for them. The length of screw which penetrates the wood depends on the size of the bowl but is likely to be between 5⁄16 in and ½ in. Screws of the maximum gauge which will pass through the holes in the faceplate should always be used.

Another aid to getting any piece of faceplate work concentric when changing from one side to another is this: to start with, screw the faceplate to the work with two screws only. Mount it on the lathe and check if it is running true or not. If not, slacken the two screws already inserted and insert the remaining two in such a way as to pull the faceplate into the central position. If, when the concentricity is checked after inserting the first two screws, it is found to be well out, it is best to start again and check more carefully.

If a small faceplate is not available, the standard faceplate provided with the lathe will have to be used, but this is likely to be larger than the base of the bowl. While such a faceplate could be screwed directly to the bowl, it restricts the space on the underside, and this makes subsequent glasspapering and polishing very difficult (see *Figure 7.24*). The answer is to

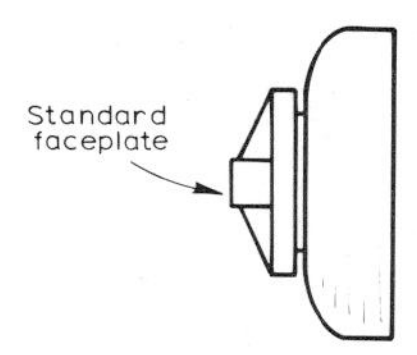

Fig. 7.24. Restricted space between bowl and faceplate

introduce a packing-piece between the two. Plywood is ideal for packing as it holds screws well and does not split. A thickness of about ½in usually gives enough clearance. It is best if the packing itself is turned to circular shape and screwed to the bowl, then the faceplate screwed to the packing. The same precautions to ensure that the bowl is always concentric must be taken.

One of the many advantages of the six-in-one chuck previously described is that the work is automatically centralised when the chuck is mounted in the dovetailed recess made for it.

Glasspapering should not take place at this stage. It is best left until all the actual turning has been completed. Glasspapering is dealt with in Chapter 11.

Completing the outside

With the work reversed, the next step is to complete the turning of the outside with scraper or gouge. This stage is shown in *Figure 7.25*. As absolute concentricity of one side of the bowl with the reverse side is in reality not easy to achieve, a certain amount of blending-in of the two curves will in all probability be needed.

An alternative way of working is to turn the whole of the outside while the block is mounted on the faceplate by its upper surface, as shown in *Figure 7.26*. This has an advantage and a disadvantage. On the credit side, the whole of the outer curved

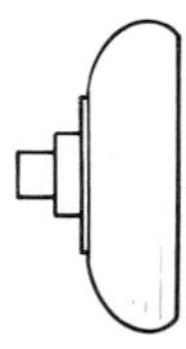

Fig. 7.25. Completion of outside

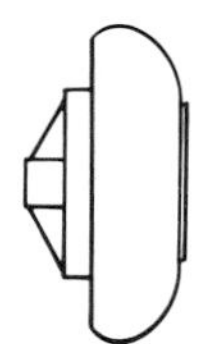

Fig. 7.26. Outside completed on large faceplate

surface will be smooth and continuous, without any danger that the upper and lower curves do not flow into each other. On the other hand, if there is a slight eccentricity when the work is reversed, this will show itself by the wall of the bowl being of varying thickness.

Hollowing the inside

Rough hollowing of the inside proceeds in stages (*Figures 7.17 – 7.21*) and these are shown in *Figure 7.27*. It is important to ensure that there is always adequate thickness at the base, especially in the early stages. If the bowl is screw-mounted, it is important to guard against removing too much wood and hitting the tips of the screws.

Depth can be checked with a rule and a straight-edged piece of wood, as shown in *Figure 7.29*. This depth must, of course, be compared with the overall thickness of the block and the amount of screw penetration.

The toolrest always needs to be fairly close to the work, otherwise the turning-tool can overhang the rest too much and thus cause the resistance of the wood to have a noticeable leverage effect. Because of this, the rest will have to be re-adjusted as wood is removed, and positioned so that it is part-way into the hollow of the bowl, as shown in *Figure 7.28*.

Fig. 7.27. Hollowing of inside with gouge or scraper

Fig. 7.28. Toolrest positioned inside bowl

Hollowing the inside should continue with the round-end scraper until, for the average-size bowl, the wall is approximately $\frac{1}{4}$in thick at the rim and gaining steadily in thickness towards the base, where a good $\frac{1}{16}$in needs to be allowed for safely clearing screw-tips.

The inside bottom of a bowl can be almost flat, depending to some extent on its size and shape. For this part, a scraper about

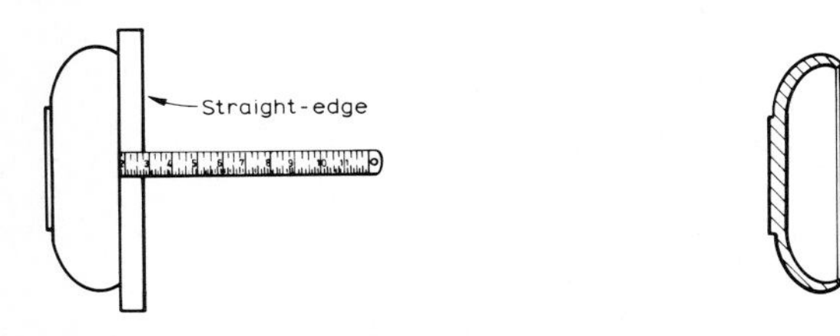

Fig. 7.29. Measuring depth of inside

Fig. 7.30. Typical section

1in wide is best for the final steps. It should be square-ended with slightly radiused corners, or a round-end one with fairly flat curvature.

Finally, the edge of the rim will need attention. A typical profile given to this part of the bowl is shown in *Figure 7.30*, which illustrates the final shape of a fairly traditional bowl.

Bowl shapes

Other typical shapes for bowls are shown in *Figure 7.31*. What must be remembered in woodturning is that the majority of items produced need to be designed so as to combine function with attractiveness, since they are likely to be on display as part of the furniture and furnishings of our homes.

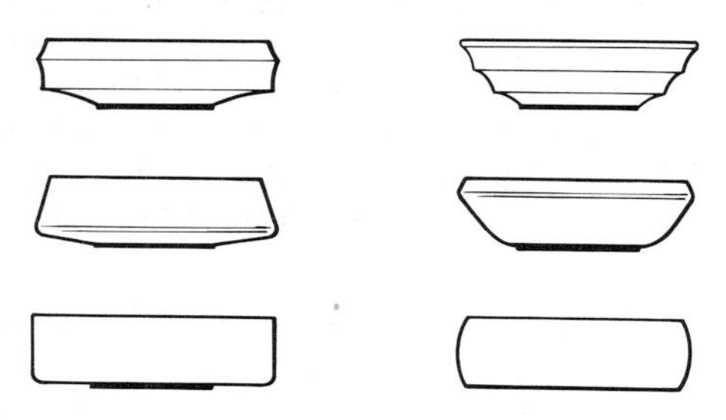

Fig. 7.31. Alternative profiles

A variety of bowl which has become popular in recent years is one specially intended for nuts and incorporating a nutcracker. It is the availability of the nutcracking fitting which has led to the popularity of this type of bowl, although older versions were made complete with a small mallet for cracking the nuts. A typical section of the modern nut-bowl is shown in *Figure 7.32*,

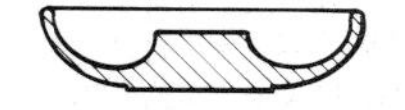

Fig. 7.32. Section through nut-bowl

but it is advisable to obtain the fitting before starting on the bowl, in order to ensure that the raised centre is made the right size. One type of fitting available requires a handle to be added; this small piece of spindle turning can be made in the same wood as the bowl.

Bowls with lids

Small bowls are often made to be used as accessories on dressing-tables, usually as containers for items of jewellery, powder puffs, and so on. Such bowls need lids.

A typical lid is shown in *Figure 7.33* without its knob. Because a lid needs to be turned and finished on all its surfaces, it presents problems of mounting. These are overcome in different ways, depending on whether or not a knob is to be added to the lid and, if so, the way in which the knob is fitted.

A lid of 4in diameter or less does not need to have a knob, as the hand will span this distance. Such a lid will need to overlap the bowl to allow for easy removal, as shown in *Figure 7.34*. The

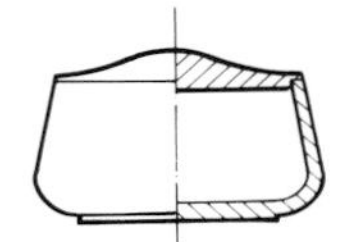

Fig. 7.33. Bowl with lid

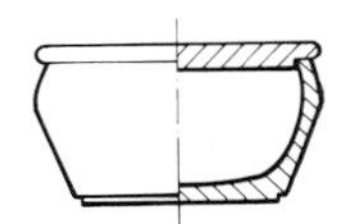

Fig. 7.34. Overhanging lid

wood for such a lid is cut square and left square. This enables it to be screwed to the faceplate, or first to packing and then to the faceplate, by the corners which are going to be waste. This enables the step to be made, to produce what is in effect a rebate.

The size of the raised centre part should be marked in pencil, making the diameter at this stage rather larger than the inside of the bowl. The slight excess allows for the bulk of the waste to be removed, when the diameter is adjusted slowly and carefully so as to produce a fit on the bowl with minimum clearance. The bowl itself is used to test the fit as turning proceeds. The lid at this stage is shown *Figure 7.35*.

The next step of turning the outer part of the lid can be tackled in more ways than one. The simplest is to mount it on a screw-chuck. For this method, the lid should be bradawled when still mounted as shown in *Figure 7.35*, while revolving: with care, this ensures that the hole is central. When reversed and mounted

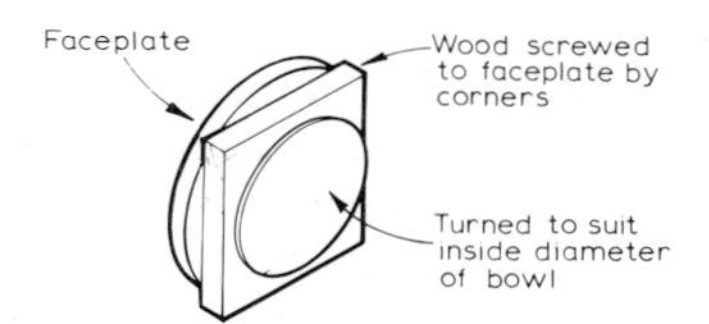

Fig. 7.35. Turning a lid

on the screw-chuck, the outside can be completed in either a plain or a decorative way. Where it is possible to use a gouge for the shaping, it will give a better surface. Some typical lid sections are shown in *Figure 7.36*.

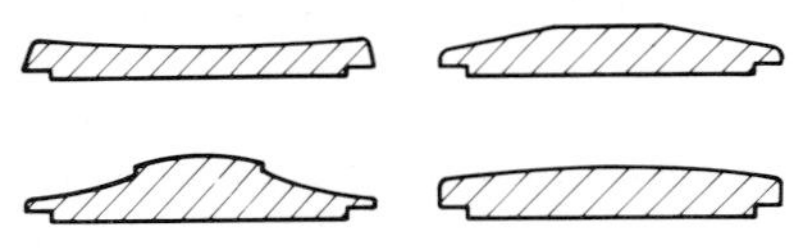

Fig. 7.36. Lid sections

Mounting a lid on the screw-chuck is simple, but it has the obvious disadvantage that it will leave an exposed screwhole on the underside. This has to be filled by gluing a small plug in the hole – a small price to pay for ease, speed, and simplicity.

To complete a lid without a screwhole, rather more work is required. A piece of ½in plywood, about 1in larger than the finished size of the lid, is screwed to the faceplate. A recess must now be formed in the plywood, so that the depth equals the extent of the step just made on the lid (see *Figure 7.37*). The important dimension is the diameter of the recess, as this must be made so that the lid becomes a tight fit in it. Depending on

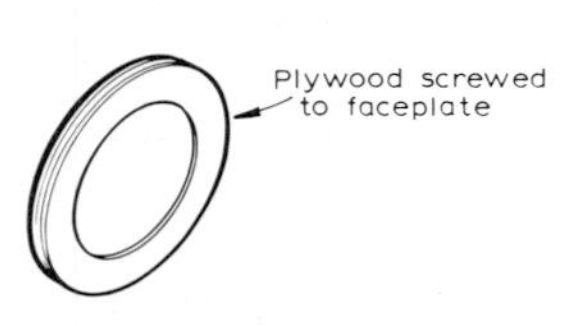

Fig. 7.37. Holding device for lid

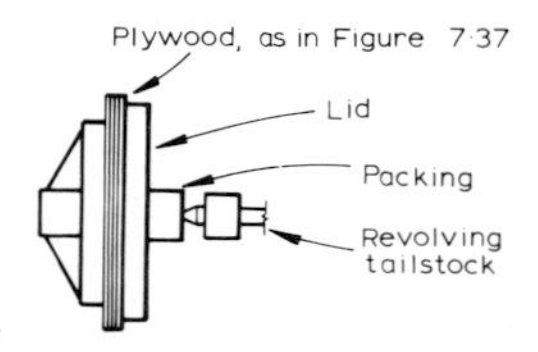

Fig. 7.38. Turning top of lid

the proposed shape of the lid, it is sometimes possible to make doubly sure that the lid is held firmly in place by the arrangement shown in *Figure 7.38*. Here the tailstock is being used to keep the lid in the recess cut in the plywood by means of an oddment of wood against which the dead centre can exert pressure. This dodge works much more successfully if a revolving centre is used.

Knobs for lids

It is easier in many ways to make a lid with a knob than one without. This is because a screw-centre can be used for mounting the work, and the knob is then a very convenient way of concealing the screwhole. There are alternative ways of going about this.

The simpler method is to cut the wood to circular shape, but somewhat larger than the final size. It is then mounted on a screw-chuck, and the underside of the lid is turned so as to form the rebate to fit the bowl. The work is then reversed on the screw-chuck, and the remainder of the lid is turned so as to form the rebate to fit the bowl. The work is then reversed on the screw-chuck and the remainder of the lid turned to the shape required. A hole is now bored completely through the middle of the lid – ⅜ in or ½ in are usual sizes, depending on the size of the knob, which is normally related to the size of the bowl.

The knob now needs to be turned as a piece of spindle-work. The pin part must be made to fit the hole bored in the lid, and sufficiently long to penetrate it. The end of the pin is then domed over, so that when glued to the lid, the section is as shown in *Figure 7.39*. Knobs may be made in the same wood as the rest of

Fig. 7.39. Knob which penetrates lid

the bowl or in a contrasting one, such as an exotic hardwood (rosewood or ebony, for example).

A second way of fitting the knob to a lid results in an underside free of evidence of the knob or of the method of mounting. The lid is started by mounting it in similar manner to that shown in *Figure 7.35*, where the square of wood is screwed through its corners to the faceplate. Here, however, it is the outside of the lid which is turned first. The work is then reversed on to screw-chuck and the work completed by turning the underside. This will leave a screwhole on the upper surface only.

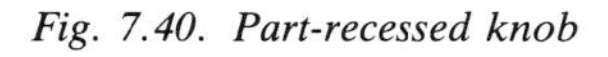

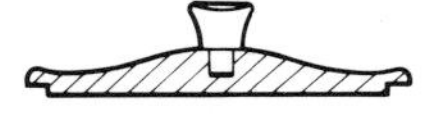

Fig. 7.40. Part-recessed knob

A hole for the pin of the knob is now bored part-way through from this side and the knob is glued in as shown in the sectional view in *Figure 7.40*. Suggested knob shapes are shown in *Figure 7.41*.

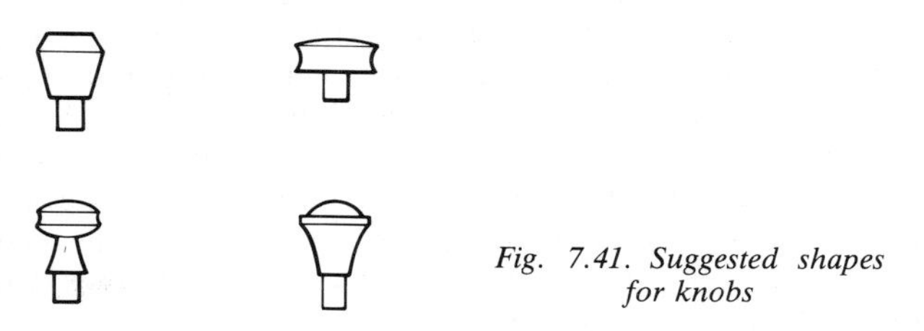

Fig. 7.41. Suggested shapes for knobs

If the method chosen is the first one, a completely different way of going about the work is available. If the hole for the knob is made at the start, the lid can be mounted and turned on a mandrel (see Chapter 3).

8 Other faceplate work

While a well-produced bowl can be regarded as a tour-de-force for the turner, there is a wide assortment of other items which can be produced on the faceplate. Many incorporate bought fittings, of which there is a large choice: circular tiles and mirrors, clock faces, glass dishes, glass and plastic liners, pen holders, and many more. If any piece of turnery is to incorporate a commercially produced fitting, it is advisable to obtain this first and make the turning to suit, especially if the fitting is to be inserted into a hole or recess.

Platters

Plates, platters, and shallow dishes involve very similar techniques to those used for bowls, but their shallowness creates special problems: because of the thinness of the base, mounting is difficult. The mounting adopted will depend on the thickness of the wood used and the design chosen for the project. Typical thickness for platters is about ⅞ in, but the diameter can be almost anything – 8 in to 9 in is average.

The design and the method of mounting must be thought of together, as one affects the other. As an example, the design shown in *Figure 8.1* is a simple one because of the relatively thick amount of wood left at the base, which would allow screw mounting. Against ease of mounting must be balanced the restricted hollowing which can take place, and the relative heaviness of the result.

For the section shown in *Figure 8.1,* the whole of the turning can be tackled from one side. Because of this, it is necessary to start with one side of the initial piece of wood planed flat. The faceplate can now be screwed centrally to this side, taking the care regarding length of screw which has previously been stressed. The first stage of working is to true up the edge or periphery, as for a bowl.

Fig. 8.1. Section through platter with thick base for screw-mounting

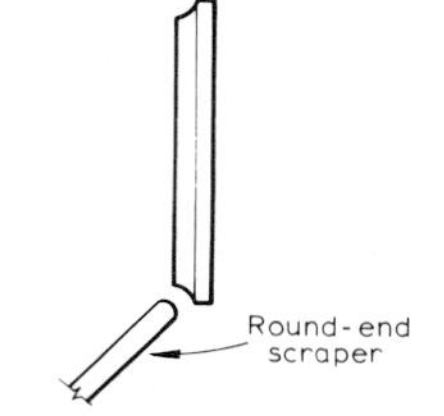

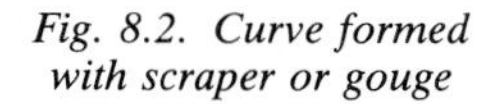

Fig. 8.2. Curve formed with scraper or gouge

The concave curve on the underside of the platter is the next to be formed, and is shown in *Figure 8.2*. Whether this is cut with a scraper or a gouge will possibly depend on accessibility. If it is a smallish platter and the headstock of the lathe is somewhat large, it may be difficult to approach the work satisfactorily with a gouge. A scraper does not require the same amount of space for the manipulation of the handle as does a gouge, so a round-end scraper will cope better if space is restricted in any way.

For the hollowing, a square-end scraper can be used throughout. Generally speaking, on work which is large in diameter but relatively thin, it is a good rule to work in such a way that the central area is not made too thin too soon, leaving a lot of wood to be removed from nearer the rim. This is to prevent the wood from losing its rigidity and thus vibrating. Removing wood from the outer parts can difficult if there is chatter. This is not likely to happen on this particular platter because an adequate thickness of wood remains throughout. The thinner the platter becomes, the more important it is to work in the correct sequence.

The best method of proceeding is to use the scraper to take light cuts only, while moving the tool across the whole of the area where wood has to be removed. In other words, the hollowing should be done uniformly, rather than by trying to take a small section to its finished depth before proceeding to the next. This is illustrated in *Figure 8.3* and *8.4,* the preferred method being shown in *Figure 8.3*.

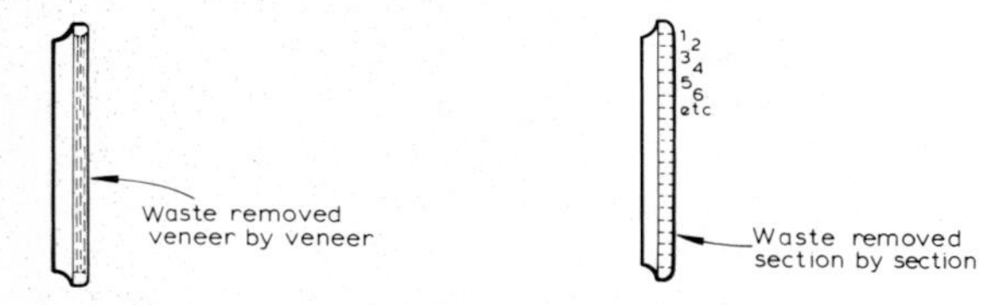

Fig. 8.3. Hollowing should be carried out uniformly

Fig. 8.4. Less satisfactory method of hollowing

As usual, where a gouge can be employed, it usually gives better results than a scraper. The plan angle of the gouge when used for hollowing is shown in *Figure 8.5*. The bevel is seen to be rubbing on the wood, and the gouge would be pointing slightly

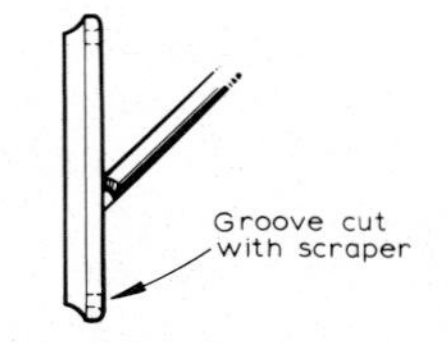

Fig. 8.5. Forming hollow with gouge

upwards. It helps a lot when using the gouge in this way if the outer limit of the hollow has been established with a scraper, as this will assist the gouge at the end of its cut, and allow a tidy corner to be produced. The last stage of the shaping is to round over the outer edge.

Mounting a thin platter

There are limited possibilities for holding a platter or similar item where the thickness is such that screwing to a faceplate is not practical. The obvious and most simple alternative is to use the six-in-one chuck. The depth of the recess required for the jaws of this chuck to grip properly need be little more than 1/16 in, assuming that the wood is fairly dense and the dovetailed edge to the recess is carefully formed. Only on exceptionally large work, or where the weight is considerable, need the depth be more than 1/8 in. This means that the chuck does not really restrict the amount of hollowing, as the thickness of wood left at the base would be greater than the depth of the recess. A typical section through a platter held in a six-in-one chuck is shown in *Figure 8.6*.

The other method of holding fairly thin work of this type is to use a block of wood glued to the workpiece. This technique is

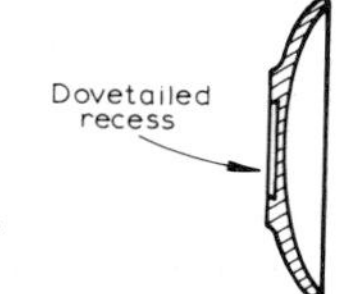

Fig. 8.6. Section through platter or dish held in six-in-one chuck

best left until some experience has been gained, because cutting needs to be fairly smooth: clumsy use of the tools could result in the work being forced off the mounting block. The technique is very dependent on care and common sense.

The idea is to add to the workpiece a piece of packing, which can then be used for screwing to the faceplate without the screws penetrating the workpiece at all. The method of working is as follows. The side of the workpiece to be hollowed is screwed to the faceplate. The underside is then shaped – and this includes skimming the central area which forms the actual base to ensure that it is as flat as possible. Flatness is essential here if the gluing is to be satisfactory.

The essence of the method is to sandwich a piece of paper between packing and workpiece. One type of paper has always proved satisfactory: good-quality brown wrapping paper of the kraft type. The packing, ½in plywood usually being ideal, is best if circular. This is glued centrally to the base with a layer of paper between. White resin (PVA) glue has also always proved to be satisfactory for mounting. The work is left for the glue to set after using hand pressure only for initial bonding. The work at this stage is shown in *Figure 8.7*.

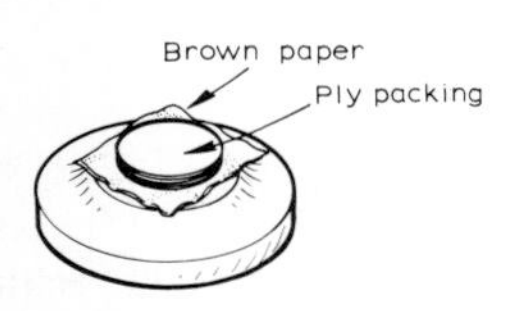

Fig. 8.7. Glued-on mounting

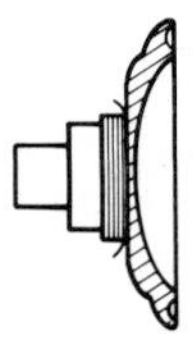

Fig. 8.8. Typical section through platter with glued-on packing

If the work is still on the faceplate, it can be remounted on the lathe and the packing trued up if needs be. The work is then reversed on to a faceplate of suitable size, checking for concentricity, as for a bowl. The upper surface is then hollowed and such decorative treatment as desired is applied to the rim.

After glasspapering and applying the finish, the faceplate is unscrewed and the packing removed. This is done by tapping a fairly large bench chisel between packing and workpiece and using the bevel as a fulcrum to prise off the packing. Kraft paper will de-laminate through its thickness, so separation is easy. Any remaining paper and glue are removed by glasspaper. A section through a shallow dish, for which this technique could be employed, is shown in *Figure 8.8*.

Breadboard

The glue-mounting technique is a suitable one to use for a project such as a breadboard. Here a thickness of ¾in is adequate, with a diameter around 9in to 10in. As the work is not hollowed, the methods of working are a little different from those used for a platter. The wood for the board needs to have at least one of its sides planed flat at the outset, and it is necessary to glue on the packing before any turning can take place. With the faceplate screwed to the packing, all the turning can be completed with one mounting.

The section shown in *Figure 8.9* provides a design which is a little more practical in use than others, as the hollow formed

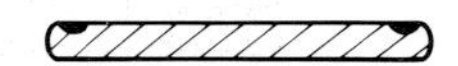

Fig. 8.9. Section through bread-board with crumb groove

towards the outer part catches crumbs. If holes on the underside are acceptable, the breadboard can simply be screwed directly to the faceplate. The resulting screw holes can either be filled with stopper or have wood plugs glued in and levelled off.

Cutting-board

A project with a practical use is a cutting-board. There is a fashion for making these into decorative items for display in the kitchen, One way in which this can be done is by providing the board with a handle. Hanging can be either by means of a leather thong passing through a small hole in the handle or by a larger hole made in the handle for hanging directly on a hook. The handle is a piece of spindle-turning.

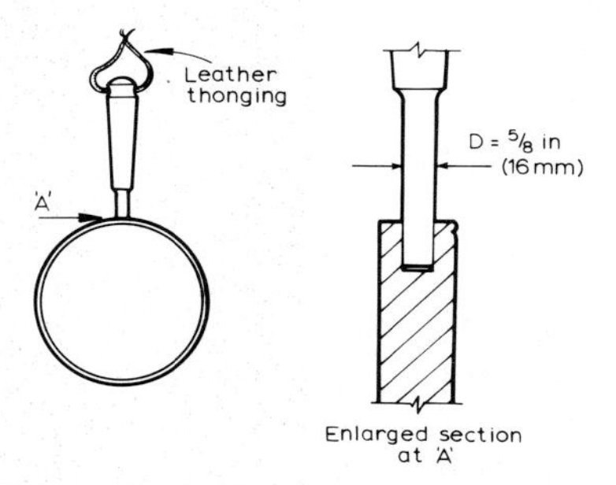

Fig. 8.10. Cutting-board with handle

A cutting board of this type is shown in *Figure 8.10*. While the diameter does not need to be as large as that of a breadboard, the thickness is best around 1¼in to allow for fitting of the handle. Methods of turning a cutting-board of this style are identical to those used for a breadboard.

Cheese-box holder

Another project is a holder for the circular box in which six triangular portions of cheese are packed. This is a job which can be turned entirely from one side while it is mounted on a screw-chuck. For the diameter needed for a project like this (around 5½in) it is important that the screw-chuck should have a face of 2½in to 3in. Small screw-chucks, with a face of 1½in, are not really suitable for a diameter as large because of the limited support they provide, wood overhanging at the periphery will be deflected under the pressure of the cutting tool.

A section of a cheese-box holder at an advanced stage is shown in *Figure 8.11*. Once again, shaping of the rim can be by scraper or gouge, and here hollowing is more simple if done with

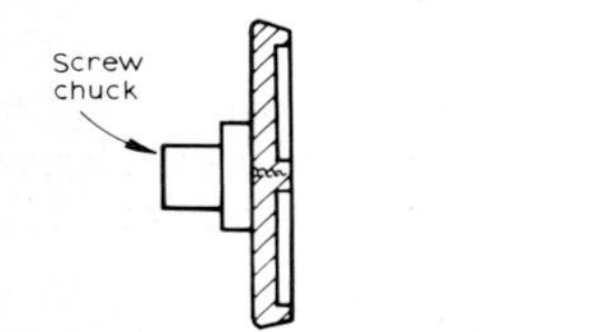

Fig. 8.11. Section through cheese-box holder nearing completion

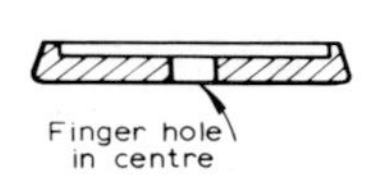

Fig. 8.12. Section through completed cheese-box holder

a square-end scraper. This is mainly because the centre is not turned away, but left on as a 'dimple'. This enables a good-size screw to be used in the chuck, the dimple accommodating the screw without danger that the turning-tools will foul it. The recess must not be too deep if the original top of the cheese-box is to be used, though these holders can be made to hold the box-base only.

The projecting dimple with its tell-tale screwhole on the underside are both removed by boring. A hole of about ¾in diameter can be used for removing the box.

Darning-mushroom

Other projects are often made in a similar way to the cheese-box holder, in that they are held on a screw-chuck and later have a hole bored in the centre. The hole may be through or stopped and is made as a circular mortice to receive a component spindle turned to fit. A simple example is a darning-mushroom. This also typifies the use to which the small (1½in) screw-chuck can be put for faceplate turning, and *Figure 8.13* shows the

Fig. 8.13. Head of darning-mushroom

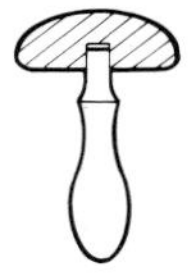

Fig. 8.14. Completed darning-mushroom

mushroom as it would be shaped on the chuck. The complete novice could form the whole of this with a square-end scraper. In this example, the hole would be bored part-way through only. The complete job is shown in section in *Figure 8.14*.

Cotton-reel holder

The manner of making a cotton-reel holder (*Figure 8.15*) is very similar to the mushroom, but the lower end of the handle should be turned so as to provide a shoulder for the circular pin. These variations will be dicussed later.

The diameter indicated allows for six reels; by increasing the diameter, pegs for eight reels can be fitted. Alternatively, the pegs on which the reels are held can be made long enough to hold two reels each. The usefulness of the holder can be increased by forming the hollow shown in the drawing, its purpose being to hold pins.

The pegs can be made in a variety of ways. The simplest is to use ¼in dowel secured in holes of the same size. There is nothing, however, to stop the enthusiast from turning up a set of

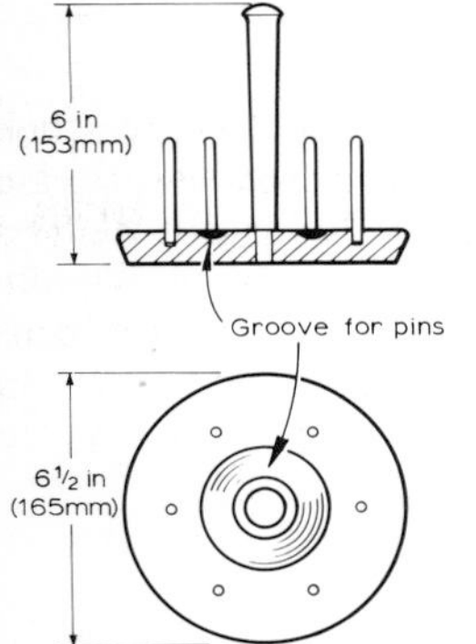

Fig. 8.15. *Cotton-reel holder*

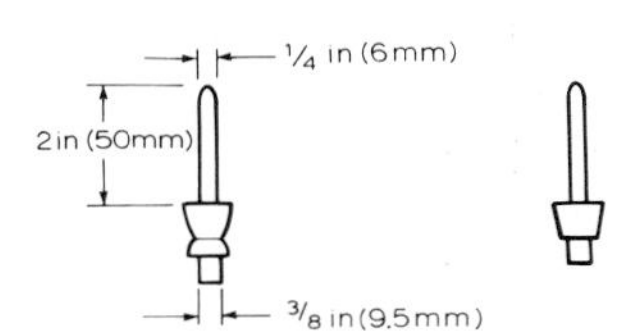

Fig. 8.16. *Pegs for cotton-reel holder*

pegs, *Figure 8.16* showing alternative suggestions. In these examples, the pins on the underside should be ⅜in in diameter.

A completely different idea is to use ¼in aluminium rods, with Araldite to bond them into the holes. If the aluminium is rubbed with fine steel-wool before fixing, the result will be a uniform satin surface.

Wall plaques

Decorative tiles for making wall plaques are readily available, one supplier listing over a hundred patterns. They can be purchased singly or in sets which follow a theme: veteran cars, butterflies, exotic birds, scenes by Constable, etc. Making a tile-holder for display purposes presents no problems, and the procedure is quite similar to a cheesebox project. The work can be held on a screw-chuck, recessing being carried out with the square-end scraper. Two typical patterns are illustrated in *Figure 8.17,* where the thickness of the wood needs to be about ⅝in. The centre is not recessed but left as shown because of the mounting-screw. The dimple of wood can simply be cut away with an ordinary bench-chisel once turning has been completed and the work removed from the lathe. There is little point in trying to produce a super-smooth surface in the bottom of the recess, as it will be permanently covered with the tile, but it does need to be flat.

The depth of the recess depends to some extent on personal preference. Tiles are usually around ¼in thick, but they can be recessed so that their surface is flush with the wood, or slightly raised, or slightly below. If the tile is below the surface, the job will have a more finished look if the inner corner of the recess is

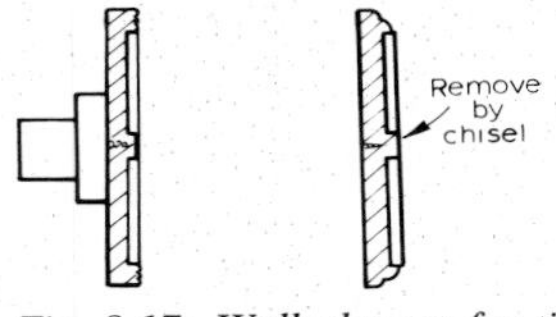

Fig. 8.17. Wall plaques for tile inserts

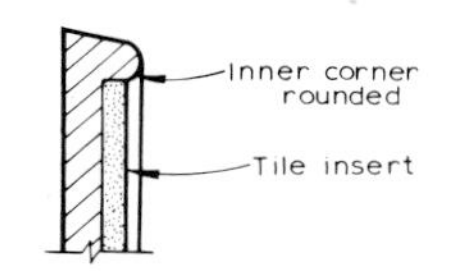

Fig. 8.18. Tile recessed below rim

rounded slightly, as shown in *Figure 8.18*. It is best if the fit of the tile is not made too tight (a $\frac{1}{16}$in allowance is suggested). This is to provide for the possibility that the wood will shrink, as even slight shrinkage and a tight-fitting tile could result in a split being formed.

Before securing the tile, provision must be made for hanging. A simple method is shown in *Figure 8.19*, where a hole of ¼in diameter is bored in the back, at a slight upward angle. A 1in panel-pin or masonry-pin driven at a corresponding angle into

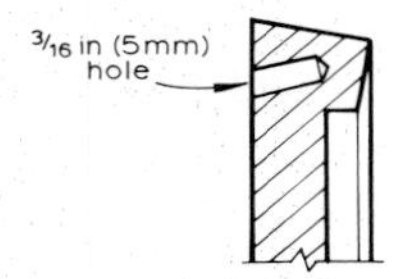

Fig. 8.19. Simple means of hanging plaque

Fig. 8.20. Hanging-plate

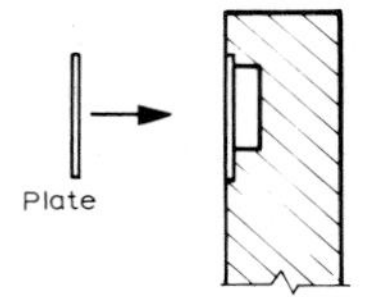

Fig. 8.21. Preparation for hanging-plate

the wall will provide adequate support. For a rather more professional job, or for larger plaques or heavier objects, such as wall-clocks, a hanging-plate should be used (see *Figure 8.20*). *Figure 8.21* shows a section through the back of an item and illustrates the preparation needed.

When making provision for hanging any piece of turnery, attention must be paid to the grain direction. When it is hung, the grain should be either vertical or horizontal: if it at an angle, it will look untidy.

When fixing the tiles in place, a rubber-based glue is recommended, as this type of adhesive has elastic properties which will help to protect the tile from cracking.

Most tiles are 6 in in diameter, but some are made with a diameter of 3½ in.

Teapot stand and cheeseboard

While tiles are intended primarily for decorative purposes, they can be used for utilitarian purposes as well. A wall-plaque can be used as a stand for a teapot or coffee pot. It is best if the tile is not fully recessed into the wood, as it is desirable to keep the base of the pot clear of the wood.

Another use for decorative tiles – once more only a variation of the wall plaque – is as a cheese board for cut cheese. Because

Fig. 8.22. Cheese board with handle

the cheese board will be passed around the meal-table, it will be much more convenient if it is provided with a handle. A section of such a cheese board is shown in *Figure 8.22*.

Butterdish and sugarbowl

Two further items of kitchenware which are examples of faceplate turning are butterdishes and sugarbowls. Methods of making are again similar to the tile plaque, although the recess needs to be made sufficiently smooth to receive the same finish as the remainder of the job. The recess also needs to be deep enough to stop the glass insert from slipping out. The corners of the recess are best rounded, assuming that the outer edge of the glass is of this shape.

The butterdish is really intended for holding pats of butter at the dining-table, rather than a large piece of butter for use in the kitchen. Because of this, a lid is not really necessary. On the

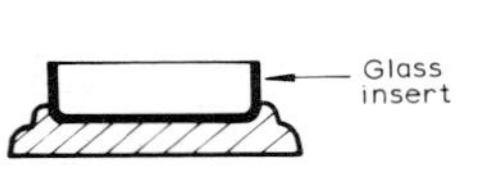

Fig. 8.23. Butterdish

Fig. 8.24. Sugar-bowl

other hand, the sugarbowl is probably better if a cover is provided. A suitable lid is made as described in the chapter on bowls. A typical section through a butterdish is shown in *Figure 8.23*; *Figure 8.24* illustrates a sugarbowl complete with lid.

Mirror-frames

It is possible to obtain circular mirrors in sizes from 3½in to 12in. Frames for these mirrors require rather different techniques from those so far described. The thickness of wood needed differs according to the diameter of the mirror and the pattern adopted. Wood about ½in thick is about right for the smallest size, and if it is less than about 8in in diameter, it can be mounted on a screw-chuck of appropriate size. Anything above this diameter will need to be screwed to a faceplate.

A section at the first stage of turning is shown in *Figure 8.25*. The groove is formed with a square-end scraper, and the diameter (D) needs to be 1/16in or so larger than the mirror. While there is no need to remove the waste in the centre part of the job, it helps if the thickness at this part is reduced by about ⅛in to allow for the mirror to be tried in place when checking the diameter.

The depth of this recess needs to be between 5/16in and ⅜in. Into the recess has to be fitted the mirror, a piece of card behind this to act as a cushion, and then a plywood back of 3mm or 4mm thickness. One slightly variable factor is the thickness of the mirror, but extra card can be placed between it and the plywood to act as packing.

At this stage, the work is unscrewed from the faceplate, ready for reversing. A ½ in thick plywood disc is now prepared for either four or six holes near its edge so that it can be screwed to the frame. The essential point is that the plywood must be fixed to the frame so that the screws enter the middle of the wood forming the rim. This is shown in *Figure 8.26*. It is advisable to check the true running of the workpiece before all the screws are

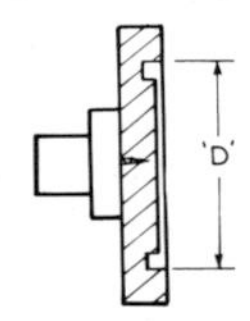

Fig. 8.25. First stage of wall mirror

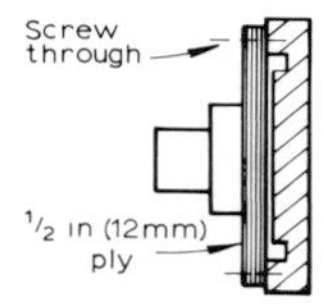

Fig. 8.26. Mirror-frame reversed on plywood backing

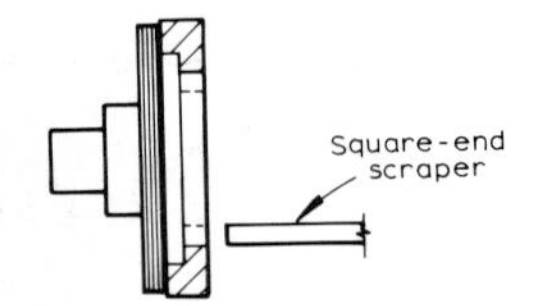

Fig. 8.27. Centre removed by forming groove from outside

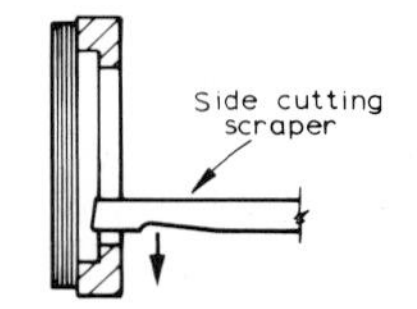

Fig. 8.28. Trimming rebate to final size

inserted, to allow for possible adjustment. Work now proceeds on the face by again using the ½ in square-end chisel. A groove is made which just overlaps the one already formed on the back (see *Figure 8.27*). Care is required at the moment of severance: The lathe should be stopped at this point and the loose piece removed from the centre. The chances that this piece will fly out are small, but as a precaution, the tailstock centre can be brought up and gentle pressure applied with it to the wood to hold it steady.

Working in this manner will produce what is, in effect, a rebate much wider than is needed. In order to reduce it to the size required (about 3⁄16 in), a side-cutting scraper is brought into use as shown in *Figure 8.28* Final shaping of the frame can be

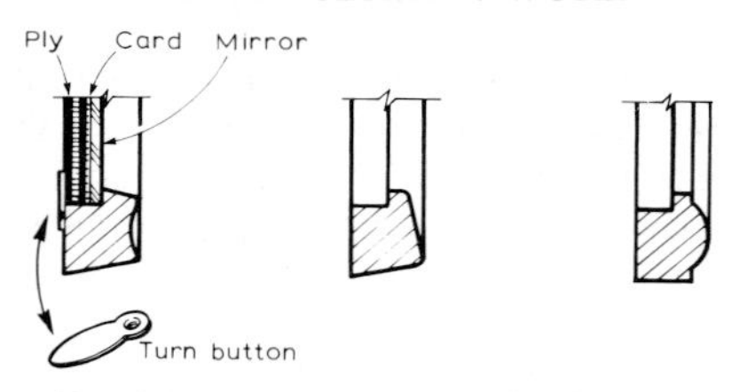

Fig. 8.29. Typical sections for frames

carried out at this stage, *Figure 8.29* showing three typical sections through a rim.

An alternative method of hanging to those suggested for plaques is the ring-and-screw fitting used for ordinary pictureframes, illustrated in *Figure 8.30*. A completely different

Fig. 8.30. Ring-and-screw

Fig. 8.31. Mirror with handle

method of hanging the mirror, which adds to its attractiveness, is to provide it with a handle. Such a design is shown in *Figure 8.31*, where the actual means of hanging can be a hook or, preferably, an eye screwed into the end of the handle or a hole bored near the end of the handle with a length of leather thonging through it.

Penholder

There was a time when a popular project for a turner was a stand for an inkwell, the more elaborate wells being made of silver and with lids. The modern equivalent of this is a stand for a ball-pen, the actual holder for the pen being known as a 'trumpet'. Trumpets are made of metal with silver or gilt finish. They incorporate a universal ball-joint and are held to the stand by a built-in bolt and nut. Turning a stand is an excellent way of using a wood offcut, a diameter of 3 in to 3½ in being about right.

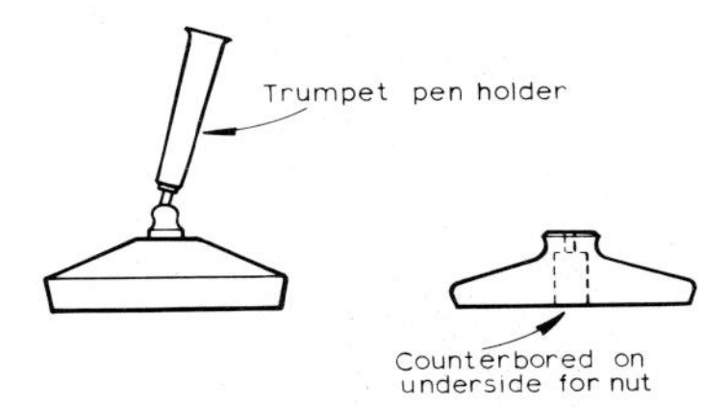

Fig. 8.32. Bases for ball-pen and trumpet

Thickness can be anything from ⅝ in to 1½ in, depending on the design. Indeed, the design can be adapted to suit the material available.

A couple of ideas for penholders are shown in *Figure 8.32*. These are further examples of work which can be carried out from one side. The screw-chuck is perfectly satisfactory for holding them.

Reading-lamp bases

It is questionable whether there are more bowls turned in a year or more reading-lamps, but reading-lamps have always been popular. Designs must be countless, but they can be grouped into two broad categories; those turned from a single piece of wood, and those where two pieces are used. One made from a single piece will be spindle turned, whereas a two-piece lamp is a combination of spindle and faceplate work. In this section, it is the base of the two-part lamp which will be considered.

After cutting the base to circular or octagonal shape, it is best to bore the hole in the base for wiring before turning is started. A ¼ in diameter hole will be adequate for standard two-core flex. It should be bored to just short of the centre. It should be made fairly close to the lower surface of the base, otherwise it may interfere with turning. Initial preparation of the base, with the flex-hole, is shown in *Figure 8.33*. Note that the hole should be drilled through side-grain: if it is made in end-grain, subsequent turning will cause splintering around the hole.

Mounting can be by a screw-chuck of 2½in to 3in diameter. If a large base is being made, it is better to use screws through the holes in the faceplate rather than to rely on the single central screw.

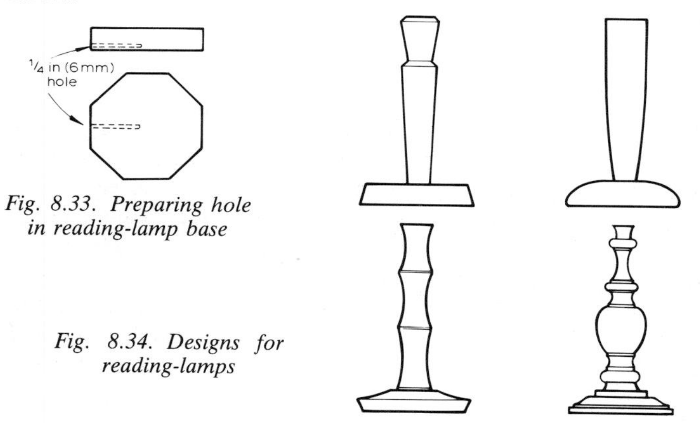

Fig. 8.33. Preparing hole in reading-lamp base

Fig. 8.34. Designs for reading-lamps

A selection of bases is shown in *Figure 8.34*. Sizes are not critical, provided that the base is in proportion to the stem. All the profiles shown can be made by scraper or gouge, but correct use of a faceplate gouge will normally give a much smoother surface. While the work is still revolving on the lathe, a small depression should be made in the centre to enable the hole to be accurately positioned later.

As well as the base and stem being in proportion, there should also be harmony between the two. A traditional stem needs a traditional base; a simple profile for the upper part should be matched with a simple base, and so on.

9 Spindle work

'Turning between centres' means just what it says – shaping the wood when it is held between the live centre of the headstock and the centre held in the tailstock. This is loosely called 'spindle-turning'. Spindle turning also embraces work held at one end only, but only if the grain of the wood is parallel to the axis of rotation. A block of wood mounted only on a screw-chuck is regarded as spindle turning if its grain is in line with the bed of the lathe. (An example would be the turning of a small knob.) So the tailstock, which is essential to turning between centres, does not have to be in use for the work to be called spindle-turning. The screw-chuck in particular is a very versatile means of holding the workpiece when it is not too large, and so it can be used for both faceplate work and spindle turning. The difference lies entirely in the direction of the grain, not in the means of holding and supporting the work.

Basic information on preparing the wood, roughing to shape, and principal cuts with the gouge and chisel has already been given. The application of those basic techniques to a variety of objects will now be explained.

Many items of spindle turning are complete projects in themselves – for instance, a one-piece table lamp. Other pieces form only part of a turned project. Spindle-turned pieces are aften made as part of a cabinet-work project or item of furniture – for instance, a set of stool or table legs.

Sometimes the ends of spindle-turned wood do not have to be attended to on the lathe. Here the tell-tale signs of the mounting are of no importance. On other examples, one end needs to be completed as part of the turning operation – for example, a handle of which one end has to be inserted into a hole. Many spindle-turning projects, however, call for the work to be turned up to both ends. Depending on the nature of the project, there are various dodges which help to achieve this, but for many jobs one end, or both, has to be completed by hand when the piece is off the lathe.

Garden dibber

The first project suggested as an exercise in spindle-turning is a garden dibber. It is a good example of the use of oddments of wood, and although hardwood is better for a job like this, one of the dense softwoods such as parana pine would be quite acceptable. Measurements and exact shape are not critical.

A piece like this, where both ends need to be finished off the lathe, raises the question of the way round it should be turned; that is, pointed end to the tailstock or to the headstock. The general rule is to keep the 'heavier' end to the headstock; in other words, the end which has to have the most wood removed should be towards the tailstock.

Let us assume that the wood has been rough-turned to a cylindrical shape, remembering that wherever possible a little excess should be left on the diameter at this stage. The next step is to mark out in pencil the overall length needed – here 9 in – and also the position of other main features – in this case the point where the conical end meets the handle. This stage is shown in *Figure 9.1(a)*.

Cutting is best started – certainly by the beginner – by using the parting tool to establish the outer limits of the piece. At this stage, the groove formed by the parting tool should be just outside the pencil-lines. The diameter within the grooves should be about ½ in. The aim is to define the ends of the work but leave sufficient diameter, and therefore strength, to allow further shaping to be carried out. (See *Figure 9.1(b)*.)

The roughing gouge can be used quite satisfactorily for removing the bulk of waste from the conical end, taking the

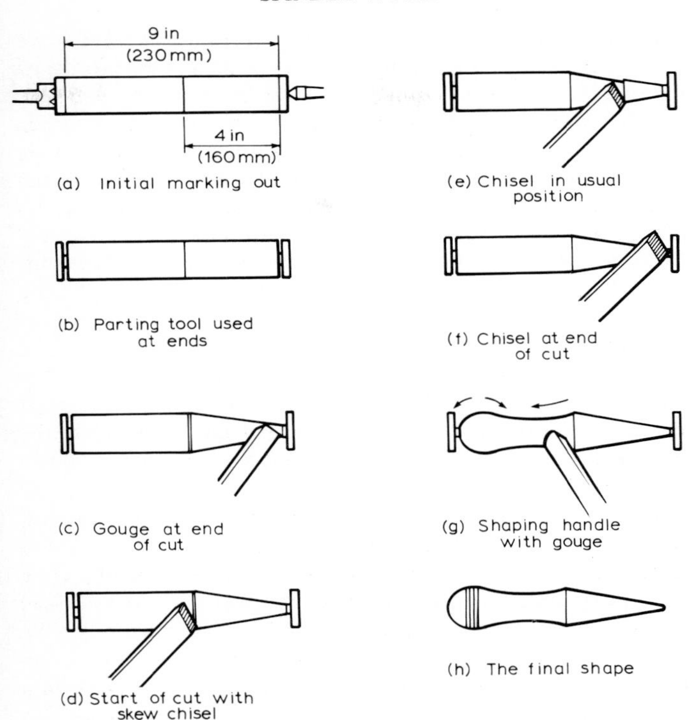

Fig. 9.1. Turning a garden dibber

diameter at the right-hand end to rather less than the ½in diameter at the bottom of the groove already formed. Remember that, in spindle work, one always works from the large diameter to the small, and that it helps if the gouge is pointed slightly in the direction of working. An advantage of the square-end roughing gouge is that it is fairly easy to produce a sharp internal angle with it, as formed at this stage at the lower end of the slope. This is achieved by rolling the tool well over to the right, so that the cutting is taking place at the extremity, rather than the centre, of the cutting edge. The gouge in this position at the end of the cut is shown in *Figure 9.1*(*c*).

A roughing gouge, when freshly sharpened, is capable of leaving a smooth surface, especially on a conical shape like this: because of the slope, cutting is almost bound to be with the grain. However, a skew chisel is the accepted tool for finishing cuts, and this is a good opportunity to gain practice in its use. Using a 1 in chisel, the start of the cut should be made with the heel of the tool as shown in *Figure 9.1*(*d*). As with the gouge, the chisel points a little in the direction of movement, and the initial movement is to pivot the tool slightly on the toolrest so as to shift the point of cutting from the heel to the centre of the cutting edge. Remember to keep the toe or pointed end well clear of the wood: the closer the toe comes to the wood, the greater is the risk that it will dig in. The chisel in its 'normal' cutting position is shown in *Figure 9.1*(*e*); *Figure 9.1*(*f*) illustrates the chisel as it nears the end of the cut, where cutting is again more with the heel. At this stage, one should leave a little wood uncut to allow for final shaping.

A gouge around ¾ in will be found to be a suitable size for forming the simple shape suggested for the handle. Its use is shown in *Figure 9.1*(*g*), following the same rules for the direction of both pointing and moving, as indicated by arrows. The rounding of the top or left-hand end of the dibber can be achieved with the gouge, by rolling it over as it follows the curve, or with a skew chisel. Decorative lines can be cut, as shown in *Figure 9.1*(*h*).

Finally, the pointed end can have its diameter reduced even further to the point of severance. If the fingers of the left hand are lightly held around the work, the skew chisel can be used until the wood is parted, and then the hand supports it as it releases itself from the driving centre. This may seem risky to the novice, but with small, light pieces which can be encompassed with the hand, the knack of catching the wood in the hand as it is freed from the centre is quickly learnt. The alternative is simply to reduce the pointed end to about 3⁄16 in and then remove the job from the lathe.

There will still be some waste wood at the end of the handle. This is sawn off, the end is rounded a little with a bench chisel and glasspapered while held in the hand. Similar treatment is needed at the pointed end if it has not been completed on the lathe. In any case, the pointed end of a dibber does not need to be sharp, but rounded over. The finished shape is shown in *Figure 9.1*(*h*).

Rolling-pin

Another project where the beginner should produce a worthwile result at the first attempt is a rolling-pin. This needs to have a working length of about 12 in, so a piece of wood about 15 in long is required. Prepare, mount, and rough-turn as already described. Next, pencil in the four lines shown in *Figure 9.2*(*a*) and use the parting tool to reduce the diameter outside the outer lines to about ½ in. The hollows which form the main part of the handles are made with a gouge of about ⅜ in size. Remember, when forming a hollow, that the deeper the hollow, the narrower does the curve of the gouge need to be. Stages of using the parting tool and forming the hollows are shown in *Figure 9.2*(*b*).

The part of the handle which lies between the end and the hollow is in effect a bead. Beads, it will be recalled, are usually formed with a skew chisel. The chisel is used as shown in *Figure 9.2*(*c*), and cutting is carried out in the direction indicated by the arrows. The centre of the rolling-pin still needs to be smoothed; because the work is cylindrical, the skew chisel is used from the middle outwards. As this surface needs to be straight, the wood should be checked with a straightedge during this final stage.

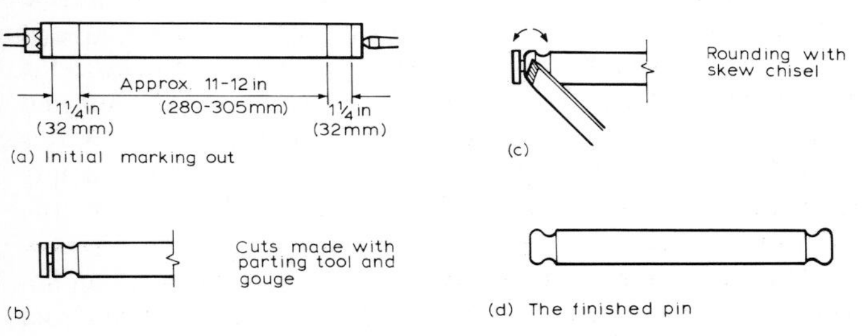

Fig. 9.2. Turning a rolling-pin

Because the rolling-pin has handles at the ends, the easiest way of completing the work is to remove it from the lathe, saw off the waste very near the ends, and finish with chisel and glasspaper. The final shape should be as shown in *Figure 9.2(d)*.

A popular novelty is a half-size rolling-pin, suitably adorned with white ribbon, to present to a bride. Another novelty is shown in *Figure 9.3,* where it forms part of an egg-timer. The

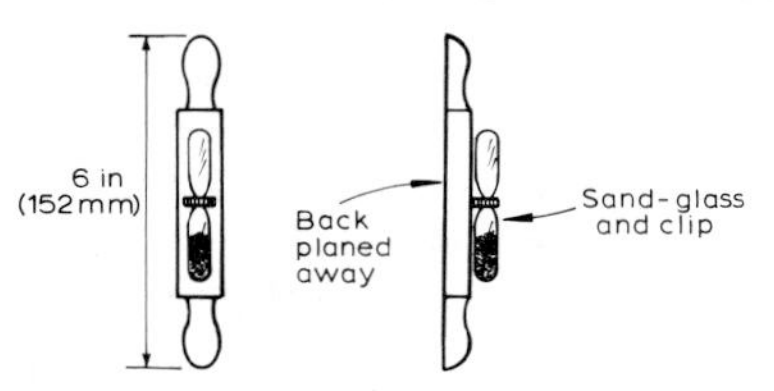

Fig. 9.3. Rolling-pin egg-timer

scale is reduced, but the suggested length is only a guide. In this design, a different pattern of handle is given. It is, in effect, only a half-turning to allow it to hang flat against a wall, This shape can be achieved either by planing away the waste or by producing two half-turnings with the cup-chucks described in Chapter 3.

Handles

Figure 9.4 shows two contrasting styles of the type of handle which might be used with, for example, the cutting-board or cheeseboard described in the previous chapter. Note that both these patterns are without shoulders on the part that enters the

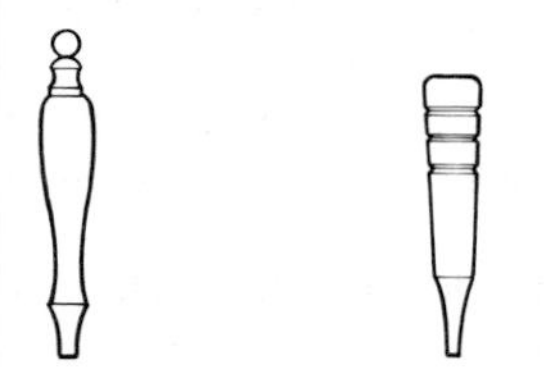

Fig. 9.4. Handles for cheese-boards and cutting-boards

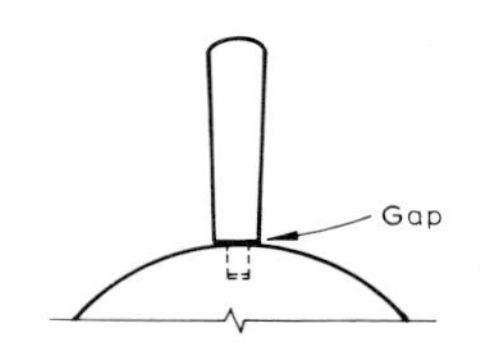

Fig. 9.5. Problem of square shoulder against curved surface

fixing hole. If a shoulder is formed on a handle which is to go into a curved edge, the result would be a slight gap, as shown in *Figure 9.5*. There is a way round this problem: counterbore the hole in the main component to enable the shoulder of the handle to sit in the counterbore. There is little advantage to this unless there are special circumstances, but a handle fitted into a counterbored hole is shown in *Figure 9.6*.

To turn the first part of handle shown in *Figure 9.4*: after rough turning, the pencil-lines are marked in to correspond to the features, as shown in *Figure 9.7*. Note that on something like

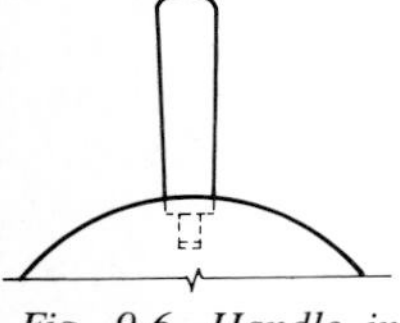

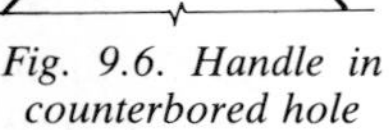

Fig. 9.6. Handle in counterbored hole

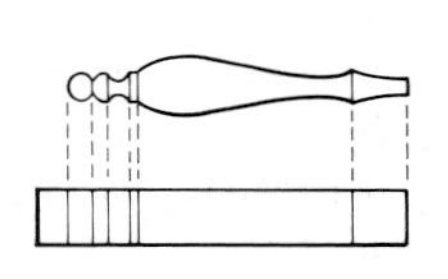

Fig. 9.7. Marking out for handle

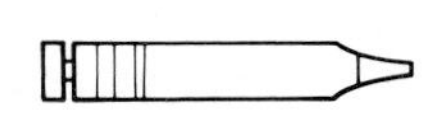

Fig. 9.8. Early stages of forming handle

a handle, where one end will eventually not be seen, and where fitting may have to be checked during the turning, waste is not left at this end.

Although the parting tool can be used to form a groove and reduce the diameter at the left-hand end, its use elsewhere is restricted, because the shape is composed entirely of curves. Where a specific diameter has to be produced, it is better to turn this part first, as a serious mistake here would mean either scrapping the work and starting again, or making a change in design to overcome the error.

Initial shaping of the right-hand end could be with the roughing gouge, almost as part of the roughing stage. Otherwise, a smaller spindle-gouge of about ¾ in could be used, as it would be for the final shaping of this part. Shaping up to this stage is shown in *Figure 9.8*.

The right-hand end should be completed with the slightest of tapers, as this ensures a cork-like effect when fitting the handle into the hole. It also helps if the extreme end is slightly chamfered. To arrive at the correct diameter for a satisfactory fit in the hole, either callipers can be used or, better still, the home-made gauge shown in *Figure 6.7.* A handle should be fitted with a slight gap between its end and the bottom of the hole to ensure good contact on the sides.

There are no set rules for the sequence of turning a handle of the pattern shown in *Figure 9.4.* The hollow towards the top is a good place to start, followed by cutting-in at the base of the spherical feature. This cutting-in is carried out by the point of the skew with the chisel resting on its edge on the toolrest. The wood immediately alongside is also shaped by the skew, used as for forming a bead. The whole of the main part of the handle can be formed with a medium-size gouge.

When turning items like handles, where the diameter at the tailstock end is fairly small, there is some danger that an ordinary cone centre will cause the wood to split. This is why a ring centre is preferred where the diameter is small, although a revolving centre, with its absence of friction on the wood, is better still.

Sometimes handles are turned with shoulders above the pin: a typical one are shown in *Figure 9.9.* Where the handle is to go

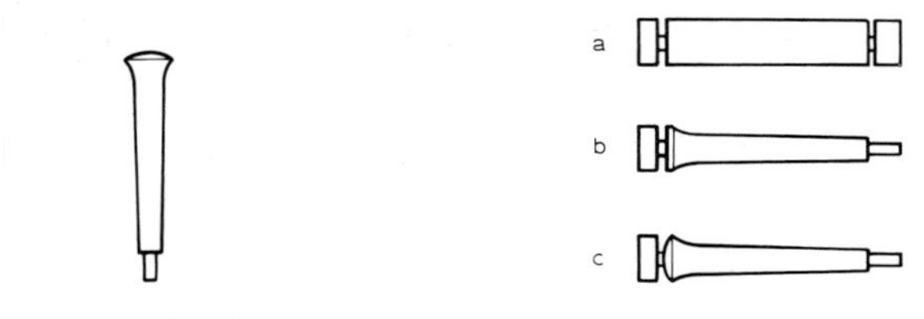

Fig. 9.9. Handle with shoulder on pin

Fig. 9.10. Stages in forming handle

into a flat surface, the gap problem shown in *Figure 9.5* will not occur. The main stages in making such a handle is shown in *Figure 9.10,* the first one (*a*) being achieved with the parting tool. The concave stem (*b*) is made with the gouge, and the dome at the left-hand end (*c*) is formed with the skew.

A job which the turner will want to do for himself before he has had a lathe very long is to make tool handles, especially for turning tools. Apart from the fact that scrapers can be conveniently made from old files, which need handles, money can be saved by buying turning tools unhandled and making the handles oneself. Brass ferrules of both $\frac{3}{4}$in and $\frac{7}{8}$in diameter can be bought, although odd lengths of tubing often come to hand and require little more than hacksawing to provide several ferrules.

When making tool handles on which ferrules have to be fitted, it helps, provided that the dimensions of the tailstock allow, to slide the ferrule on to the tailstock centre. This enables the ferrule to be instantly used to check the diameter at this end as the handle is reduced, thus enabling a good fit to be obtained. A

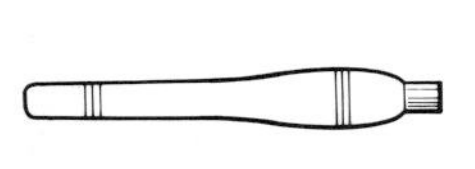

Fig. 9.11. Typical turning tool handle

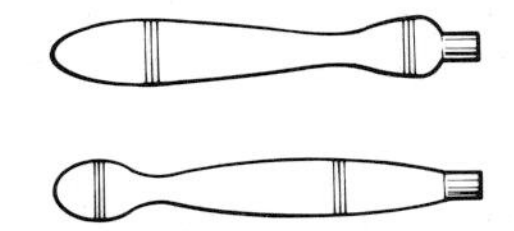

Fig. 9.12. Alternative turning tool handles

typical handle for a turning tool, where the overall length can be anything from 6in to 12in, is shown in *Figure 9.11*. Alternative shapes are shown in *Figure 9.12*. While shapes should strictly speaking be formed with the skew chisel, in practice these can be made quite well with a medium-size gouge, which means that all the shaping can be completed with this tool.

Mallets

A too! which can be produced entirely by turning is the mallet. A traditional carver's mallet, made from a single piece of dense hardwood about 3in square, is shown in *Figure 9.13*. For a larger, heavier size, the shaft will need to be turned separately. The head is then a piece of faceplate turning. The shaft is made so that the part which enters the hole in the head is without a

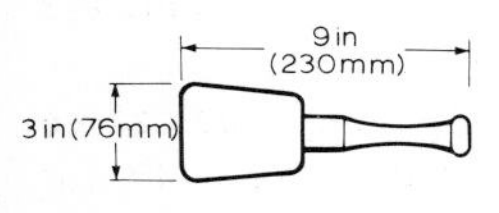

Fig. 9.13. One-piece carver's mallet

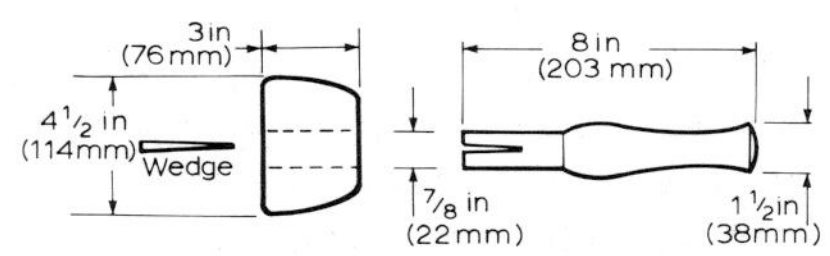

Fig. 9.14. Two-piece carver's mallet

shoulder but has a slight taper towards the grip. This enables the head to be driven on tightly. It is secured by driving a wedge into a cut prepared at the end of the shaft. Details are shown in *Figure 9.14*.

A mallet for general purposes is illustrated in *Figure 9.15*. Sizes are only approximate; a slightly smaller one, with a head around 2in in diameter, would be ideal for camping purposes. With such a mallet it is better to bore the hole first, taking care that is goes through the axis of the points of mounting at the ends. The wood turned up to cylindrical form and with the parting tool used at the ends is shown in *Figure 9.16*. The parting

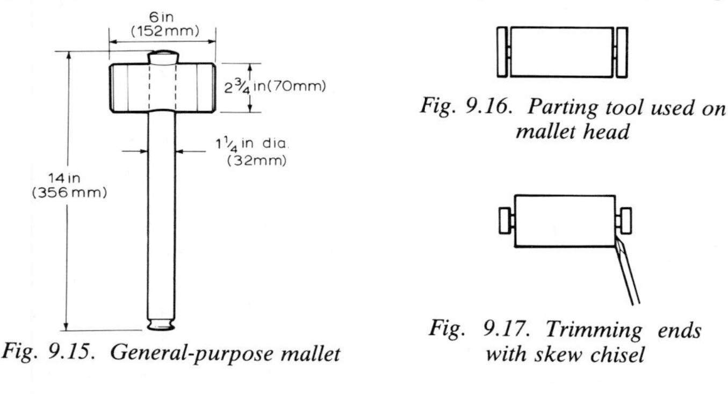

Fig. 9.15. General-purpose mallet

Fig. 9.16. Parting tool used on mallet head

Fig. 9.17. Trimming ends with skew chisel

tool does not give a particularly clean cut, but the slight tearing of the grain which it creates does not really matter for a project like a mallet. However, this is a good project on which to practise using the skew chisel to get a cleanly cut surface at the end of a piece of turning.

The chisel in use is shown in *Figure 9.17* where, to make room to manipulate it, waste on the outside of the parting-tool groove has been removed. This is easily done with either the parting tool or a gouge. When using the skew, cutting is carried out with the toe of the tool by moving it towards the centre. It is essential, though, to have the chisel very slightly twisted, so that the cutting edge is just clear of the wood. If more of the cutting edge than the extreme end comes in contact with the wood, it is almost certain to dig in.

The mallet used by auctioneers and chairmen of meetings is known as a gavel. Gavels are frequently quite ornamental and are often made as presentation pieces. A suggested design is shown in *Figure 9.18.* Again, when turning the head, it is better if the hole is bored first. The extent to which turning can be taken before the head is removed from the lathe for final finishing of the ends by hand is shown in *Figure 9.19.*

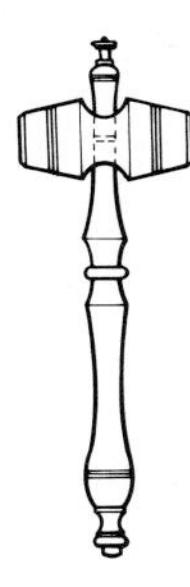

Fig. 9.18. Chairman's gavel

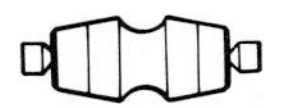

Fig. 9.19. Extent of turning gavel head

In this design it would be impossible to make and fit the handle with its projecting top all in one piece. The top is really a dummy, as the mallet will never be put to serious use. The main part of the handle should hold sufficiently well if a good fit is achieved, and glue used.

Brief reference to design balance has already been made in connection with reading-lamps. This gavel is another example where the design should be thought of as a whole, so that one part or feature matches the other. Careful study of the drawing will show that the top of the handle is a smaller version of the lower end, and that the three rings on the handle are repeated on the head. Small rings in the form of vee-cuts are made by first making a cut with the toe of the skew, then removing the wood on either side with the heel.

A gavel is used to strike a block. This is usually a piece of faceplate turning, so in order to complete the set, a suggested profile for the block is shown in *Figure 9.20.*

Yet another version of the mallet is the one used in the kitchen for 'tenderising' steaks prior to cooking. The striking faces of the mallet are of metal and are bought in pairs consisting of one plain end and one spiked end. Here the smoothness of the ends of the turning is of no great importance, but they must be true, with the diameters made to match the striking faces. Because such a mallet is used relatively gently, there is no need to make the handle pass right through the head, so the hole is bored

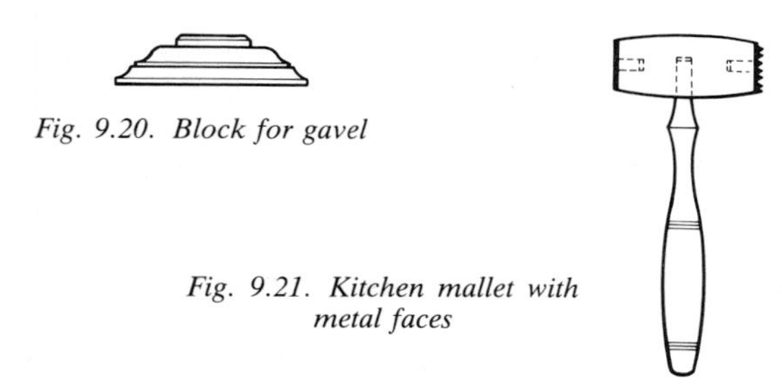

Fig. 9.20. Block for gavel

Fig. 9.21. Kitchen mallet with metal faces

part-way only. The metal faces have spigots on them, for which holes must be made in the head ends, and final fixing must be made with an adhesive such as Araldite. A waterproof glue should also be used for bonding the handle to the head as, obviously, a meat mallet is going to be washed as often as it is used. Details of a typical mallet are shown in *Figure 9.21.*

Vases

Thanks to the availability of glass liners, small flower-vases make pleasant little projects for the turner. The liners are around 4½ in long and ⅞ in in diameter and are intended to take a single flower. Three different profiles are shown in *Figure 9.22*. This is a job where, provided the wood blank can be crosscut accurately with the ends square, there is no need to leave waste on the length. The work should be mounted on a screw-chuck but supported at the other end with the tailstock centre.

The work should be rough-turned and, if need be, the right-hand end skimmed as described for the mallet-head. For the second and third suggestions in *Figure 9.2,* it is advisable at this stage to carry out some prelimiary shaping so that the outline

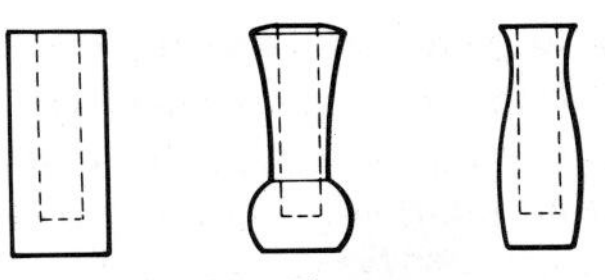

Fig. 9.22. Flower-vases

is near to the final one. At this stage the hole is bored and the final skimming to shape carried out with skew chisel and gouge, according to the profile.

Larger vases can be made to accommodate tall and slender drinking glasses.

Candle-holders

An item similar to a vase is a candle-holder. Three designs are suggested in *Figure 9.23*. In all of them the upper end has been kept as wide as possible and the top surface hollowed a little so that molten wax will not readily overflow. This hollowing should

Fig. 9.23. Candle-holders

Fig. 9.24. Undercutting at top of candle-holder

be done while the tailstock centre is still supporting the wood, as otherwise the leverage effect when working at the end could force the wood off the screw-chuck. The hollowing does not have to extend to the middle of the wood; *Figure 9.24* shows what is required, as the uncut spigot in the middle is removed when the hole is bored. (For a modification which can be made to a drill for boring candle-holders, see Chapter 10.)

Corkscrews

For a corkscrew with a turned handle, only an oddment of wood is needed, and so this is an excellent way to use up an offcut with unusual colouring or grain. Various ideas are shown in *Figure 9.25*. It is on small items like these, and where the wood is one of the denser species, that the turner often has to use scraping techniques. The harder the wood, the more likely it is to respond to scraping, and some woods are so hard that chisel and gouge cannot be used.

Because these handles require finishing at both ends, the turning has to be reduced at these points to the minimum

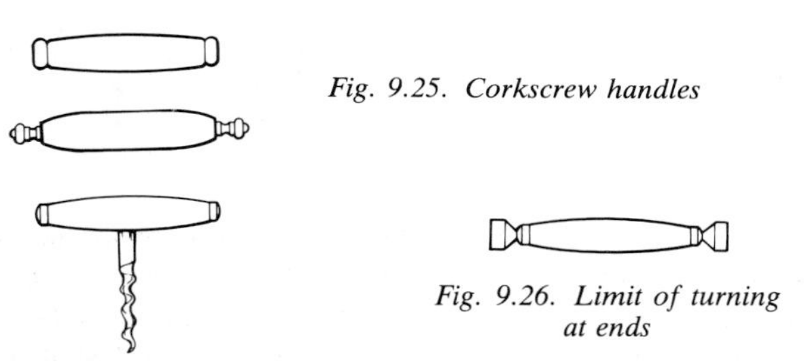

Fig. 9.25. Corkscrew handles

Fig. 9.26. Limit of turning at ends

thickness consistent with retaining enough strength to prevent failure. The ends should therefore be turned last, enabling the main part to be tackled while there is ample wood at the extremities. The limit to which the ends can be turned is shown in *Figure 9.26,* after which completion is best carried out off the lathe.

Bottle-stoppers

To reclose wine or similar bottles, turned stoppers can be made with what are known as 'optic corks', which are bored down their centres to a diameter of about 7⁄16 in.

To turn such a stopper, start with the work between centres and turn it to cylindrical form. The parting tool is next used to cut in the shoulder, making the distance from the end to the shoulder approximately equal to the length of the cork and the diameter slightly more than that of the hole in it. Wood between shoulder and end is now removed to produce the stage shown in *Figure 9.27*. The spigot at this end needs to be trimmed down by skew chisel or scraper so as to provide a good fit in the cork.

These stoppers are good examples of work which, in the absence of a collet-chuck, can be held in a drill-chuck. The wood at this stage should be reversed so that it is set up as shown in

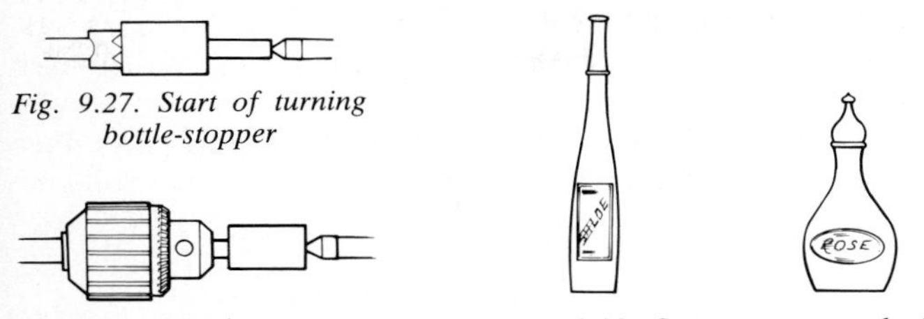

Fig. 9.27. Start of turning bottle-stopper

Fig. 9.28. Bottle-stopper reversed into drill chuck

Fig. 9.29. Stoppers to match the bottles

Figure 9.28, when turning can be completed. It always helps in a situation like this if the support of the tailstock is retained for as long as possible. So the main part of the stopper is turned first, with the actual top of the stopper, which is adjacent to the tailstock, turned last of all. If the stopper is a fairly large one, it is not wise to actually part through at the tailstock end and expect the wood to be sufficiently secure for cutting to continue when it is held at one end only.

It is not difficult to match the design of the stopper to the shape of the bottle. This idea applied to bottles of quite different shape is shown in *Figure 9.29.*

Cabinet knobs

Knobs, too, offer the turner an opportunity to evolve a design not commercially available or seen elsewhere, whether they be for a piece of cabinetwork made by himself or for a turnery project such as a bowl. There are two main methods of securing knobs in place. The most simple is by screwing – ideal for drawers, as the screws cannot be seen. The alternative is to turn a pin on the end of the knob so that this can be glued into a hole of matching diameter.

For a knob which is to be screwed in place, the screw-chuck offers the easiest method of mounting. As the diameter of the base of the knob is almost certain to be less than the diameter of even the smallest screw-chuck, a piece of plywood packing about ¼in thick should be placed on the chuck before mounting the wood. This ensures that the turning tools will not come into contact with the metal of the chuck. A selection of knobs which can be turned on a screw-chuck is shown in *Figure 9.30*. Because of their small size and limited overhang from the chuck, these can normally be turned without support from the tailstock.

Fig. 9.30. Knobs turned on screw-chuck

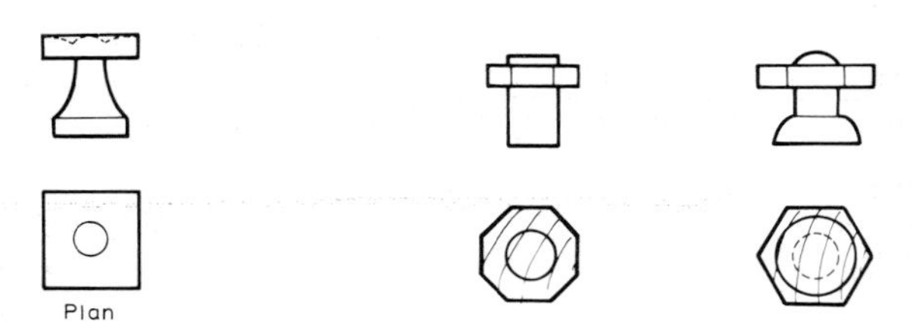

Fig. 9.31. Combined turned and square knob

Fig. 9.32 Hexagonal and octagonal turned knobs

Knobs can be made as a combination of a turned part and a part which is of another shape. A simple example of this is illustrated in *Figure 9.31*. To make such a knob, the wood must be accurately prepared to a square section and carefully cross-cut to length. A pilot-hole needs to be made to assist in mounting on the screw; this must be exactly in the centre of the wood, otherwise the square top of the knob and its turned base will not be in line with each other. Similar ideas can be based on the hexagon and octagon: two possibilities are shown in *Figure 9.32*.

Knobs with pins are made in very much the same manner as bottle-stoppers, by turning the pin first, with this towards the tailstock. As an alternative to holding the workpiece in a drill-chuck when it is reversed, home-made collet-chucks are simple to make; a pattern often used is shown in *Figure 3.40*.

Reading-lamps

For the style of reading-lamp which involves a separate base, the base will have to be bored at its centre with a hole between ¾ in and 1 in in diameter to take the pin on the stem. Once the stem has been rough-turned, the next stage is to turn the pin on the end. The techniques of producing this pin are the same as for handles and bottle-stoppers, but a dodge worth the little trouble it takes will ensure a good fit where the pin has a diameter larger than the barrel of the tailstock. An oddment of plywood, around 2 in or 3 in square, is bored in its centre with the bit used in the lamp-base. This piece of plywood should be slipped over the protruding end of the tailstock before the wood is mounted in the lathe. When the pin is being turned down to size, as well as using callipers and any other measuring device, the plywood can be slid along the tailstock and on to the pin to check the fit between pin and base. This set-up is shown in *Figure 9.33*.

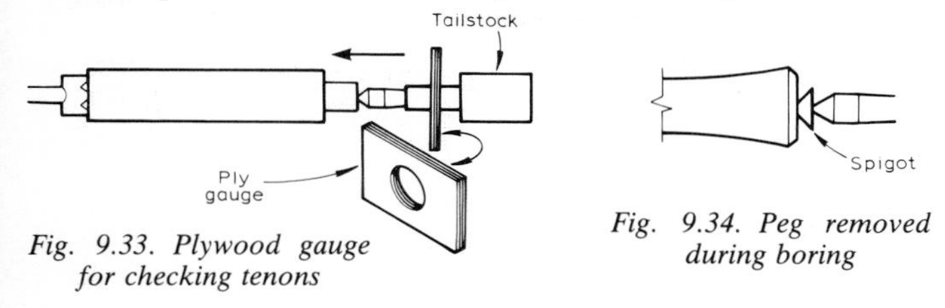

Fig. 9.33. Plywood gauge for checking tenons

Fig. 9.34. Peg removed during boring

It is a matter of preference whether the remainder of the shaping is carried out with the wood as first mounted or whether it is reversed so that the pin engages with the headstock centre. The second way enables the top end of the lamp to be more readily attended to with the turning-tools, and turning should proceed until only a small pin is left, as shown in *Figure 9.34*. Provided that this pin is less than the 5⁄16 in diameter of the hole to be bored through the stem, it will be removed when boring takes place.

An alternative way of proceeding is to bore the hole after the pin at the end has been turned. When the stem is reversed, the tailstock centre then engages in the hole just bored, which also ensures that all stages are concentric. The slight disadvantage of this method is that when turning what is to be the top of the lamp, the tools are again working right up to the metal of the tailstock centre.

A selection of profiles appears in the previous chapter (p.136).

One-piece reading-lamps require a rather different procedure, and this depends on the size of the lamp and facilities available for cross-cutting. This is because it is essential to have the end of the wood which is secured to the faceplate flat and square. If this can be achieved before turning takes place, then the wood can be mounted directly on the chuck. For the smaller sizes of lamps, a screw-chuck can be used, provided that additional screws can be inserted. However, before mounting, it is best to bore the small hole for the flex. This should be about ¼in in diameter and made as near to the bottom as is possible. It is desirable with work of this type to use the support of the tailstock for as long as possible, and only light finishing cuts should be made without this support if the height of the lamp is more than minimum. Suggested designs are shown in *Figure 9.35*.

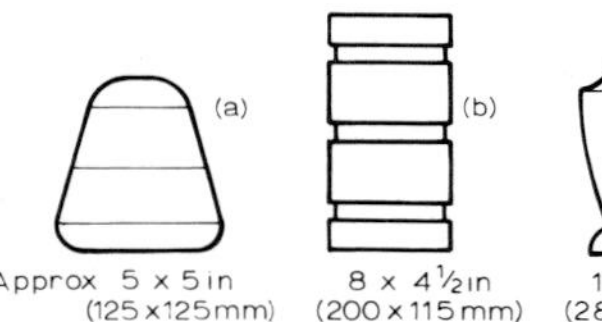

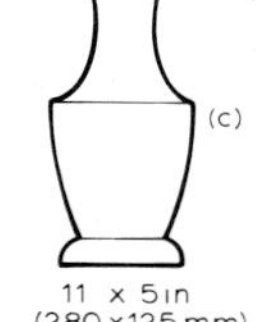

Fig. 9.35. One-piece reading-lamps

If the design of the lamp necessitates using a block of wood about 5in or 6in square, truing up of the lower end in readiness for chuck or faceplate mounting can be carried out on the lathe. After rough turning, the parting tool is used at the tailstock end to true up what will be the lower surface. The parting tool does not have to be used at a distance from the end so that a groove is formed – it can be employed very close to the end so that only enough wood is removed to give effective truing-up. It is possible to mount wood for a particularly large reading-lamp either on a chuck with split rings, such as the six-in-one, or by screwing directly to a standard faceplate (though large work held entirely by screws into end-grain must be treated with care because of the limited holding power of such screws).

Boxes

Turned boxes with lids can be made in several ways, but the method described here is both straightforward and simple. A block is prepared large enough for the box and its lid, and sufficiently long to allow for both mounting and cutting through between lid and box. For small boxes, mounting on the screw-chuck is sufficient; otherwise the blank has to be treated as described for reading-lamps.

After rough turning, the right-hand end is trued up. This is to be the underside of the lid. Ideally, the hollowing – or at least the bulk of it – should be carried out by boring (see Chapter 10).

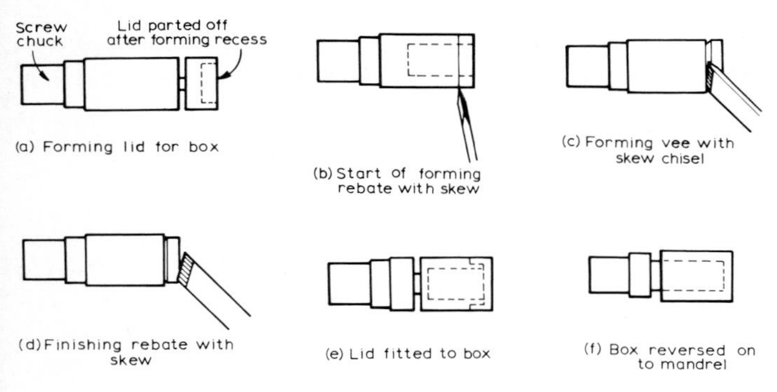

Fig. 9.36. Turning boxes

Normally, there is no advantage in making the lid too deep; a typical depth is ⅜in. By using end- and side-scrapers, this hole can be enlarged if needs be, and the lower surface cleaned up. Reference to the final shape, shown in *Figure 9.36(e)*, will indicate the nature and purpose of this recess. The parting tool can now be used to separate the lid; the work at this stage is shown in *Figure 9.36(a)*.

The end of the remaining wood is now trued up. This end also is best hollowed mainly by boring and the hole cleaned up or enlarged by scraping. In the absence of a suitable boring bit, all the hollowing can be done with scrapers.

The step, or rebate, for the lid should now be made. This is the stage where maximum care is needed to produce the right fit. The skew chisel is used. *Figure 9.36(b)* shows the first cut, which is made by the toe of the tool, angled in such a way that the left-hand bevel is square to the wood. By reversing the chisel so that it is heel-down and moving the handle to the right, a second cut is made with the heel so as to produce a distinct vee-shaped cut, as shown in *Figure 9.36(c)*. By using the chisel as when cleaning up a cylinder, but mostly with the heel, the waste is removed from the rebate as shown in *Figure 9.36(d)*. The lid must be as tight as possible without risk of splitting.

The outside of the box is turned while the lid is in place, hence the need for a good fit of the lid on its box. It helps if the underside of the box is almost parted through, and this stage is shown in *Figure 9.36(e)*. It is a matter of choice whether the joint between lid and box is slightly tapered or the meeting surfaces are left dead square so as to reduce the joint to a hairline. The fit of the lid can be adjusted, if necessary, by glasspapering.

To give a well finished surface to the underside, a supporting mandrel has to be turned. This is simply a block mounted on the screw-chuck and carefully turned to cylindrical shape so that the box will be a friction fit on it. This is shown in *Figure 9.36(f)*. The underside can then be trimmed up to complete the box.

Stool-legs

Sets of legs do not particularly call for any techniques not so far mentioned. It is likely that legs will need to be morticed. The mortices should be cut first if the legs are to be turned from end to end. Because of this, the wood needs to be accurately prepared and mounted on the lathe, as inaccuracies here will be reflected in the mortices. Modern trends in turned legs are for great simplicity. An example is given in *Figure 9.37,* where the slight narrowing at the lower end is the only variation from a plain cylinder. A second example is shown in *Figure 9.38.*

There are two methods of fitting a tenoned member in a mortice. One is to prepare a flat surface alongside the mortice so

Fig. 9.37. Modern leg of restrained design

Fig. 9.38. Further example of modern leg design

that the overall width of the flat is equal to the thickness of the tenoned piece: this is shown in *Figure 9.39*. The second method is to cut the shoulder of the tenon to match the leg. While, in theory, this should be a concave curve, in practice a bevelled shoulder produces a fit which is perfectly satisfactory. This method is shown in *Figure 9.40*.

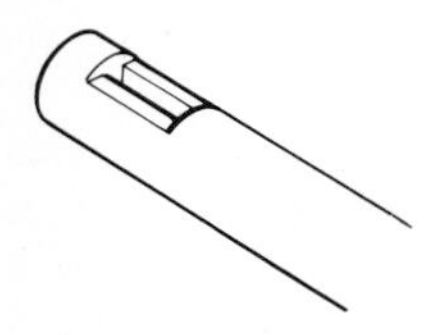

Fig. 9.39. Leg prepared for square-shouldered tenon

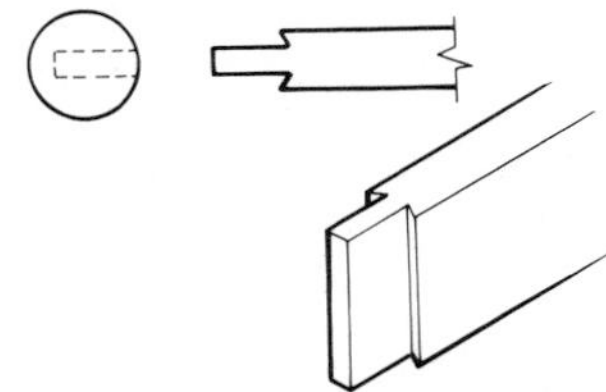

Fig. 9.40. Tenon with bevelled shoulder

Legs are often required with parts left 'in the square' (not turned), to have rails tenoned into them. It does not matter whether the mortices are formed before or after turning. A typical leg of this type is shown in *Figure 9.41,* which includes alternative ways of treating the lower end.

Wood for this sort of leg must be planed square at the start. Next, the limits of the turned and non-turned parts must be marked out. For accuracy as well as speed, it is best to mark all four legs at the same time while they are held together by cramps or in a vice. Marking should be done in heavy pencil lines and the lines then squared across all faces. These lines are then visible during turning. Centering at the ends needs extra care, and mounting is between standard centres.

With square stock on the lathe, it is very important to revolve it by hand first to ensure that it clears the toolrest. The ends of the square parts are always cut first, and this is started by the toe of the skew chisel, as shown in *Figure 9.42*. The first cut should

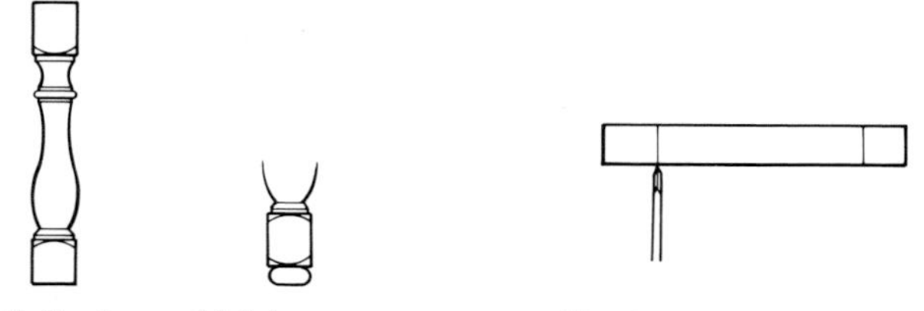

Fig. 9.41. Legs which incorporate squares

Fig. 9.42. First cut to form shoulder

be no more than a nick in the corners. The lathe should now be stopped, to ensure that these nicks are uniform on all four corners. If not, the work is not quite centrally mounted, and it should be adjusted until the nicks are equal.

The chisel is next reversed to take up the position shown in *Figure 9.43* and is moved by rolling it to the left to give a rounded cut. This is repeated from the other side. It is unlikely that the cut formed will be sufficiently deep at this stage, so it will

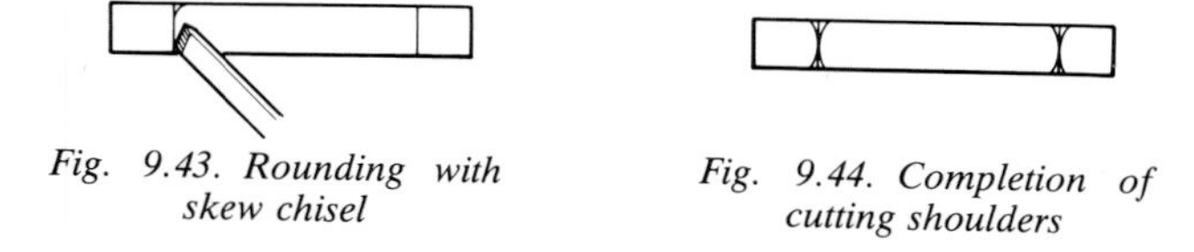

Fig. 9.43. Rounding with skew chisel

Fig. 9.44. Completion of cutting shoulders

probably be necessary to cut in deeper with the toe and to repeat the whole operation until the cut encircles the wood. This is the stage shown in *Figure 9.44*.

The next step is to turn the wood between the shoulders to cylindrical shape. A 1¼in roughing gouge can be used for this, although some turners may prefer a smaller size. The best way of proceeding is to tackle the parts adjacent to the shoulders. By rolling the tool to left or right, as appropriate, the surface being turned can be kept quite clean and smooth. With the ends attended to, the wood between is now made cylindrical and kept to as large a diameter as possible. The work is now ready for turning to the required shape.

When turning sets of legs, it helps when forming the actual profile to keep the diameter of the various features slightly on the full side. This allows for a little final trimming, if needed, to ensure that all legs are reasonably identical. More wood can be removed, but it cannot be put back!

10 Boring on the lathe

One operation, apart from actual turning, which can fairly readily be carried out on the lathe is boring. Holes of one sort or another are used a great deal in turnery, and the use of the lathe for boring leads to speedy, easy, and accurate work. It is also possible to use the lathe for boring holes in components which are not themselves turned, but such use of the lathe is outside the scope of this book.

Most bits used for boring will need to be held in a chuck. A typical three-jaw drill-chuck is shown in *Figure 10.1*. The

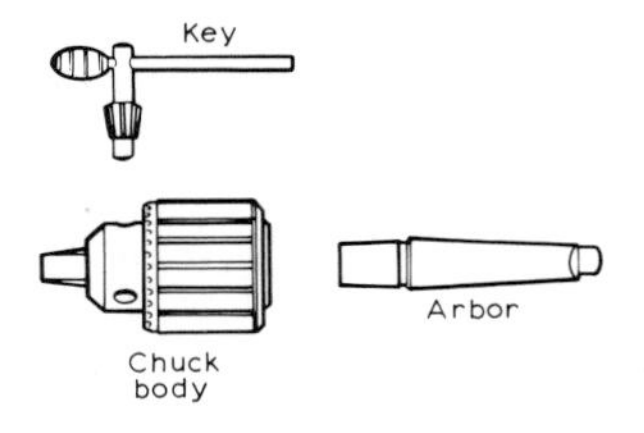

Fig. 10.1. Drill-chuck

standard chuck has a capacity of ½in, but one pattern closes down to zero while another will only close down to 5⁄64in. The arbor is separate from the actual chuck and must be obtained with a morse taper to match that of the lathe. The chuck can then be used in either the headstock or the tailstock mandrel.

Bits

The most popular pattern of bit for machine use is the sawtooth variety shown in *Figure 10.2*. This bit bores very cleanly both with and across the grain, and also at an angle. Because of its efficient cutting action, it absorbs the minimum of power. It is available is sizes from ⅜in to 3½in. Because of its small point, deep blind holes can be made without fear of penetrating to the opposite side.

For holes which are particularly deep, the Jennings bit is to be preferred (*Figure 10.3*). These bits have an overall length of 9in and are available in sizes from ¼in to 1in. The advantage of this bit is that, for deep holes, the chips are readily ejected by the spiral fluting, so the problem of choking, which can occur with some types of bit, does not arise. These bits are made with a screw-nose which assists in drawing the bit into the wood. This works well where the wood is secured and can move only in a controlled way, but there is a danger of overboring if the wood is free to move on to the bit. For lathework, it helps if the threaded point is lightly filed so that it cannot cause the turner to lose control when the wood is hand-held.

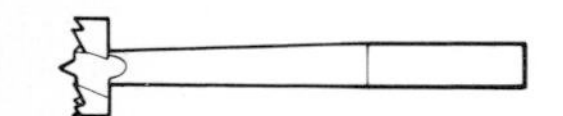

Fig. 10.2. Sawtooth machine bit

Fig. 10.3. Jennings pattern twist-bit

Fig. 10.4. Lip-and-spur bit

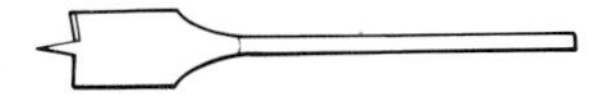

Fig. 10.5. Flatbit

Another pattern of bit which works well for general purposes is known as the 'lip-and-spur', shown in *Figure 10.4*. Such bits are particularly useful for boring deep holes in small diameters.

Flatbits were originally designed for use in portable electric drills; one is illustrated in *Figure 10.5*. They absorb very little power, are easy to sharpen, and, although they work by what is really a scraping action, they cut a reasonably clean hole. They work well in the lathe, but for most purposes, the bit will be better if it is modified slightly. These bits have particularly large points – essential when the bit is used freehand in a drill. But, because the bit is held in a positive way when used in the lathe, the large point is no longer essential, so for lathe-work these points can be filed down considerably, which reduces the amount of wood which it is necessary to leave at the bottom of a blind hole to avoid breaking through.

A feature of flatbits is that their edges can be filed so as to reduce their diameter to a specific size. For example, for a hole

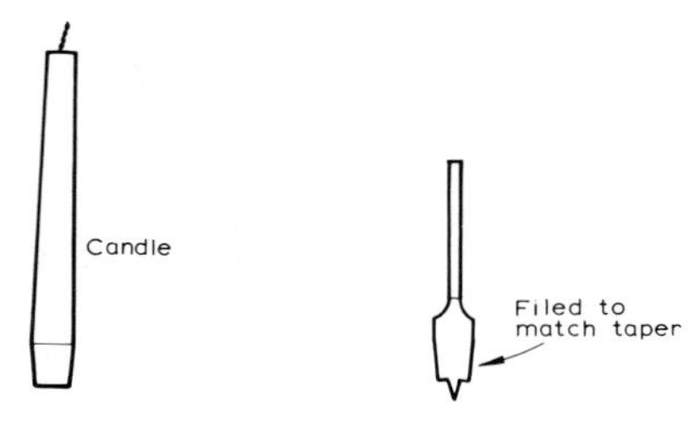

Fig. 10.6. Flatbit modified for candle-holder

of 1¹⁄₁₆ in diameter (which is not a standard size for the other bits mentioned), a flatbit of 1⅛ in diameter can be modified by filing.

A flatbit can also be modified to bore a hole which has tapering sides to match the lower end of most decorative candles. A bit of ⅞ in. diameter is needed, and *Figure 10.6* shows the way in which it should be filed to match a typical candle. For tapering holes which are as shallow as this, a further small modification is to cut down the length of the shank by about half. This makes the bit much stiffer in use.

Morse drills

Ordinary engineers' Morse drills can be used in the drill-chuck, and are useful because of the variety of small diameters which can be obtained. It is particularly important when using Morse drills to make a slight indentation in the wood with a bradawl or otherwise to ensure that the hole is made exactly where needed. This is especially necessary when drilling into a curved surface as, because there is no definite point on Morse drills and also because smaller sizes can bend slightly, the drill can easily skid off-course before penetration starts.

A turner will often have to carry out small batches of repetition work or, over a period of time, will produce an oft-repeated item on his lathe. When many holes of a specific depth are required, a useful dodge is to file a small notch on the drill-shank at a distance from the cutting edge equal to the depth of hole required.

It is possible to obtain Morse drills which, instead of a parallel shank, have a Morse taper. These are intended to be mounted directly into the head- or tail-stock. They seem to have been more popular in the past than at present and were intended for engineering trades. Sometimes they can be picked up second-hand and are always worth the small amount they usually cost.

Boring techniques

The most common method of boring on the lathe is to mount the bit and chuck in the tailstock and advance them to the work. It always helps if the centre of the work is marked. This is best done with the point or toe of the skew chisel while the work is revolving, so that a tiny recess is made. This will ensure that the point of the bit locates itself accurately and the hole will be made truly central.

Certain precautions are needed. First, high speeds are not necessary, and can lead to burning. A speed around 1200 r.p.m., or the second slowest, is about right. Second, where the work is mounted on the screw-chuck, it must be checked that the screw will not foul the bit: bits can be badly damaged if forced against metal. Finally, and especially if the work is held by a single screw, boring must be done slowly and gently – more so with larger diameters. If an attempt is made to bore the wood too quickly, the resistance of the bit can become greater than the grip of the screw, with the result that the wood is wrenched off the chuck.

Reading-lamp base

It is often convenient, or even essential, to have the bit held in the headstock and feed the wood on to it. An example is the base of a reading-lamp which has been turned on a screw-chuck and where the hole is required right through the centre in order to take the pin of the stem. Another example is the hole for the flex in the same lamp-base.

Figure 10.7 shows how the flex-hole in the lamp-base is tackled if a sanding table is available. Sanding tables are usually about 9 in square, made of ½ in plywood, and are held by a pin, attached to the table, in the toolrest holder. A suitable pin is listed in the catalogue of at least one turnery supplier.

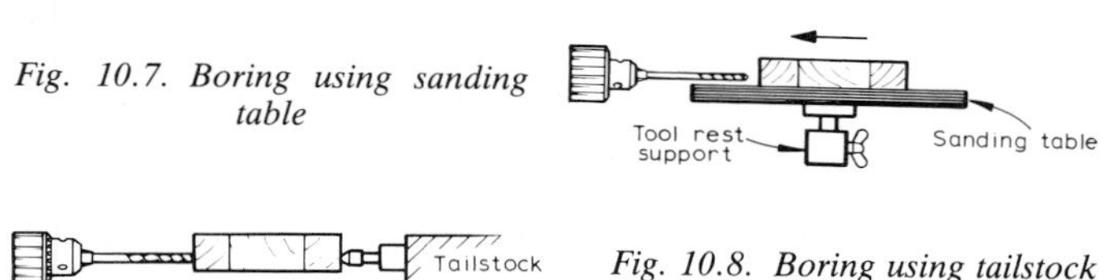

Fig. 10.7. Boring using sanding table

Fig. 10.8. Boring using tailstock

The height of the table is adjusted so that the block from which the base is to be turned can rest on it at the right height. The wood is then advanced on to the bit by hand and, by looking down on the wood, it can be accurately controlled so that the hole is made exactly in the centre.

An alternative method dispenses with the sanding table. The position for the hole is marked on one edge of the wood and a corresponding mark is made directly opposite. The tailstock with cone-centre is then positioned so that the wood can be held with one of the marks on the centre and the point of the bit on the other mark. This stage is shown in *Figure 10.8*. The wood is then fed on to the bit by turning the tailstock wheel. This method can give accurate results but it depends on the initial marking out.

For boring the hole in the centre of the base, some form of boring-pad at the tailstock end is needed. The small faceplate shown in *Figure 3.43* is ideal, but it needs to have a piece of scrap wood screwed to it so that when the bit penetrates the workpiece it will not strike metal. As these small, taper-mounted faceplates are difficult to obtain, there is a simple alternative. Into the centre of a block of wood about 4 in square and 2 in thick is bored a hole about half-way through, of a diameter exactly equal to the barrel of the tailstock. The block is then slipped over the tailstock barrel, the workpiece is held against the block, and the whole is then advanced on to the bit revolving in the headstock. This arrangement is shown in *Figure 10.9*.

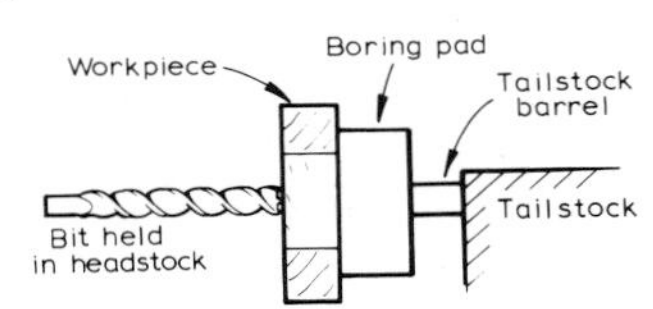

Fig. 10.9. Using boring-pad on tailstock

It is essential for the block to fit on the tailstock without any play if boring is not to be out of true. If a good fit between block and tailstock cannot be obtained by boring the locating hole, the block can be mounted on the faceplate and the hole made with the square-end scraper.

Reading-lamp stem

The hole down the stem of a reading-lamp needs to be 5⁄16 in in diameter, assuming that a screw-in brass nipple will be used to hold the lampholder. For a lamp of average height, boring must take place from both ends. A Jennings bit will cope with this job, or a Morse drill of the 'long shank' type can be used. The method is to fit the drill-chuck in the headstock and hold the work between the bit and the tailstock centre. The tailstock hand-wheel is used to advance the wood. Because of the depth of boring needed, it will probably be necessary to re-position the tailstock when the end of the tailstock thread is reached, and also to repeat the whole operation from the opposite end. With practice and care, the workpiece can be held and advanced on to the bit entirely by hand. The wood must be kept in line with the bed of the lathe to ensure that boring takes place on the axis of the work; to be certain of this, the workpiece should be rotated through 90 deg two or three times as boring proceeds.

When inserting the brass nipple to the hole, it is easy to damage the thread if pliers or similar tools are used. But if a kerf

Fig. 10.10. Making saw-kerf in brass nipple

is cut in the top with a hacksaw, as shown in *Figure 10.10*, a screwdriver with a large blade can be used to screw the nipple into the hole.

Tool handles

Another common boring job is to make the hole required in the handle of a turning tool. In this case, the hole needs to taper, or at least approximate to a taper. The tangs of turning tools vary in size and so the size of hole required for a particular blade has to be estimated. The following procedure will suit blades of average size. The work should be held between tailstock and drill. First, bore a ⅛in diameter hole as deep as possible. Next, enlarge this small hole to a depth of about 2in. with a ¼in drill. Finally, enlarge this hole to ⅜in and about 1in deep. Small, lightweight tools might need the drill sizes to be scaled down a bit; extra large ones are likely to require the three-stage hole to be both wider and deeper.

When fitting the tool to the handle, grip the blade in a vice and rotate the handle on to the tang. The fairly sharp corners of the tang will act rather like a reamer and will both smooth out the steps inside the hole and enlarge it if rotating is continued. Finally, the handle is tapped on to the blade with a mallet.

When making stepped holes as described with Morse drills, it matters little if the stages are carried out from the small diameter to large, or vice versa. This is not so when using a sawtooth drill, Jennings bit, or flatbit. The hole shown in *Figure 10.11* is known as counter-bored (as distinct from countersunk), and here the large hole must be bored first. This is because all these bits must

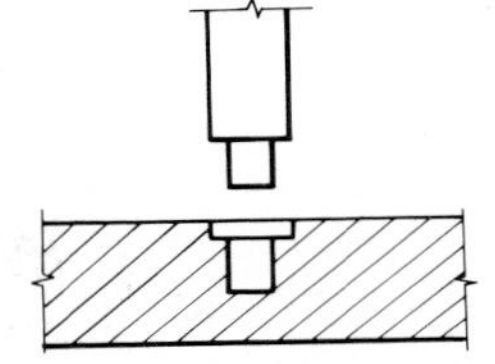

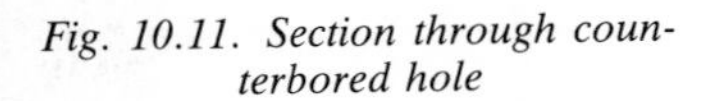

Fig. 10.11. Section through counterbored hole

have solid wood on which their points can rotate, and this would not be the case if the small holes were made first and then an attempt made to enlarge them.

Stool tops

In some boring operations, the holes have to be made towards the edge of a piece of faceplate turning, rather than at the centre. A simple example of this is the top of a three-legged stool, which needs to have holes near the edge and spaced equidistantly. These holes are almost certainly to be bored at an angle so as to splay the legs, and they may or may not need to be bored right through. How the centres for the holes are marked out is shown in *Figure 10.12*: the circle is made by compasses, and the same setting of the compasses is stepped off around the circle. This will give six equally spaced divisions, of which only alternate ones are required.

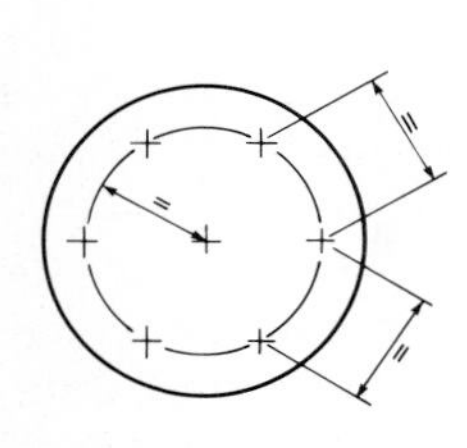

Fig. 10.12. Marking-out for three or six holes

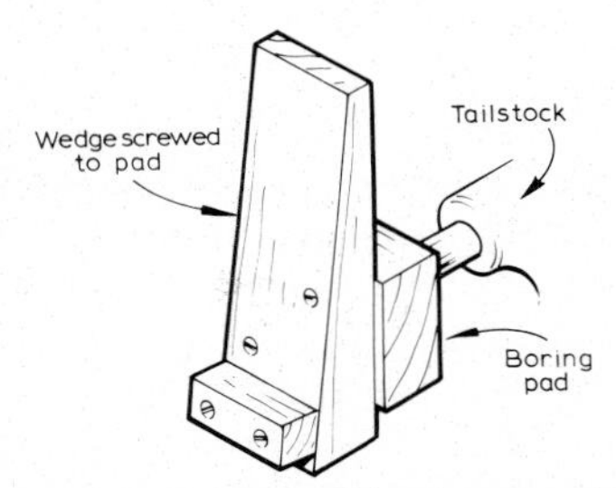

Fig. 10.13. Jig for boring at angle to face

In order to facilitate boring the holes and ensuring a consistent angle, the arrangement shown in *Figure 10.13* is needed. The angle of the wedge-shaped block corresponds to the splay required for the legs. While the small block at the lower end of the wedge is not essential, it is an aid to accuracy as well as giving support to the piece being bored. The wedge is screwed to the boring-pad already referred to, although it could be bored on its rear surface for mounting directly on the tailstock mandrel.

Fig. 10.14. Splayed underside of stool

Fig. 10.15. Stool with flat underside

If, when turning the top, the underside is bevelled as shown in *Figure 10.14*, the holes for the legs are made at right angles to this bevel. While this will still necessitate using the jig shown in *Figure 10.13*, the result is that the pins on the top of the legs can be shouldered without counterboring being necessary, as it would be in the example shown in *Figure 10.15*. Also shown in *Figure 10.15* is the complication which can arise when fitting a component into an angled hole.

Morticing a spindle

Sometimes it is necessary to bore into the side of a spindle-turned component, such as a leg, in order that the end of another spindle-turned part, such as a rail, can be fitted in. How the boring-jig is adapted to cope with such an operation is shown in *Figure 10.16*. Holes of this type usually have to be of a specific depth, as the parts which are fitted in do not have shoulders. This means that the end of the rail must make contact with the bottom of the hole in order to maintain the overall dimensions.

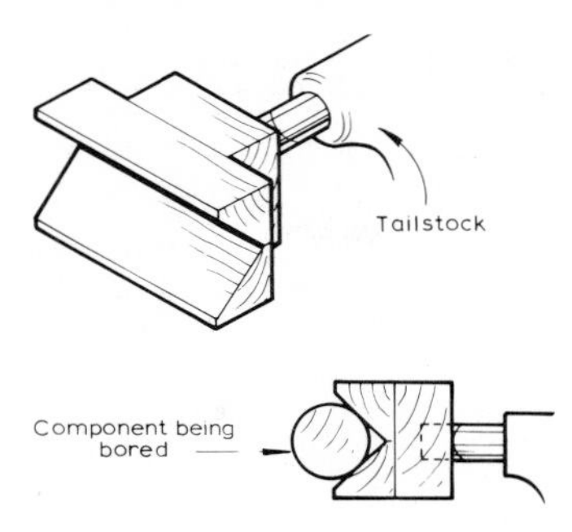

Fig. 10.16. Jig for boring into side of turned part

Only a small selection of basic boring methods has been described, but, as in most operations on the lathe, the scope of what can be achieved is governed very largely by the ingenuity of the turner. Master the operations described and you will never be lost for an answer to a boring problem.

11 Finishing

In all branches of woodworking, the term 'finishing' refers to the application of some kind of coating to the surface of the wood. The reasons for doing this are to seal the grain and keep out dirt, thus preserving the natural colour of the wood; to provide a durable surface that will withstand the use to which the object will be subjected; and to enliven and enhance the beauty of the grain. Most polishes, lacquers, and waxes give a gloss or semi-gloss finish, but matt finishes are available.

Opaque finishes such as oil paint are not likely to be much used by the turner. Some items of turnery, such as rolling pins, are best left without any kind of surface finish.

Before any type of finishing process can be carried out, the surface of the wood must be in a fit state to receive the finish. It has been stressed throughout this book that proper techniques with the tools will lead to cutting the wood 'cleanly' – that is, leaving the surface relatively smooth. Conversely, incorrect use of the tools – expecially when cutting tools are used in a scraping manner and when scrapers are not correctly sharpened or used – results in the wood not being properly cut and the grain being torn out. This leads to a rough surface which makes subsequent stages more difficult. It must be stressed, however, that some woods cut more cleanly than others, whatever techniques and tools are used.

Sanding

Even with species which respond well to the cutting action of the tools, it is rare that a surface can be produced directly from the tools which is sufficiently smooth to receive a finish. Further smoothing is carried out with glasspaper or other abrasive material and is usually called 'sanding'. (The name comes from early types of abrasive paper, which were coated with sand.)

It is a mistake to assume that sanding is a satisfactory substitute for good tool-manipulation. Sanding will make a good surface better but will rarely make a poor, badly-torn surface into a good one.

Sanding is normally carried out by holding the paper in the fingers and, to minimise the risk of injury, the toolrest should first be removed or swung well clear so that there is no danger that the fingers will be trapped between it and the wood. Another precaution is to hold the paper in such a way that the fingers are pointing in the direction of rotation, so that they will not be forced back on themselves by the rotating wood. This applies particularly when sanding the inside of small bowls and other hollowed items, and wherever the fingers are working in a restricted space. On spindle-work, the fingers will be under the work, not on top of it.

When sanding a piece of spindle-turning, the glasspaper should not be moved quickly sideways. Rapid movement of the abrasive paper from one end to the other will result in spiral marks on the work, especially when a moderately coarse grade is being used.

Coarse glasspaper should be avoided wherever possible on spindle-work, as it will probably do more harm than good. It must be remembered that with between-centres work, abrasion always takes place across the grain, so some scratching is inevitable. The secret of good sanding is to keep it to the minimum, and do it with progressively finer grades and with nothing coarser than medium grade.

A danger with excessive sanding is that corners which are intended to be sharp become rounded – indeed, it is possible to reshape small details of the turning by careless abrading. For fine detail work, it sometimes helps if the glasspaper is wrapped around a suitable piece of scrap wood and this used with a light filing action on the rotating wood. The forward movement is only to avoid concentrated use of a small part of the paper, as this would quickly render it useless and could lead to scorching of the wood if much pressure was being used.

Faceplate work is almost certain to require rather more sanding, partly because of the inevitable areas of against-the-grain cutting, and partly because scrapers – however skilfully used – are not likely to leave the surface as smooth as cutting tools will.

Ordinary cabinetmakers' quality glasspaper can be used perfectly well on the lathe, but its life is very limited. Machine-grade abrasive paper, on which the grit is usually aluminium oxide, will retain its cutting ability far longer. Strips of this type of abrasive are readily available in packs for small orbital (or 'finishing') sanders. Even such strips of paper discarded from power sanders as worn out will be found to have plenty of life in them for lathework if there is no resin, paint, glue, etc, clogging the grit.

Some woods do not respond well to glasspapering, as the grain tends to be pulled out so that the surface becomes almost furry. For such 'woolly' woods, only fairly fine grades of paper should be used. A good preparation for sanding woolly wood is 'sanding sealer'. This is used by marquetarians and should be obtainable from suppliers of marquetry gear. The sealer is applied to the revolving work by a pad; when it has dried out, ordinary sanding follows. Any finish can subsequently be used.

Care with sanding will pay dividends once the finish has been applied. Clear finishes will not conceal blemishes; indeed, they have the reverse effect. Slight imperfections which cannot be easily spotted before applying the finish sometimes become all too obvious once polishing starts, expecially if a high shine is required.

Staining

Unless there is a special reason for staining a piece of turnery, as when restoring an antique and colour-match is important, staining is not recommended. These days, most people prefer to see wood in its natural colour, and staining has generally gone out of favour for furniture as well as turnery. When staining is called for, it is strongly suggested that ready-to-use proprietary stains be used. Stains from the same maker can usually be intermixed to provide almost any shade, and they also have the advantage of being very even in their staining action. Application is with a cloth pad, the surplus is wiped off, and the job is then left a few hours to dry.

The question of compatibility will crop up. Spirit and naphtha-based stains are not too good if they are to be followed by shellac polish. Polyurethane polishes must follow stains formulated for them. Wax, which can follow shellac, is not good on naphtha – and so on. Water-based stains are compatible with most finishes, but they tend to raise the grain, so light, fine sanding is needed after the stain has dried.

Oil finishes

For items which are used for serving food, such as salad bowls and cheese boards, olive oil provides a suitable finish. This is applied while the work is still on the lathe. Two or three applications are given with a cloth, using a second cloth to remove excess oil and to burnish the surface. Oil of any kind will impart only a hint of a shine (although it will bring out colour and figure), but it is easy to apply and can readily be renewed at any time.

Wax polishing

One of the most popular finishes for turnery is wax polish. Although carnauba wax is often suggested for this purpose, it is so hard that if used directly on the wood it can bruise the softer species. Moreover, also because of its hardness, carnauba wax softens with the friction created by applying it to the revolving work only to a very limited extent. The result is that the film of wax deposited is very much on the surface, with little going into the pores of the grain, so a pure carnauba wax finish just flakes off.

After a lot of experimenting with wax polish for lathework, the following formula has been found to give the best all-round results.

Mix two parts of crushed carnauba wax and one part of beeswax together in a shallow tin. The carnauba wax is best crushed by wrapping it in strong cloth then hammering it on a convenient surface. Beeswax can be shredded with a chisel. Add enough turpentine to just cover the bottom of the tin, and heat gently until the waxes melt. Heat must not be applied directly to the tin or there will be a risk of fire: an asbestos mat can be used to isolate the tin from direct flame. Stir well when mixed, then allow to cool. When the wax mixture has set, it can easily be broken into pieces while in the tin, and pieces removed as required for use.

The wax is applied directly to the revolving wood, using a fair amount of pressure until it melts. A soft cloth is then used with moderate pressure to even out the film and burnish it. Too little pressure from the cloth will fail to soften the wax and thereby even it out and burnish the surface; too much pressure will cause so much heat that the wax will completely melt and be driven fully into the grain, leaving insufficient on the surface for a satisfactory shine. Some turners burnish with a handful of shavings: the method is worth a try.

Lacquer

A polish suitable for lathe work where a top-class finish is required has been developed by several manufacturers. It is generally called 'catalyst lacquer' and is cellulose-based, with a high viscosity. It requires the addition of a catalyst, usually in a ratio around 1:20, to react with the lacquer and cause it to harden. The mixture is liberally brushed on the work while it is revolved by hand, and allowed to set. Once the two components are mixed, setting commences and is irreversible, so only sufficient for the job in hand should be prepared and application must be started right away.

Medium-grade wet-or-dry abrasive paper is then used, with the lathe revolving, to smooth the surface ready for a second coat. Water or white spirit can be used as a lubricant. When the wood is dry and clean, the second coat is applied. Two coats are usually enough to provide a substantial film of lacquer, as the build-up is considerable. The second coat is again flatted down, this time using fine (400 grade) wet-or-dry paper, until the surface is quite smooth and uniformly dull. The shine is now brought up by using burnishing cream, usually supplied with the lacquer, to give a mirror-like gloss with the surface completely sealed.

Although catalyst lacquers involve a little more time and trouble than most other finishes, they are ideal for lathe work because the task of rubbing down and burnishing is done by the lathe itself. Two coats are sufficient to fill the grain completely. The finish is impervious, not affected by normal household liquids, and heatproof up to boiling point.

This lacquer can be given a semi-gloss finish (also known as eggshell or satin). The work is completed as already described. The gloss is then reduced by the use of fine steel wool (grade 000) dipped in an ordinary soft wax polish, which acts as a lubricant. The degree of dulling depends on the amount of abrasion by the steel wool.

A finish specially formulated for lathe work, also cellulose-based, is called 'Craftlac'. It is available in two varieties, 'standard' and 'melamine', the later being formulated to give a heat- and waterproof finish. It is applied with a soft brush or cloth and allowed about ten minutes to dry. Light flatting with very fine abrasive follows, after which the second coat is given. Burnishing with a soft cloth imparts a good finish which is particularly pleasant to handle.

French polish

French polish and similar types of finish consisting of shellac dissolved in alcohol can produce a beautiful finish with great depth of colour and shine. Generally, the grain has first to be filled and allowed to dry, then the work is carefully sanded with fine garnet or similar paper.

Fillers, already stained to match certain species of wood or 'clear', can be obtained ready-mixed or in powder form to mix with water. They are applied with a damp rag and rubbed firmly into the grain while the work revolves.

After drying, the work is again mounted and the polish is applied with a pad or 'rubber'. A wad of cotton wool is impregnated with polish, laid on a clean square of cotton fabric (old cotton shirts are ideal), and rolled into a pad. The pad is held lightly against the work and moved over it, increasing the pressure gradually as polish is used. Several coats are required – the more the better – but each coat must be thinly applied and allowed to dry before the next. The polish dries quickly. A few drops of linseed oil on the pad reduce the risk of sticking or dragging, but this must not be overdone. When the polish has built up, a wad of wool is moistened with methylated spirit, wrapped in clean cotton, then very lightly and swiftly worked over the job. This is a polishing technique which requires skill and care but it produces a glorious finish.

12 Timbers for turning

If a species of wood is capable of being worked by hand or machine – and few of the world's timbers are not – then that wood can be turned. However, some species respond far better than do others, and may species are not likely to be chosen for turning purposes. Broadly, timbers of medium density are the easiest to turn. Softwoods, and some of the softer hardwoods, can be turned quite well between centres, when the tools remove wood by a cutting action. ('Hard wood' and 'soft wood' mean what is stated. 'Hardwood' is timber from trees which bear broad leaves and usually shed them annually. 'Softwood' is from trees that have needle-like leaves and usually are evergreen. Yew is a softwood but it is quite hard and dense; obeche is a hardwood, but it is quite soft.) Faceplate turning of the softer woods requires extra care and it is difficult to leave the surface of the wood in a reasonably clean state. Soft-textured timbers do not respond well to scraping, and the grain can finish up badly pitted.

Yew is botanically a softwood but is generally (but incorrectly) regarded as a hardwood because it is so dense and stable. It is normally available only in small sizes, as the log, when converted, tends to have many faults. It is light-brown in colour with pale sapwood and is much used for ornamental pieces. It turns very well and finishes beautifully.

Elm, a hardwood traditionally used for the hubs or naves of wooden wheels, is obtainable in fairly large sizes and so lends itself to bowl-turning in particular. The wood is an attractive mid-brown colour, with a fairly wild grain which gives it added appeal. The wood tends to dull tools more quickly than most other species as there are occasional small areas of a gritty deposit in the grain which has a noticeable and rapid effect on the sharpness of tools. These areas can often be seen as whitish patches. Because of the interlocking grain, elm is difficult to split and so it is ideal for the tops of three-legged stools.

Oak is usually very hard but it turns well. It is renowned for its pronounced medullary rays, which, when seen on the surface, are known as 'silver grain' and are one of the beauties of oak. On spindle-work the rays are sure to be visible somewhere on the surface. Oak is favoured for ecclesiastical work of all types and domestic items as well. It is renowned for its attractiveness, strength, and durability.

Ash is usually paler than oak but it can have dark streaks in it. It turns cleanly and, as well as being suitable for general turnery, it is one of the most resilient woods there is. It is also quite strong. Its particular qualities make it specially suitable for sports goods like cricket stumps and croquet mallets, and it is the wood almost invariably used for handles for spades and other digging tools. It is an excellent wood for handles of small tools and bench mallets.

Sycamore is an excellent wood for turning. It probably responds to sharp tools and experienced hands better than any other wood. Continuous shavings several yards long can be removed and a very smooth surface produced at the same time. It is one of the whitest woods there is, apart from holly. Sycamore is the wood to use for kitchenware such as rolling pins and breadboards. Its whiteness and its freedom from odour and closeness of grain – which prevents foodstuffs from sticking to the wood – makes it suitable for kitchen use.

Chestnut has a similar colour and grain to oak (but without the silver grain), for which it can be used as a substitute, especially if the work has to be stained dark, as for reproduction Jacobean furniture.

Beech, if English, is off-white in colour, tough, and dense. It is a very good wood for both spindle and faceplate turning, and its close, compact grain means there is little tearing of the fibres even when scrapers are used. It is not a highly decorative wood either in colour or grain, but it lends itself to legs and rails, for which it was used in vast quantities by the chairmakers of the 18th and 19th centuries. Beech has strong medullary rays, but they are not as pronounced on the surface as on oak. However, the rays have reinforcing effect on the grain, which makes beech quite strong across the grain and quite difficult to split. This, and its hard, tough nature, make it an excellent timber for tool-handles and similar functional things.

European beech is much more pinkish in colour than the English wood, the colour being caused by a steaming process it goes through during seasoning in a kiln. It is usually referred to as 'steamed beech' and, although it is not quite dense as English beech, it is a little more uniform in texture.

Mahogany is a name very loosely applied these days and it seems to be given to even distant relatives of the family provided they are reddish in colour. Main varieties include Brazilian, Philippine and African. True mahogany is quite scarce now, and costly. Most of the mahoganies now available tend to be a little woolly in the grain, which means they do not respond well to the scraping techniques used on faceplate work. Some mahoganies have a quite rich colour and look their best when given a glossy finish.

Teak has become a popular species for furniture in recent years but, like the real mahoganies, true teak is scarce and costly. It is of a mid-brown colour, with occasional black streaks. While it turns well in one sense, it is notorious in another: it is extremely abrasive to tools because of a silica-like deposit in the grain, and so tools need to be constantly re-sharpened during turning. Although it has an oily nature, it sands well and is generally regarded as looking its best when given a matt finish or burnished with 'teak oil' formulated for finishing teak and leaving it with a natural look.

Other species Afrormosia and iroko come from Africa and both are frequently used as substitutes for teak. Although colours are similar, afrormosia has a rather finer texture than teak, whereas iroko is rather more coarse, with an open, more irregular grain. Neither has the same dulling effect on tools as has teak, but iroko can be a little brittle, and it has happened when turning a bowl in iroko that it has shattered for no apparent reason when the walls were being reduced.

Although they are expensive, it is possible to obtain a range of woods broadly referred to as 'exotics'. Partly because of their rarity and high cost, they are normally available only in fairly small sizes, but they are ideal for the special job which is itself fairly small: knobs and handles in particular. Among the better known timbers of this group are box, which is pale yellow in colour; ebony, which is very dark and can be jet black; and rosewood, which is rich, dark red and sometimes variegated with brown to black streaks. Other exotics include laurel, padouk, bubinga, cocobola, and palisander.

Specialist firms sell blocks and discs for turning, but good stock can sometimes be found in country timber yards. Fruit and nut tree timbers turn well and have attractive colours and figure. Holly, hawthorn, and many other hedgerow trees provide fine decorative timber which is worth collecting and seasoning.

Squares and strips of different coloured woods can be prepared and glued together to make blocks and lengths for faceplate and spindle turning. This technique, known as 'laminating', can produce beautiful effects when turned.

13 Safety rules

The following list of points to observe when turning is not intended to be exhaustive but rather to act as a guide which will give the turner an awareness of the need to be safety-conscious. Lathes are relatively safe machines, as it is the wood which revolves, not the cutters, as in most other woodworking machines. There is, however, some potential danger where there are any moving parts.

Install the machine according to the maker's instructions and the electricity-board requirements.

Ensure that the motor is earthed and that the electric cable is in sound condition before each session. Isolate the machine from the mains when carrying out any repairs or adjustments.

Check that the mounting of the work is secure, and rotate the work by hand to ensure that it is free to revolve.

Check that the toolrest is secure and, for spindle work, that the barrel-lock is tightened.

Clothing should be tidy, a tie should be removed or tucked into the shirt, cuffs should be gathered at the wrist or rolled back.

Keep the toolrest close to the work to reduce the leverage effect which the wood exerts on the turning tool.

Safety glasses should be worn, especially when grinding tools.

The hand holding the blade of the turning tools should, wherever possible, also lie on the toolrest so as to maintain control of the tool.

Where fingers come into close proximity with work which is revolving, as when glasspapering, hold the fingers in the direction of rotation.

Wear a breathing-mask when sanding woods, such as mansonia, whose fine dust causes nasal and bronchial irritation.

Index